PENGUIN CANADA

THE LIFE

Steve Paikin is co-host of *Studio 2*, TVOntario's highly acclaimed current affairs program, now in its eighth season. He also hosts *Diplomatic Immunity*, a weekly foreign affairs program, now in its fourth season. A graduate of the University of Toronto and Boston University, Paikin began his career as a city hall reporter for CHFI and CFTR in Toronto. He spent seven years at CBC-TV working as a news reporter, Queen's Park correspondent and, eventually, anchor of the six o'clock news. *The Life* is his first book.

THE LIFE

THE SEDUCTIVE CALL OF POLITICS

Steve Paikin

PENGUIN
CANADA

PENGUIN CANADA
Published by the Penguin Group
Penguin Books, a division of Pearson Canada, 10 Alcorn Avenue, Toronto, Ontario, Canada M4V 3B2
Penguin Books Ltd, 80 Strand, London WC2R 0RL, England
Penguin Putnam Inc., 375 Hudson Street, New York, New York 10014, U.S.A.
Penguin Books Australia Ltd, 250 Camberwell Road, Camberwell, Victoria 3124, Australia
Penguin Books India (P) Ltd, 11, Community Centre, Panchsheel Park, New Delhi – 110 017, India
Penguin Books (NZ) Ltd, cnr Rosedale and Airborne Roads, Albany, Auckland 1310, New Zealand
Penguin Books (South Africa) (Pty) Ltd, 24 Sturdee Avenue, Rosebank 2196, South Africa

Penguin Books Ltd, Registered Offices: 80 Strand, London WC2R 0RL, England

First published in Viking by Penguin Books Canada Limited, 2001
Published in Penguin Canada by Penguin Books, a division of Pearson Canada, 2002

Published in this edition, 2002

10 9 8 7 6 5 4 3 2 1

Manufactured in Canada.

NATIONAL LIBRARY OF CANADA CATALOGUING IN PUBLICATION DATA

Paikin, Steve, 1960–
The life : the seductive call of politics / Steve Paikin.

Includes index.
ISBN 0-14-029370-1

1. Politicians—Canada. 2. Women politicians—Canada.
3. Canada—Politics and government—1935–. I. Title.

FC26.P6P335 2002 324.2'2'0971 C2002-903367-5
F1034.3.A2P35 2002

For Shirley Sibulash,
a great grandmother

THE TABLE OF CONTENTS

THE INTRODUCTION

When William Grenville Davis retired as the longest-serving premier of Ontario in the twentieth century, he was at the top of his game. He was enjoying unprecedented popularity, which is saying a lot for a man who'd already won four elections and held one of the most coveted political jobs in the country. There was no question that, had Davis decided to run for a fifth mandate, it would have been his.

And yet, on Thanksgiving weekend in 1984, Davis told his family he'd had enough. He'd been at Queen's Park for twenty-five years, fourteen of them as premier. He knew he could stay on and win another election. But he also knew he could never look the public in the eye and commit to serving even close to a full term. It just wasn't in him any more. So rather than call the election which would certainly preserve an already four-decades-old Tory dynasty in Ontario, Bill Davis quit politics with barely a thought as to what he'd do next.

Two years later, in October, 1986, I sat down with Davis in his new professional surroundings—the law offices of Tory Tory DesLauriers and Binnington, on the thirty-second floor of the Toronto-Dominion Centre. The first thing one notices is that Bill Davis's office as premier of Ontario is about ten times the size of Bill Davis's office as a senior law partner. It's strange to see the man who was premier since I was eleven years old in such under-whelming surroundings.

Nevertheless, we do our interview for CBC-TV on whether there's life after politics for Bill Davis. Apparently, there is.

"I think I maybe exaggerated a little bit in my own mind the extent of the trauma," he tells me. "As a result, I've been pleasantly surprised because it has not been as difficult for me as I thought it might have been."

The unprecedented way in which this former politician has been courted by the business community has, no doubt, eased the transition. Less than two years out of office, Davis is already firmly ensconced in one of the country's most prestigious law firms. He's sitting on eleven different boards of directors. He's jetting all over North America for meetings. He's probably earning more than he ever thought he would—probably at least three times his salary as premier. And best of all, no cranky reporters or opposition politicians to answer to.

I tell him, from where I'm sitting, things presumably couldn't be better.

"Steven, let me tell you something," he starts. "This job on the most exciting, interesting day can't touch being premier of Ontario on the dullest."

Excuse me? How can a life that provides a huge salary, where you rub shoulders with the most influential movers and shakers in the private sector, where you're still revered as an historic figure of influence... how can that not compare to the discredited world of politics?

Davis reminds me that during his six years of leading minority governments, "There was nothing more thrilling than coming to work every day, knowing the entire government could collapse if you made a mistake."

Even Brian Mulroney, whose success in the private sector both before and after he became prime minister is unrivalled in Canadian political history, shares Davis's view.

"I'd have to agree with Bill," he told me over the phone, as we tried to nail down a time to meet. "If you've been the prime minister or the premier, your agenda is the country's agenda. In the private sector, your agenda is of little consequence to anyone but you."

Peter Lougheed, perhaps the only provincial first minister of the last quarter century with a record equal to or better than Davis's, echoes the sentiments.

"I think Bill puts it very well," Lougheed says. "I would say the most insignificant day being premier of Alberta for fourteen years was still more interesting than any other day that I've spent before or after."

I've covered politics in Canada for almost twenty years now. I've spoken to thousands of people engaged in the political process. But that comment of Bill Davis's has consistently intrigued me.

What is it about public life that's so alluring to so many? From the outside, it often seems like a miserable, thankless job. Voters hate politicians and the feeling is often mutual. Media coverage frequently portrays politicians as slimy, unprincipled egomaniacs who are only out to feather their own nests, their constituents' needs be damned.

So what's the attraction?

When I told Floyd Laughren, Ontario's finance minister from 1990–95, that I intended to interview nearly one hundred current and former politicians for this book, he answered, "Why would you want to spend a year talking to a bunch of psychopaths?" I think he was only partly kidding.

David Goyette, who's served as a political consultant to more than seventy politicians over the years, calls public life "an emotional addiction."

"It's an addiction about ego, about the exercise of power, about being perceived as an important person in your community. It's self-aggrandizement, and that's a good thing. You can't survive without it. You can't be a leader without an ego—being able to say how I think the world should be."

Well, here's my dirty little secret which no self-respecting journalist is ever supposed to admit.

I like politicians—at least, the vast majority of the ones I've met. It's certainly more fashionable—and will sell more newspapers—to focus on the stupid things of which some of them are guilty. Every time an elected member does something indefensible, it makes one question their motives and fitness to represent us.

But there is an unmistakable lure to "The Life," as former New Brunswick premier Frank McKenna called it, which they clearly crave. If you've ever wondered what that is, keep reading. Their stories, I hope, will make you understand what "The Life," the seductive call of politics, is all about.

Steve Paikin
Toronto, Canada
October, 2001

THE LIFE

THE CRUSADERS

It was October 30, 1995, and Lewis MacKenzie found himself at home in Bracebridge, Ontario, watching his big-screen TV. MacKenzie was the closest thing Canadians had to a genuine war hero. He'd been in the service for more than three decades and garnered international acclaim for himself and his country, thanks to his United Nations peacekeeping efforts in Bosnia. He had everything most Canadian military men I've known didn't have: an infectious personality, rugged good looks, impressive leadership skills, and most important in this day and age, tremendous poise and ease on television. The guy had done *Larry King Live* on CNN—what more need be said?

MacKenzie had watched countries tear themselves apart all over the world, but always enjoyed the security of knowing his own homeland wasn't like that. Canadians had always managed, through a mix of intelligent leaders or plain dumb luck, to avoid becoming the next Yugoslavia, Cyprus, or Czechoslovakia. Sure, we'd flirted with disaster but somehow always stepped back from the brink.

But MacKenzie sensed that this night was different. He was watching televised coverage of Quebec's second sovereignty referendum and he was feeling an incredible amount of anxiety.

For anxious hour after hour, he watched the TV graphics nudge past 50 per cent for Quebec sovereignty, then retreat back ever so slightly against it

"I was a limp rag by the time midnight came around," he says. "The barest of majorities in favour of holding the country together...."

The next morning, while shaving, MacKenzie took a good look at himself in the mirror. He realized his military service had provided him with a wealth of knowledge on how countries stay together or break apart. "I understood that I had this fluke of exposure because a whole bunch of good soldiers had made me look good over the years," he says. "And I wasn't doing anything with it as far as the country went. Sure I was going across the country and saying 'Rah rah Canada' and talking national unity, but it was more of an entertainment platform. So I said, 'Okay, what are you going to do?'"

A few years earlier, MacKenzie had flirted ever so briefly with entering politics after he retired from the military. The Liberal, Conservative, and Reform parties had all approached him to be a candidate in the 1993 federal election. Jean Chrétien invited him to the opposition leader's official residence, Stornoway, to give his pitch added oomph. Both the Grits and Tories assured him he could run in one of their safest seats.

"Funny thing was," MacKenzie recalls with a laugh, "they were both promising the same seat."

In any event, the retired major-general decided politics was no life for a soldier, so he put it out of his mind—until the morning after those results appeared on his television set.

Lewis MacKenzie's story is a good one because, eventually, he was motivated to enter the political arena for all the right reasons. He wasn't pre-occupied with what cabinet position might await him at the end of the day. He chose to run for the Tories in the 1997 election, having been impressed with party leader Jean Charest's gutsy leadership. The notion that Charest could promise him anything with a straight face, given that his caucus consisted of two MPs at the time, seems a bit unlikely. MacKenzie didn't stash his personal beliefs in his back pocket, then opportunistically hitch his wagon to whatever party was leading in the polls at the time, as many "star" candidates do. And he certainly didn't enter the fray, confident that his participation would pay dividends in the business community somewhere down the road. He saw an issue, and had just enough ego to think he might be able to make a contribution to the public agenda. He wasn't Mother Teresa. But his motives for seeking public office seem altruistic enough.

Voters today no doubt think altruism has disappeared as a factor motivating people to get into politics. Those voters would be mistaken. Don't misunderstand. These candidates are not without ego. They can also play political hardball with the best of them. But their reasons for entering the arena are decent. Their hopes for what they can achieve for people are even noble. And surprise, surprise, they're not all New Democrats (although a lot of them are).

IN CANADIAN POLITICAL CIRCLES, the year 1968 means one thing and one thing only. It's the year the country's justice minister transformed politics into rock 'n' roll. He took the Liberal Party, and then the country, by the sheer force of his personality and his ideas.

In London, Ontario, fourteen-year-old Frances Lankin was preparing to be part of Trudeaumania. She was the colour-guard captain in a drum and bugle corps, which local Liberals had just hired for the new prime minister's big campaign rally at London Gardens.

"I knew that everybody loved Trudeau, and everybody screamed everywhere Trudeau went," she remembers. Lankin thought she was too young to have truly appreciated the Beatles, but this would be the next best thing.

"When he came through, he shook my hand," Lankin says. "And I was so amazed at this." A simple handshake from the man who would dominate Canadian political affairs for the next decade and a half was certainly enough to enlist thousands of Canadians in the Liberal cause. What happened to Frances Lankin as a result of that handshake?

Nothing. Despite the attraction to the individual, her political awakening did not happen that night. She came to realize it was just an encounter between a young girl and a television personality. She would not be swept up, either by the Trudeau magic or the thousands of partisan Liberal supporters in attendance.

Her real political awakening came three years later during a provincial election campaign. At an all-candidates debate at her school, Oakridge Secondary, the New Democratic candidate, William Murdock, who was blind, started to speak about social justice issues in a way Lankin had never heard before.

"Something touched me. I was awed. I was inspired," she says.

"All of a sudden, something mattered to me outside of just the normal stuff of being a kid."

Lankin volunteered to distribute some leaflets. And she put up a sign on the front lawn of her home, forgetting for the moment that her father, George Ollmann, was staunchly pro-Conservative.

"He came home and saw an NDP sign on his lawn, and came in fit to be tied," Lankin says.

"What the hell is that?" he asked angrily.

"It's my sign," she told him.

"What gives you the right to have that sign?" he snapped back.

Father and daughter proceeded to have their first political discussion of some significance. She explained her "awakening" at the all-candidates meeting, mentioned her volunteering efforts, and obviously convinced her father of her commitment. His response surprised Lankin.

"Well, what's really important in life is that if you find something that you believe in, and you believe strongly in it, that's good," he said. "But if you don't do anything about it, it doesn't amount to anything, Frances. So if you believe something and you're prepared to go and do something about it, then even if I disagree with you I'll support you in that.

"You can have your sign."

Lankin was surprised and delighted. Not that the sign was likely to sway many votes. The Ollmanns lived at the dead-end of a country road, and the only folks likely to see the sign were one neighbour and a lot of cows. But it was her first lesson about fighting for your principles.

DESPITE ITS RECENT FORTUNES, there are some parts of Canada where being a member of the New Democratic Party actually means a lot. In many legislatures, NDP politicians continue to be effective opponents to the government of the day. And in a very few provinces, such as British Columbia, Saskatchewan, and Manitoba, the party either is in power or has historically remained a viable option to form a government.

Such has never been the case for New Democrats in Alberta. To be "an ND," as they're called in Alberta, is to take on a particular vow of political chastity. You never win elections. You never elect very many members. Your job is to pick your crusades carefully, then survive to fight another day.

Pam Barrett did that and much more. Hers is one of the truly unique stories in Canadian history. A trip to the dentist transformed her from an obscure provincial politician to the bright lights of the national stage. New Democrats have experienced numerous political deaths in this country. But Barrett has done it in a way no one ever has or ever will again.

Pamela Trainor Barrett remembers as if it were yesterday the moment she knew she wanted to be a politician with the New Democratic Party. It was 1961, and she was living in Shilo, Manitoba. Tommy Douglas's government in neighbouring Saskatchewan introduced North America's first Medicare plan, to a firestorm of protest by the province's doctors, who promptly went on strike. What did eight-year-old Pam Barrett make of all this? "All I could think of was, 'Oh, Mummy, I wish we could move to Saskatchewan, because we're so poor,'" she says.

And poor they were. Barrett grew up an army brat, one of seven children to Agatha and Raymond Barrett. Her father was a Canadian armed forces private. Three of her siblings were triplets, meaning her mother at one time was dealing with seven kids under the age of five, virtually single-handedly. Agatha Barrett could frequently be found at the kitchen table, crying over her chequebook as she tried to make her unworkable financial situation work. But there was Saskatchewan, right next door, a kind of beacon of hope, for this family close to distress.

"I knew right then and there," Barrett says, "gee, if the NDP government will do such a good thing for people regardless of how much money they've got in their wallet, then we should have an NDP government everywhere."

Four years later, as a twelve-year-old in social studies class near Edmonton on another armed forces base, Barrett was told by one of her teachers that the opposition Liberals and Conservatives in Saskatchewan helped orchestrate the doctors' strike. She was enraged. Not that she needed much more prodding, but she came home that day and declared to her family that she was absolutely, positively, inalterably, and unquestionably committed to the New Democratic Party.

"That's interesting," her mother said.

"You'll get over it," added her Uncle Fred Trainor, her mother's younger brother, visiting from Greenland.

But they were wrong. She never did get over it.

DERWYN SHEA'S APPEARANCE IS SURPRISING. It shouldn't be, because he's been a prominent presence in Toronto politics for almost two decades. Every time the public has seen Shea, he's been dressed like a politician—usually a modest-looking blue suit, plain shirt and tie, never anything too loud or fancy.

But today Shea is in Toronto's west end at St. Hilda's, the Anglican parish and residential care facility he runs. And he's wearing his priestly collar. Shea was an Anglican priest while he was in municipal and provincial politics. His politics were known to be moderate to conservative. But as we sit down to lunch in the St. Hilda's dining room, I'm about to discover a multitude of things about a man I thought I knew, but really didn't—about a man whose political aspirations and accomplishments were modest, and ultimately couldn't compete with his pulpit.

Derwyn Spencer Shea's life began in 1937 as a mistake and got a lot worse before it got better. With fourteen years between his next oldest sibling and himself, he suspects his unanticipated arrival was the straw that broke the camel's back, or to be more precise, broke up his parents' marriage. In what must have been a shocking development in the Hamilton, Ontario, of the 1940s, his mother, Kathleen, left his father.

"She took me, two dollars in her pocket, and a box of chocolates," Shea says. "She hitched a ride to Toronto, gave the driver who gave her the ride the box of chocolates and she had two bucks to start with."

If a busted-up marriage, a two-year-old kid, and virtually nothing to her name weren't tough enough for Kathleen Shea, something would happen three years down the road that would truly break her heart. Her oldest son, David, who was the youngest pilot to graduate from his base in Hamilton, was sent off to war. Little Derwyn was almost six years old when David was shipped out from the grounds of the Canadian National Exhibition in Toronto, and went to fly Spitfires in World War II. He was shot down and killed over the skies of Britain. Shea still goes to the Brookfield Cemetery just outside London every two years to see David's grave. David's participation in the war was a family tradition. Kathleen Shea's two middle names were Ladysmith and Mafeking—two major battles in the Boer War, in which her father fought and died.

Shea never knew his father. He was always told John Joseph Shea was dead. Until one day at his middle brother Gerald's wedding, "Somebody came up to me and said, 'Now, son, do you know who I am?' It was a helluva shock."

And there were more surprises to come.

NOW THAT HE'D MADE THE DECISION TO GET IN, Lewis MacKenzie needed to find a place to run, and it was here that he committed his first political mistake. The pros in the Conservative party told him he should seek a seat in Toronto.

"I said, 'Absolutely not,'" MacKenzie recalls. He and his wife had put down roots in Bracebridge, a lovely tourist community in the heart of Ontario's cottage country, two hours north of Toronto. It was bad enough he'd have to live in an apartment in Ottawa during the week. When would he see his constituents? The politicos assured him he could drop in to his Toronto riding for a couple of hours after Question Period on Fridays, and that would suffice.

MacKenzie's response? "Yeah sure. You've got a whole frigging riding and you're just going to drop in on Friday night? Not bloody likely. So I said I'd run where I live."

That meant contesting the riding of Parry Sound–Muskoka. After all, he lived in one of the riding's biggest towns, which was also his wife's hometown. He'd been going to the area for the past twenty-five years to see her and her family. A worthy decision, perhaps, but this old soldier didn't count on the kind of warfare he'd encounter on the political battlefield.

For example, in his first local newspaper interview, he told the reporter he'd lived in thirteen different homes in seven different Canadian provinces and served in eleven countries overseas. That should make you a more attractive candidate because it suggests some knowledge of the country and its place in the world.

But to the local media in Muskoka, Lewis MacKenzie was a parachute candidate of the worst kind. "The article came out that 'General MacKenzie has seven residences in Canada and occasionally visits the one in Bracebridge.' My wife wanted to go down and kill the editor," he says.

It didn't take MacKenzie long to realize something no candidate ever wants to face, even on election day. He was going to lose and he knew it. With only two sitting MPs, the Tories needed MacKenzie to go all over the country and shirk his own riding, where they naïvely hoped his star power alone would be enough to carry the day. The candidate himself knew the strength of the Reform Party, particularly in Parry Sound, and he could do the math. Still, he got out there and did his thing. When he was in the riding, he somehow found the time to do five or six coffee parties a day (where he was almost always the youngest person in the room). And he travelled the country, using his own experiences in the Canadian armed forces as an example of how anglophones and francophones, working together, could achieve great things on the world stage.

"I talked about national unity," MacKenzie says, "and I raised a piss-pot full of money for the party. And that was my contribution."

Meanwhile, the local newspapers in Muskoka helpfully reminded their readers that the PC candidate wasn't in the riding when the writ was dropped, missed an all-candidates debate, and provided a list of all the other parts of Canada in which MacKenzie had campaigned, rather than attending to the needs of his own backyard. It was mean-spirited, small-town reportage as its pettiest.

He also experienced some of the stupidity that's often a part of election campaigning. "People would actually say to me, 'This campaign is war.' And twice I had to say, 'You have no idea what war is. These are fellow Canadians with whom we have a small difference of opinion on how we should achieve things in this paradise called

Canada. It's not perfect, but it's better than anywhere else. This is not war. These are our friends, for God's sake.'"

However, MacKenzie did love the hustings. Senator Norman Atkins, one of the best political organizers in Canadian history, took a liking to MacKenzie and shepherded him through a campaign swing in the Maritimes: Halifax, Wolfville, Kempville, Sydney, Saint John, Oromocto. He saw the way the crowds reacted to MacKenzie and thought the general should have sought a seat in Fredericton.

"Frank McKenna kept telling me I was the second-largest employer in the province behind him," MacKenzie jokes, referring to the former New Brunswick premier and MacKenzie's own time at Base Gagetown in the late 1980s.

"He was terrific," Atkins recalled. "If we had run him in Fredericton, he'd have won." Given the fact the Progressive Conservative party did stage a partial rebirth in Atlantic Canada by winning thirteen seats in the '97 election, Atkins's boast may not be without merit. However, if MacKenzie *had* run and won in the Maritimes, would his marriage have survived it all?

"Probably not," Atkins responded.

And what does MacKenzie think?

"Had I listened to the pros, my wife would have probably left me by now," he says. "She's only moved twenty-seven times in twenty-four years. I promised her a little bit of stability when I left the military."

Instead, in Parry Sound–Muskoka the Liberals' Andy Mitchell took almost eighteen thousand votes. MacKenzie came second, more than six thousand votes behind. He edged the Reform candidate by five hundred votes.

And with that, the political career of Major General Lewis MacKenzie (retired) was over. It had lasted five months.

After the 1997 election, Lewis MacKenzie had a chance to kick back and think about his brief, yet exhilarating career in politics.

"I wanted to make a small contribution to holding this country together," MacKenzie says. "That was the motivating factor for getting into it. Once I got into it, my strongest critics were right. They were Liberals, obviously, and said, 'This guy, with what he's seen and what he's done, probably isn't cut out to be worrying about the responsibility for water waste in Muskoka.' They'd stand up there and say, 'He's going to try to become the minister for external affairs.' And they were probably right."

Lewis MacKenzie's political career may have been a short one. But it was long enough for him to have experienced what the lure of The Life is all about.

His best day in politics started in Saint John, New Brunswick, where he was assigned to watch a "real" politician work—Elsie Wayne, whom he'd first met in 1990 when she was the mayor of Saint John and he was the commander of Base Gagetown.

"I was in awe," MacKenzie remembers of his personal tour of the local market courtesy of Wayne. "She worked that town. Even if she hadn't the faintest idea of who someone was, she told me about their background, how many kids they had. I'm sure she was making some of it up." (Incidentally, I checked with Elsie. She *was* making some of it up.)

Next was a stop at the Opera House where MacKenzie gave perhaps the best speech of his life, a *cri de coeur* for national unity. "Had a lot of tears going for Canada," he recalls. "I still get letters for that presentation."

Next stop, pinch-hitting for party leader Jean Charest at a CBC-TV debate. He and Norman Atkins hopped on a Falcon, much like a Learjet, to fly from Saint John to Montreal "and the friggin' heater went in the Falcon about ten minutes after we took off. I've never been so cold in my life. Parachuting into the Arctic Circle wasn't that cold."

The group landed in Montreal only to discover they were running behind schedule. Fortunately, as MacKenzie describes it, "Jacques Villeneuve's long-lost brother is driving. At least he thinks he's Jacques's brother."

Meantime, the other candidates and the CBC's Hana Gartner were all waiting on the set for MacKenzie to arrive. When he finally did, he made a quick pit-stop to the makeup chair, where he was told to be ready to give an opening statement, but prepared notes were not allowed. Eventually, he got to his seat and checked out the lay of the land: the Liberals' Stéphane Dion was on his left and Reform's Preston Manning on his right.

"And Hana Gartner says, 'I'll turn to you first, General MacKenzie.' And I see Manning has an upper-case, double-spaced speech in front of him. I look over at Dion and he's got some hand-written notes and I've got nothing. So I figure, okay, a good defence is a good offence and I start going after Manning for the 'No Quebec Prime Minister' ads. I said at the end of my comments, 'You have stepped over my line in the sand.' Everyone was clapping."

MacKenzie had discovered one of the things he loved most about public life: "Turning an audience on, whether 'live' or on television. Absolutely."

Preston Manning had to speak next. He decided to ditch his script and go after MacKenzie.

"I had good fun with Manning, but it was self-destructive if you believe in party politics, because those were the two right-wing parties tearing the shit out of each other."

Later in the debate, MacKenzie had it out with his Liberal opponent, the architect of the government's Clarity Bill, its "get tough" approach with Quebec. "I remember saying to Stephane Dion, 'When I walk in to negotiate in Bosnia between people who are trying to kill each other, I don't take my bloody pistol out and slam it down on the coffee table and say, 'Here I am,' which is what you guys are doing with Plan B.'"

Would MacKenzie ever run again? He seriously doubts it. He's enjoying life in Bracebridge again. He's got more time for his passion for auto racing. (At age sixty-one, he loves driving the Ultima Mark III and still races thirteen weekends a summer.) He is a busy professional speaker, mostly on peacekeeping, the United Nations, or leadership. He does the occasional television interview. He speaks out on behalf of the troops whenever he can. He sees his thirty-four-year-old daughter, Kimm, who, ironically, married MacKenzie's former aide-de-camp from Central America. ("He started looking after my daughter better than he was looking after me.") And he's devoting time to three charities he loves: the Special Olympics, Parkinson's, and Can-Far, which does AIDS research.

He figures it would take another national emergency to prompt him to re-enter the arena, and he's hoping none is on the horizon.

Now that he knows what politicians go through to get elected, he has a lot more respect for what they do. And in hindsight, he admits the political pros were right. They told him if he ran in a rural area, he'd be expected to attend every birthday party, corn roast, and christening. They told him to run in the city, get his mug on TV once a week, and his constituents would think he was doing a good job. Maybe it wouldn't have mattered. After all, the Liberals did win every seat in Ontario, save two.

"So, was it worth it?" I ask him, just before he takes off to one of his charity fundraisers. To answer that, MacKenzie tells me a story about a social event he and his wife attended while he was attached to the Third Battalion of the Queen's Regiment in Lemgo, Germany, almost thirty-five years ago.

"My wife was dancing with the British Adjutant," MacKenzie says. "And my wife said, 'What does the Adjutant do?' And this supercilious twit said, 'It's a job to have done.' And I'd say the same thing about politics. It's something to have done. It's part of the education process of life."

It doesn't sound supercilious when Lew MacKenzie says it.

AFTER WINNING THE SIGN WAR WITH HER FATHER, Frances Lankin's interest in social justice issues began to deepen. Enrolling at the University of Toronto's Scarborough College, she began to work for feminist causes and against apartheid in South Africa. Her work after university at a private child-care centre, and the appalling lack of interest the owners took in the welfare of the children, resulted in her becoming one of the founding members of the Ontario Coalition for Better Child Care. "I ended up breaking out in hives, I hated going to work so much," Lankin remembers. "This guy was ripping the parents off. He was paying the staff low wages. The food wasn't fit to be eaten by the kids. I just knew it was wrong."

The opportunities kept coming. Lankin became a prison guard at the Don Jail in Toronto. As such, she joined the Ontario Public Service Employees' Union, which gave her exposure to issues such as employment equity, pay equity, and workers' rights. She joined the NDP executive of her riding association and the provincial executive of the NDP. There seemed no end to the passion ignited in that fourteen-year-old school girl from London. And in Frances Lankin's world, it was a good time to be a New Democrat. She lived in the Beaches neighbourhood of Toronto, where the MP, MPP, both city councillors, and school board trustee were all members of the NDP.

Eventually, someone asked the obvious question. "Some of the women in the party said to me, 'Well, when are you going to stop encouraging other women to run, and when are you going to run?'"

Being "the candidate" was never part of Lankin's plan. She was always more comfortable in the backrooms, encouraging others to step into the spotlight, rather than wanting it for herself. However, when New Democrat MPP Jim Renwick died, opening up Riverdale riding right beside the Beaches, Lankin stepped forward to seek the nomination. And she lost.

"It was a really good learning experience," she says. "I mean, I was outgunned from the beginning—really green in terms of being a candidate." But the experience did convince Lankin she could be more than an organizer—that she could be "the candidate." Next time around, things would be different—in ways Lankin could never have imagined.

Two days before the 1990 Ontario election—Frances Lankin's first as a candidate—her campaign manager told her to take the day off. This was, to say the least, rather unorthodox advice, and the candidate for the Beaches–Woodbine riding didn't take it too well.

"Excuse me?" she said.

"I want you to go shopping," said Joanne McNiven, one of the NDP's top campaign managers, having run several of former national leader Ed Broadbent's campaigns.

Lankin was tired and irritated. "What are you talking about?" she said. "Get to the point here. Don't play games with me. I've gotta get out there."

"I want you to go and buy some cabinet minister clothes," McNiven said.

Lankin thought McNiven was off her rocker. So she ignored her, grabbed a fistful of leaflets and went canvassing. She was so focused on winning her own seat that she somehow hadn't let the province-wide picture infiltrate her consciousness. And province-wide, the NDP was doing just fine, thank you.

Unfortunately for Lankin, she didn't get the kind of pre-election night briefing I got. Or if she did, she ignored it. My job on September 6, 1990, was to co-host CBC-TV's election night coverage with my friend and colleague Lyn Whitham. While Frances Lankin was being told to go buy cabinet minister clothes (and not believing it), Lyn and I were in a private meeting with the CBC's unrivalled guru of election coverage, Elly Alboim. Before he left the Mother Corp. to work for an Ottawa political consulting firm, Alboim had produced countless national and regional election broadcasts. I've never met a journalist before or since who knew as much about the intricacies of politics.

"I wanted to talk to you two because you need to get your head around some critical issues so you don't look foolish on election night," Alboim said to us. He said a CBC Alberta anchor was unprepared for the strong showing the Liberals had made in a recent election, so much so, the host nearly said "Holy shit!" on the air as the Grits started to win seats.

I promised Elly I'd do my best not to be profane on Her Majesty's airwaves and could he please tell us what was so urgent as to require this behind-closed-doors session. And then he said something after which you could have knocked me over with a feather.

"The NDP is going to win a majority government and David Peterson is going to lose his seat."

I was speechless. Unlike Lankin, the latest polls had registered with me, so I knew the NDP was doing well. But certainly not well enough to form a majority government. Not even well enough to win the biggest number of seats, I thought. And the premier lose his own seat? In Ontario? No politician, elected premier by the public and seeking re-election, had lost an *election* since 1923, let alone his own seat. It was impossible.

"How do you know?" I asked Alboim.

"Trust me. I just know," he said. "Now get your head around that."

I didn't know it at the time, but two days later on election night, I made Frances Lankin's life quite miserable. Sure enough, Alboim was spot-on, and within twenty minutes of our having gone on the air, I had the unprecedented task of saying, "Based on the returns received so far, our CBC Decision Desk has determined the NDP will form a majority government. Bob Rae will be the next premier of Ontario." That was all well and good, but an hour later, having gone through much of the province seat by seat, I still hadn't mentioned that, oh yes, by the way, Frances Lankin won her seat in Beaches–Woodbine.

"I refused to leave the campaign office until I saw it on television—'til someone made it official for me," Lankin tells me ten years later at her Queen's Park office. "And I think back now and I must have been a total basket case in that last period of the campaign. I'd never experienced anything like it in my life. I probably never will again. It's just raw emotion, exhaustion, and adrenaline that was happening there."

Those are the moments politicians live for. It's why they knock on thousands of doors, engage in endless small talk with constituents, and put up with the internecine battles within caucus and with their opponents. Because there can't be any greater feeling than bucking the odds, confounding the experts, winning your first election, and going shopping for "cabinet minister clothes."

And for Frances Lankin, on September 6, 1990, there wasn't.

It was pretty apparent from the get-go that Lankin was going into cabinet. She was a woman, she represented a Toronto riding, and she had deep roots in the union movement. In the New Democratic Party, those are all good things.

What ministry she'd get was a little more complicated. The new premier's first intention was to take advantage of her background in corrections by making her minister of correctional services and solicitor-general, together. Putting a woman in what's always been considered a macho portfolio would make a strong statement on how Bob Rae's government would be different. But there was a problem. When she was in the jail guards' union, Lankin put the motion on the floor to conduct Ontario's first and only illegal corrections' strike. She told the new premier that could prove embarrassing to the government somewhere down the road.

Apparently Rae agreed, because a day later he called Lankin back and offered her the education portfolio. But that didn't last long either. For reasons Lankin never learned, Rae called back a third time—this time, the day before the swearing-in—and offered her an impressive trifecta: chair of management board, minister of government services, and chair of cabinet. Was Lankin ready for the task ahead?

"I was scared shitless," she admits. "I ran to be the goddamned best member of opposition they'd ever seen, right? To actually end up in cabinet and have to think about being part of running a government and actually overseeing a portfolio in a ministry, I mean it was really scary."

And funny. The first time one of her staffers answered a question with "Yes, Minister," Lankin burst out laughing, unable to think of anything except the British sitcom of the same title.

"I said right from the beginning, 'My name is Frances.' I couldn't handle being called 'Minister,'" she says. (In others, I'd be tempted to see this as false modesty. However, Lankin was once booked to appear on a TVOntario program I was hosting. She arrived by herself—no hangers-on, almost unheard of for cabinet ministers—having taken the subway from the legislature to our studios.)

She may not have been able to handle being called "Minister," but she loved the gig. Reading briefing books until 4 a.m., having every minute of every day jam-packed with discussions about issues, and a car and a driver available, if not always used.

"People would schedule you to end one meeting at ten o'clock, begin the next meeting at ten o'clock and it's two buildings over," Lankin remembers. "I had bladder infections several times during the first years because there was never enough time to go to the bathroom!"

One of the most dramatic incidents during the Rae government's term was the bombing of Henry Morgentaler's abortion clinic in downtown Toronto. The clinic's destruction had an impact far beyond the obvious—an end to providing abortion services. As the first free-standing clinic in the province, it was a highly emotional symbol, even a shrine, to women who'd spent years fighting for abortion rights. One of those women was Frances Lankin, who happened to have been shuffled to the Ministry of Health just before the incident took place.

"It was such a shocking thing to hear about the bombing," she says. "And I immediately went to the clinic, not as a minister. I went as a woman who'd spent years in demonstrations. And it was a sadness that our clinic had been bombed."

She soon learned the difference between being an activist and being the person who gets to decide what happens next.

"To be able to go into cabinet and say, 'We're not going to let this stop women from getting access to a legal health service. We have to respond as government,'" she says, still visibly moved. "And then to realize, I can do something about this. And do it."

Lankin formed a kind of tag team with Ontario's first female attorney general, Marion Boyd. The health minister ensured the dollars were there to rebuild the clinic at another location. The attorney general attended to the security side, by getting an injunction against pro-life pickets.

"There are things that I'd spent years dedicated to achieving as a lobbyist, and all of a sudden there I was, able to do it as a minister," Lankin says. "It was all the dreams of an organizer/activist/feminist come together in this world of politics."

Unfortunately for Lankin, she'd soon experience the other side of The Life—the side that takes a bite out of your soul, chews you up, spits you out, and leaves you on the side of the highway like roadkill.

As Audrey McLaughlin, the former NDP leader, put it, one has to be philosophical about being a New Democrat in Ontario. "We're very good at losing and rationalizing it."

So it's perhaps a cruel twist of fate that the first ever NDP government in Canada's richest province found itself elected on the eve of the worst recession since the Great Depression. So many of the projects New Democrats had championed all their lives were simply out of the question. Every time the finance minister, Floyd Laughren, saw the bureaucrats from the revenue section of his ministry coming down the hall, he wanted to hide. Government revenues were constantly plummeting, with no end in sight.

The government determined it needed to save six billion dollars or the deficit would be right through the roof. It was already in the attic. The solution was a three-pronged approach: two billion dollars in tax increases, two billion dollars in spending cuts, and finally, the two billion dollars that ripped apart the heart and soul of the NDP—the Social Contract.

"The absolute worst time ever in government, the hardest, most difficult, blackest and the worst day, all wrapped up around the Social Contract," says Frances Lankin.

The idea was simple. Rather than lay off thousands of public sector workers to find the last two billion in savings, the NDP would ask everyone to put a little water in their wine. The government itself employed about eighty thousand people, but the broader public sector—people who worked for schools, hospitals, and municipalities—brought the number closer to one million. If they could be convinced to take some unpaid days off work, no one would have to be fired to realize the savings. Given how many thousands of people in the private sector had already lost their jobs because of the recession, it seemed a reasonable way to protect both jobs and services.

"I remember being so hopeful that people would see there was an opportunity here to do something different," Lankin says.

Lankin hoped the NDP's special relationship with the labour movement would count for something. But the relationship wasn't as special as she thought.

"Their first reaction was, 'Your numbers are bullshit. You're lying to us,'" Lankin says. So labour leaders were called in for special briefings from Finance Ministry officials. The numbers suggested that without the mix of tax increases, spending cuts, and the Social Contract, the deficit would hit sixteen billion dollars. The labour reps responded by saying the government shouldn't be blaming them for its own mismanagement. The union recommended other ways of saving money, but in the end, it didn't amount to nearly enough. Major confrontation seemed imminent.

"But I kept believing, God, someone's got to understand and buy into the big picture here," Lankin says.

But no one did. None of the public-sector unions was prepared to play along. The public was treated to the extraordinary sight of the president of the Ontario Medical Association holding hands with his fellow "trade unionists" singing "Solidarity Forever" as the negotiations broke down.

The question for the province was, what next? Could the Ontario government unilaterally abrogate collectively bargained contracts and impose the two billion in savings? Could an NDP government do that?

Frances Lankin hoped not. She fought against the idea in caucus, at the cabinet table, at meetings of the powerful priorities and planning committee—the so-called "inner cabinet." And she argued against it in private meetings with the premier, the premier's secretary to cabinet, his top policy people, and the list went on. At one point, during a caucus debate, she was hooted down by her fellow MPPs. Clearly, the political winds were blowing another way.

The cabinet held a special meeting at Queen's Park. Lankin drove down from her cottage on Lake Simcoe and arrived with her mind made up. She was going to resign from cabinet. The premier's principal secretary, Melody Morrison, intercepted her on the way into the meeting.

"Frances, I need to talk to you," she said.

"Mel, I need to talk to you," Lankin shot back. "I need you to know I'm going in there to resign. I want you to find Bob for me. I want to talk to him outside of the cabinet meeting and then I'm leaving. I've got to get out of here."

"No," Morrison came back. "Bob has come around in his thinking and thinks that legislating this isn't the right way and that we've got to find something else here."

So, there was still hope. Lankin entered the meeting and did hear the premier talk about finding another way. "The political downside with our own folks is too high," Rae said.

But in the end, there were simply more votes at the cabinet table to confront the unions and legislate the two billion in savings. In caucus, the support for legislation was even higher and more enthusiastic, so intense was the anger at the union leaders for pulling the plug on the negotiations. Lankin was still prepared to resign, but now several union leaders were urging her to hang in there, to make sure the legislation was drafted with their concerns in mind. That, plus her own guilt over what her colleagues might think, persuaded her to stay and tough it out.

"It was a horrible, hard thing to decide to walk out of something like that," she says. "You feel like you're betraying people. You know it's going to be a political issue. You know it's going to cause the premier all sorts of problems."

At one o'clock in the morning, the night before the vote in the legislature, Lankin received a phone call from one of her closest allies in the union movement. Julie Davis was both one of the most prominent members of the Canadian Union of Public Employees, and president of the Ontario NDP. She'd been one of Lankin's best friends for years, so much so, the pair had rented a cottage together on Lake Simcoe for a decade. Davis was in Whitehorse with Audrey McLaughlin, but absolutely had to talk to Lankin, regardless of the time. Predictably, Lankin picked up the phone after one ring. It may have been 1 a.m. but she wasn't asleep.

Davis begged Lankin to vote against the proposal, or at least not show up for the vote. "She was very upset and distressed, as was I," Davis recalls. Lankin felt as if she were in the middle of a violent tug o' war. "What do I do now?" she asked herself.

(Incidentally, after she got off the phone with Lankin, Davis rang up Ontario's premier, Bob Rae, even though it was now two o'clock in the morning. She made similar pleadings to pull the bill, saying it would wreck labour's relationship with the NDP for a decade. Rae told her the train was too far down the tracks and there was no turning back.)

The next morning, Frances Lankin had one last private meeting with Premier Rae and his closest cabinet colleagues. Lankin ended up furious and in tears. One cabinet minister, Karen Haslam, did resign rather than support the package. But Lankin had already crossed her Rubicon.

"I had become part of, complicit in all of this, and hated every minute of it," she says. When it came time to vote in the legislature, Lankin virtually went numb. She tuned out. When her name was called, someone had to prod her to stand up and be counted. She was in a daze. "And tears were streaming down my face as I stood up to vote and I went out into the lobby and another caucus member, trade unionist, a good guy, and I sobbed in each other's arms for five or ten minutes before we could leave the members' lounge that night. It was a horrible day."

Frances Lankin survived that horrible day. Eventually, she and Julie Davis would reconnect at the cottage on Lake Simcoe, pull an all-nighter with a major heart-to-heart talk, drink much wine and cognac, cry a lot, and rebuild their friendship.

But Lankin wasn't done experiencing the heartbreak of politics. After Bob Rae resigned as NDP leader following the 1995 election, all eyes in the party were on her. To friends, foes, and impartial observers, it was a given that she'd run for the vacated NDP leadership. And that was part of the problem.

"I was so ambivalent," Lankin says. "I went back and forth and back and forth in my own mind. And I should have listened to that. That probably was a good sign that maybe this wasn't the right thing for me to do."

Lankin, herself, may have been struggling with the decision to run, but nobody else was having any of that. Her friends insisted she run because she was the best candidate to replace Rae. Her enemies were sure she was nakedly ambitious in her heart and weren't buying her entreaties for more time to decide. The media saw a savvy, well-spoken woman with a solid base of support in Toronto, and couldn't understand why she wouldn't run. Of course, Lankin was going to run. Everyone had decided she was the favourite.

Everyone, that is, except the candidate herself. "I was scared. I was scared of rejection, scared of failure," she admits. But she got in anyway. She had to. Everyone expected it.

The campaign to replace Bob Rae featured plenty of surreal moments. Lankin's chief competitor was fellow cabinet minister Howard Hampton. The two couldn't have been more different. While Lankin's riding was half an hour from Queen's Park, Hampton's was so far away, it was in a different time zone (Rainy River in Northwestern Ontario—same time zone as Manitoba). Where Lankin came up through the union and women's movements, Hampton was a lawyer and former varsity hockey player at the

University of Toronto. Lankin was married, then divorced, then in a common-law relationship, then separated from that. Hampton was married to fellow caucus mate Shelley Martel, whose father, Eli, was also an MPP twenty years earlier.

What they had in common was that they both served in Bob Rae's cabinet. But somehow, Lankin came to be seen as Rae's preferred candidate, which was the kiss of death for her. Somehow, she was forced to defend the Social Contract to angry NDP delegates who hated the policy, even though she actually argued against it in cabinet. Meanwhile, Hampton became the champion of the "outs," even though he supported the Social Contract in cabinet.

"There was a lot of stuff that happened that just wasn't fair," Lankin says. "I felt offended. But that's life in politics."

On convention day, Lankin actually topped the first ballot. But her numbers were well below what they needed to be to assure victory. Hampton won on the third ballot.

"There was nothing in that process that I can say I learned from and I'm a better person for having experienced that," Lankin admits regretfully, "other than continuing to learn how to be gracious in defeat."

Lankin survived the leadership convention experience and the following general election, which was even worse. Her first campaign victory was straight out of a fairy tale. Her final one, the 1999 election, was a horror story. She was one of just nine New Democrat MPPs to survive in Mike Harris's Ontario. She pursued her passion for public life for two years, then received an offer to head the United Way of Greater Toronto that was just too good to refuse.

"Politics is the most amazing experience I have had in my life," she says. "It is the greatest honour that I will ever have bestowed upon me. I learned more than a whole lifetime of learning would have provided me in other settings.

"This place is addictive," Lankin says of the Ontario legislature. "There are the inane theatrics to this place. But there's a drama as well."

PAM BARRETT MAY HAVE DECIDED THAT SHE was going to be an NDP politician, but her body had other ideas. On April 1, 1974, doctors diagnosed she had Hodgkin's disease—cancer of the lymph nodes. She was twenty years old. By the time her doctors caught it, she was already in the final stages of the illness. It was April Fool's Day but she didn't much like the joke. "I was told to get ready for the box," she says in her typical don't-sugarcoat-it style. Her medical team offered to make her a guinea pig and so she agreed to seven months of a new kind of experimental radiation therapy. That, plus two months of surgery and recovery time, and somehow Pam Barrett pulled through. Did the brush with death change her mind about her future? Not in the least. Barrett decided to pursue post-secondary education (University of Alberta in Edmonton, Glasgow University in Scotland) to learn the best way to defend social democracy.

Now she was ready to apply her academic experience to the real thing. Barrett returned to Alberta and worked her way into a research job in the office of the NDP leader, Grant Notley. She loved the gig and admired the leader, who'd been a mentor to her since he won his party's leadership in 1968.

But then the Alberta Federation of Labour came calling. They wanted Barrett to help organize Solidarity Alberta, a broad-based coalition of organizations opposed to the anti-labour posturing of the provincial government. They offered her a $10,000 raise to help her make up her mind. It helped. She took the job.

One day, Barrett found herself racing to a convention in Calgary to speak to a gathering of plumbers. She was running late, so she dashed in, gave her address, and brought the crowd to its feet with an emotional oration. What she didn't realize in her haste was that she breezed right past Notley on the way to the stage.

He spoke after she did. "Now you know why we need to elect people like Pam Barrett to join me in the legislative assembly!" Notley said, bringing the crowd to its feet again.

And then Grant Notley pulled a fast one on Barrett. In June, 1984, he organized a lunch at a Calgary restaurant with a man named Davis Swan, who worked at Petro-Canada. Notley wondered if Barrett wanted to tag along and help convince Swan to move to Edmonton, where he'd be a star candidate for the NDP in the next election. Swan had previously run unsuccessfully in Calgary, but

Notley thought the candidate would have a better shot at winning if he moved to Edmonton Centre.

What did Barrett think of Swan? "Best-lookin' guy in Calgary, man," as only Pam Barrett can say it. "I mean, oooh, yum."

Notley was also using Swan as a bit of a misdirection trick on Barrett. Every time Swan questioned whether he could win Edmonton Centre, Notley suggested if Swan couldn't do it, Pam always could.

After teasing Barrett with that possibility a few times, Notley watched Barrett slam her fist down on the table and say, "Grant, if I run anywhere it's going to be in [Edmonton] Highlands. That's where I've lived all my life."

The bait was dangled, and taken.

Seeing Notley again also reminded Barrett of how much she loved what he stood for and how much she missed life at the legislature. So she took the pay cut and in August, 1984, returned to Notley's office as senior researcher, with a not-so-secret view to running some day. "I needed the ability to work again with the guy I thought was the best politician in Canada since Tommy Douglas," she says.

Soon, Barrett announced she'd seek the NDP nomination in Edmonton Highlands and proceeded to work tirelessly selling memberships to the meeting, which would be held on January 30, 1985. It didn't leave much time.

And then, the worst possible thing happened—even worse than staring down cancer, which she'd done more than a decade earlier.

On October 19, 1984, Pam Barrett's world fell apart. Her mentor, her idol, her hero, Grant Notley, died in a plane crash near High Prairie, Alberta. He had been a one-man caucus for eleven years, keeping the NDP flame alive. He was completely integral to Barrett's involvement in politics. And now he was gone.

"When he became leader in 1968, I went to every meeting I could," Barrett recalls. "Grant was a spark, man. He had a way with words. I was one of those young little hippies that wanted inspiration, and I got it from him."

"And after he was no longer there to provide that inspiration?" I ask.

"Well, I cried myself to sleep every night from the day we found out he was killed, until Christmas Eve that year, 1984," she says. "And that whole period was just a blur for me, a complete blur."

Just as beating cancer inspired Barrett to rededicate herself to her cause, Notley's death achieved the same outcome. Barrett won her party's nomination in January, 1985, and captured the Highlands seat in the election the following year. All told, her campaign for her first run at elective office lasted twenty months—knocking on doors three times a week in the winter, and four times a week in the warmer weather.

In many respects, it was the most extraordinary election for the NDP in Alberta history. The party went from two seats in 1982 to sixteen in 1986, under new leader Ray Martin. The Tories, under Don Getty, still won the election, but lost fourteen seats in the process.

After she was sworn in, Barrett wrote two personal commandments to herself on a piece of paper, and taped them to her desk in the legislature. That paper stayed taped on her desk for seven years.

She promised herself that before she ever opened her mouth, she'd always remember on whose behalf she was speaking. And second, she would always ask herself whether she was doing the honourable thing.

Grant Notley would have wanted it that way.

One of the first things Barrett discovered is that politics can be even trickier in the front rooms than in the backrooms. She was appointed to the board of internal economy, a kind of board of directors for the legislature itself. Within a couple of years of her election, the issue of a possible pay raise for MLAs came up. Barrett thought a pay hike seemed reasonable, given that it had been ten years since the last one. But she wanted an agreement from the other parties that if politicians' salaries went up, so too would workers' compensation and welfare rates.

Barrett thought she had a deal. But she didn't. "I got sucked into believing that they would [raise all the rates]," Barrett says. In fact, the government raised the other rates by 3 per cent, and MLAs' salaries by 10 per cent. The electorate was furious, particularly with her. Rules didn't permit her to change her vote. The optics were terrible.

"I don't criticize anybody for giving me flak over that," Barrett says. "I was too naïve. The public had greater faith in me, and I hurt that faith, and they were right."

In fact, a combination of factors was leading Barrett to face some tough realities about her time in politics. She was routinely putting in eighty- to ninety-hour weeks when the house was in session. Even when the legislature wasn't sitting, she'd log sixty-hour weeks. She caught the flu and for six months couldn't beat it. She was dramatically overdoing it. This was a woman who'd already had a run-in with cancer, which left her immune system in pretty bad shape.

Ultimately, Pam Barrett concluded she just couldn't hack it any more. She needed a break in the worst way. So she decided not to stand in the next election. She removed the piece of paper with the two commandments from her desk in the legislature and returned to journalism with a daily television and radio show, and a weekly column in the *Edmonton Sun*.

"That's where I started off, honey," Barrett says. (She loves calling me honey. I suspect she loves calling everyone honey.) Barrett's post-graduate work was in media. She'd previously worked for CBC Radio. "So it was almost like going home for me," she says.

But nothing went according to script in Barrett's career, and this departure from politics would be no exception. When the New Democrats were wiped out in the 1993 election, all eyes started to focus on Barrett. Party members started a Draft Pam Barrett campaign to pressure her back into The Life.

"Eventually I caved in to the pressure," she says.

Why did she succumb?

"I got bugged, bugged, bugged, and gee, just a little more bugging."

But it wasn't just that. Barrett could read the tea leaves as well as anyone. The Conservative government, now under Ralph Klein, was making deep cuts to spending programs, without, in Barrett's view, any opposition from the Liberals. She became convinced that the cuts would continue unless there was an NDP presence in the legislature, and the party's pollster had already told her there wouldn't be a New Democrat in the legislature unless she were the leader.

"It was ultimately my social conscience that dictated," Barrett says. "I didn't want to say yes, but my conscience would not let me say no."

How badly did the New Democrat want Barrett at the helm? Badly enough to give her 73 per cent of the votes on the first and only ballot of her September, 1996, leadership convention.

In politics, timing is everything, and in Alberta in 1997, the tide was with Ralph Klein. The former mayor of Calgary and television reporter breathed new life into the Alberta Tory party, bringing its seat count from fifty-one under Don Getty to sixty-three in that March, 1997, election. The good news for Barrett was that the NDP did not get shut out again. Barrett won back her seat in Edmonton–Highlands, and Raj Pannu took Edmonton–Strathcona. But that was it. A caucus of two. The New Democrats had been there before. And they were there again.

"It's actually pretty easy if you've got the fire in your belly and you've got the compassion in your heart," she says. Maybe so, but it still adds up to only one question during a fifty-minute Question Period.

And then, Pam Barrett did it again. Less than two years after that '97 election, she surprised everyone by asking for a temporary leave of absence as NDP leader. She needed time away from politics to deal with an accumulation of personal problems. On June 8, 1997, her mother died. A year later, one of her closest friends, Larry McClure, committed suicide. McClure's friends, including Barrett, needed lots of time to work through the shame and guilt of his suicide. And Barrett was going through a difficult divorce. It was all too much. So she sought professional psychological counselling and learned to meditate.

But Barrett struggled through her problems and returned to politics to enjoy, perhaps, her finest moment. On March 10, 1998, the Alberta government introduced a bill which reminded Barrett why she needed to be in public life. The bill attempted to limit the rights of those who had been wrongfully institutionalized and sterilized from the 1930s, all the way up to the 1970s. Limits would be placed on any individual claim. And the government vowed to use the "notwithstanding clause" of the Constitution to void any court interference and defend its plans.

Barrett had other plans for Question Period that day, which she promptly scrapped. She read the bill lightning fast and raced downstairs to consult with party staffers.

"I didn't even write out the questions," she says. "I just flew back up into the house. I went white in horror. And I brought the government down that day."

Not quite, but you get the drift. Barrett's pit-bull opposition to the bill caught the government off guard. They tried to have her question ruled out of order, but failed. She knew the rules. Attack she did.

At a news conference later that day, Premier Klein was deluged with questions from reporters. It became apparent the government underestimated the criticism the bill provoked. So Klein pulled the bill the next day. And Barrett complimented the government for doing so.

"When you've centred your entire life fighting for the underdog, and you win it in triple force, there is no high like it," Barrett says of that experience. "My soul soared in joy."

Barrett's high was *so* high because she'd been fighting for fifteen years on behalf of one particular victim—her next-door neighbour.

"He was filled with gratitude," she recalls. "His cup runneth over. He couldn't believe the audacity of what the government had tried to do, and he was delighted that I had stood them down. It was magic. Oh, honey, did I win big!" Barrett explodes with laughter.

The NDP leader eventually saw victims get much better compensation packages. And it probably wouldn't have happened had Pam Barrett not been in the Alberta legislature.

Things had really turned around for Barrett. She had confronted and defeated the personal problems which temporarily took her away from politics. She had put the Alberta New Democrats back on the map, doubling the party's membership and making them a relevant force in the legislature.

And then came the most famous visit to a dentist's office that any Canadian has ever taken.

Pam Barrett celebrated the new millennium resolved to get herself shipshape for the next Alberta election. She was forty-six years old, still working too hard, and dealing with the effects of a long history of health problems. One of the things Barrett decided she needed was a nicer smile on her campaign posters. So she made an appointment with her dentist, twenty-five-year veteran David Oyen, to have some veneers placed on her teeth. Dr. Oyen proceeded to give Barrett an anaesthetic to numb the pain.

Barrett suffered an extreme allergic reaction to the injection and went into convulsions. Her entire body went numb, her throat swelled up, and she found she couldn't breathe. She told her dentist "I'm going. I'm dying," and even though a lapsed Catholic, made the sign of the cross across her chest.

Then Pam Barrett died, at least, she felt as if she had died, just for a second. And then she came out of it. Her dentist immediately performed mouth-to-mouth resuscitation and tried to keep her calm, until help arrived.

She was raced to the Royal Alexandra Hospital, still fighting convulsions, and suffered two similar blackouts in the hospital. During one, she remembers holding a nurse's hand and feeling her soul leave her body. Her spirit looked down from above, seeing her body still with the nurse. And then suddenly, it was over and her soul returned.

She didn't see God, which for a moment, made her wonder whether she might be headed in the other direction.

Once she recovered her bearings, Barrett called the president of the NDP, Les Steel. She asked him to come to the hospital, which he did. She got into a wheelchair so she could go for a smoke. As Steel wheeled her outside, he made a joke about the thrill of finally being able to push the leader around. Then Barrett told him what had happened. He disputed her account. But he also saw a haunted look on Barrett's face and knew something had happened.

Three hours after she'd entered the hospital, fearful she was about to die, Pam Barrett went home. The incredible events of that day led the NDP leader to one conclusion—she had to find a new path. God was telling her she could understand life so much more profoundly if she quit politics and did something else. And so, on February 2, 2000, Pam Barrett once again stepped away from the all-consuming life of politics, just two weeks before the Alberta legislature was to reconvene, and Barrett was to lead the fight against Premier Ralph Klein's controversial health reforms.

"I'm on a mission, darlin'," is how she now describes her life.

"What's the difference between dying and being dead?" I wonder.

"Dying was not fun, believe me," she says. "That was scary. There's nothing like it. Being dead is just fine. Being dead was being in a wonderful, warm, grey mist of endless love, endless comfort, pure relief."

The out-of-body experience was different. A few minutes after Barrett's spirit reunited with her body on that hospital gurney, she was convinced God was telling her to find her soul. Barrett wants to spend the next phase of her life enlightening others, promoting love, and improving the collective good.

"So I have come full circle," she says. "I'm back to my socialist principles, you know what I mean?"

She's still friends with David Oyen, the dentist in whose chair her adventure began. And no, she hasn't boycotted dentists. In fact, she's received four different opinions as to what might have caused the dramatic reaction she experienced—everything from an adverse reaction to the anaesthetic in the injection to the latex in the dentist's gloves.

As we wrap up our conversation, she takes a long drag on her Gitane cigarette. I ask her how it tastes. Her answer is as much about life as it is about the tobacco.

"Wonderful, honey!"

WHEN WAS THE MOST INTERESTING ERA to be hanging around local politics in Canada? Ask any veteran, and chances are they'll say the 1970s. Reformers, rather than developers, were carrying the day at city halls across the country. In Toronto, the battle over whether to build the Spadina Expressway crystallized the war between the city and the suburbs. It was simply a marvellous time to be active in municipal affairs.

It was in this atmosphere that Derwyn Shea's interest in politics began to manifest itself. Although he was now an Anglican priest at the Church of St. Clement–Riverdale, and working to create continuing studies programs at Humber College in the city of York, he accepted an appointment to Toronto's planning board. Apparently, he did a creditable enough job during his ten years on the board (four as chairman), because Mayor David Crombie and company were telling him to dive deeper into local politics. Shea kept saying no. They kept saying, do it.

Finally, in August, 1982, he went to Humber College's president and apologized for what he was about to tell him. "I've done something really untoward," Shea recalls telling Gordon Wragg. "I've agreed to run for city council."

Wragg smiled. "Do you have a chance of winning?" he asked.

"Not a hope," Shea answered. "There's no vacancy."

"Well, why don't you do it, and put it down as an interesting experience," the president told him.

I pursue this issue with Shea, because I've heard the same story too often from too many candidates. They run for office, convinced they're going to lose, but they do it anyway. Why does anybody undertake anything if they're convinced it's going to end in failure?

This is one aspect of public life most voters can't understand. But people who stand for office in hopeless situations do so for a few simple reasons. First, campaigning can be fun. The act of putting together a team, unified in common cause, can be exhilarating. Second, a great deal of wisdom can be gained, not in spite of a loss, but particularly in a losing effort. And finally, lightning does strike in politics. Upsets do happen. Bob Rae did become premier of Ontario. As they say in the lottery business, if ya wanna win, ya gotta buy a ticket.

So, did Shea really think he had no chance of winning?

"Not a hope. Not a hope. Not a hope," he insists.

Each ward elected two city councillors, and it's true, Shea was up against two incumbents, and in local politics, incumbents virtually always win.

So why run? First, Shea was convinced a whole host of local issues—taxes, the environment, community development—weren't being properly addressed by the two incumbents on council. Second, the opportunity was personally interesting.

"I thought it was important to at least let me experience the electoral process from the other side," he says straightforwardly. "Not from the side of the electorate, but as someone whose name is on a lawn sign, and let me really feel the intimacy of that process so that, in future, if I ever teach or talk about it, I can at least honestly say: 'Been there, done that.'"

The first thing Shea discovered about campaigning? It's a lot different from preaching. Modesty is out. Brass is in. The first time he saw his name on a lawn sign, he was embarrassed. "I thought it was just too much ego flying," he says. Shea does have an ego. To preach in front of hundreds of congregants takes some ego. However, unlike other politicians, he thinks he may have been able to keep his in check, "because every Sunday and mid-weeks I had to kneel before the altar and remind myself that I was accountable to someone much higher than myself. So that I think was a saving grace for me."

When election day rolled around in November, 1982, one thing became apparent. Derwyn Shea's powers of prognostication weren't very good. He vaulted past both incumbents and came first. He was now an Anglican priest *and* a politician. His mother must have known this day would come. After all, she named him Derwyn after Archbishop Derwyn Owen, a former primate of the Canadian church. And she gave him Spencer as a middle name—the same as Winston Churchill's.

However, now Derwyn Shea was living a bit of a double life. At city hall, he represented the reasonably prosperous High Park and Swansea neighbourhoods of Toronto in the west end, where his mother lived. And on Sundays, he'd preach at St. Clement's, in the poor, working-class part of Riverdale in the east end. "Never mix parish and politics," he says.

Before long, he found himself taking on more and more responsibility. He became the first politician in modern times to be president of the Canadian National Exhibition, a post which no doubt carried with it some emotion. The CNE was, after all, the last piece of Canadian soil his oldest brother would have trod upon before dying in battle.

He was on Metropolitan Toronto's executive committee, a prize usually reserved for heavy-hitters or close associates of the Metro Chairman. He became chairman of O'Keefe Centre, the thirty-two-hundred-seat performing arts complex, over which the city had taken responsibility. The O'Keefe turned in a surplus to Toronto taxpayers every year Shea was its chairman.

"What I did may not have made the front page of the paper, but I enjoyed serving," Shea says.

But he didn't like everything about the job. When it involved service or grappling with issues, it was terrific.

"I hated the politics, *hated* the politics," he says, rolling his eyes. "I hate the posturing and I hate the egos that start clashing. I find it a real waste of time and energy."

Conversely, he loved the little moments The Life had to offer, for example, giving a public service award to a constituent who was a housewife. The woman had spent years caring for the sick and disabled.

"She justified my faith in the essential goodness of people," he says. "It justifies all the garbage you have to put up with. You say to yourself, 'You know what? That was good.' Historically it will never amount to a footnote, in a footnote, in a footnote. But it was the right thing to do at the right time. So when you finish, you finish having a sense of some integrity and you can look at yourself in the mirror and say, I really tried. I may not have been the greatest member of council, I don't think I was the worst. And then you have a sense that it's time to move on."

During our entire conversation, Shea rarely betrays any anger at his former political colleagues, except when the issue of "moving on" comes up. He evidently thinks too many politicians hang around too long.

"Some may get so caught up in the attraction of the position or in some cases even the perks and that's regretful," he says. "I'm still not impressed by people who say, 'I've been on Toronto council for twenty years.' My response is, can't you get a job? I don't mean that unkindly, but perhaps it's time to move on."

After ten years on the planning board and twelve years in elected office, it was time for a change, or as Shea puts it, "move up or out." He'd always been a fiscal conservative and liked what he was hearing about the Common Sense Revolution. When he was approached in 1993 to seek the PC nomination in High Park–Swansea, he went for it.

On the surface, it looked like appalling political judgement. No one was taking the Tories seriously. They were at 20 per cent in the polls and so off the political radar screen in Toronto, Shea won his nomination by acclamation. In a riding of eighty thousand inhabitants, not a single person, other than Shea, wanted to run as a Conservative.

"Everybody's word on council was, 'Goodbye, Shea,'" he recalls. "'He's gone, he's toast, he's finished,'" he says, betraying just a bit of a chip on his shoulder.

And yet, history repeated itself. His hopeless venture paid off. And best of all, his ninety-four-year-old mother was able to come to Queen's Park and watch her son be sworn into office as a member of the legislature. "I think for her that was a very special moment," Shea says. He is at his most solemn in our conversation as he recalls that day. His mother had just died a few months ago. She was almost ninety-nine years old.

Because the Conservatives won so many seats in the 1995 election, a dozen Tory MPPs had to sit on the opposition side of the house. There just wasn't enough room for the entire PC caucus to sit on one side. Shea refers to himself as "the leader of that rump," whose members took it upon themselves to offer mock grades when cabinet ministers responded during Question Period.

"Those collegial moments were really special for me in the house," he says. "We'd all quietly turn around and say, 'Eight-point-five' or 'Four,' or we'd put our heads down in embarrassment."

The dream of every elected parliamentarian is to sit at the cabinet table. Except Derwyn Shea? Can there really be so little ambition inside the man?

"An arrangement I had with my area bishop was that I would not go into the cabinet," he says. "If I went into the cabinet, I'd have to give up my parish. If the premier called me and said, 'I want you in my cabinet,' I'd have to say, 'I've got a problem. I've been a parish priest all of my working life. As much as I'd love to have served, I'd have to decline.' First and foremost, I'm a parish priest. Always have been. I can tell you straight out, my altar would have come first."

Maybe so, but Shea pushed the envelope with his bishop. He accepted a parliamentary assistantship from Premier Mike Harris. Back in his city hall days, the head of the Toronto Transit Commission, Al Leach, had to come before the executive committee and answer tough questions from politicians like Shea. Now, in an ironic twist, Shea would be answering to Leach, who'd quit the TTC, run for the Tories, and won an appointment as the municipal affairs minister. Shea became his parliamentary assistant. The reversal of roles probably didn't sit well with either man, given the many personal and professional disagreements they endured.

Notwithstanding that bad blood, Shea felt good about his service. He managed to get a private member's bill through the house—no mean feat in itself—designating Toronto's Humber River for special reclamation status.

"That was a really exciting moment to get that through parliament," Shea says. "I'm very proud of that. It gives us a chance to really make sure that river gets improved. That really made my day."

Unfortunately for Shea, there wouldn't be many more great days.

When Mike Harris became premier of Ontario, he forecast that there wouldn't be a blade of grass on the south lawn of Queen's Park that would not be trod upon by demonstrators by the time he was done implementing the Common Sense Revolution. The premier's forecast was accurate, and then some. No region of the province reacted with as much hostility to Harris's agenda for Ontario than its capital city. And Derwyn Shea was right in the middle of it. The war to amalgamate Toronto into a new "Megacity." Market value assessment of property tax rates. New rent-control rules tilting the balance for the first time in twenty years towards landlords. And huge education reforms prompting a province-wide strike by 120,000 teachers. Shea found himself on the opposite side of his government on some of these issues; on others, he quarrelled with the means by which the Tories were implementing the policies.

"Toronto has a style of proceeding with things and the government didn't reflect sensitivity to that style," Shea says firmly. Take property tax reassessment. For years, governments have tried but failed to level the playing field in Toronto, where some homes in the oldest part of the city were still paying taxes based on half-century-old assessment rates. Conversely, the newer suburbs, with their newer assessments, were carrying a disproportionate share of the burden. The Tories were determined to fix the inequity once and for all, but in Shea's view, were doing it with a sledgehammer. He quite correctly pointed out in private meetings with Ernie Eves, the minister of finance, that the government's policy could result in 400 per cent property tax increases for some of his constituents. People would have to sell their homes, unable to pay the new, higher taxes. Small businesses would simply go under. The conversation got ugly.

"Ernie has never forgiven me for those battles," Shea says. "We had shouting matches in his office. I went in there and I'm the one that kept pounding the table and yelling and screaming and saying, 'This is damn well not good enough.'"

"You yelled and screamed?" I ask. I've never seen Derwyn Shea yell and scream.

"I did," Shea says. "He yelled and screamed at me and I felt it was fair enough that he'd established the ground rules and so I was allowed to do the same thing, in mutual respect." Of course.

"Did you use profanity?"

"Yes."

"The 'F' word?" I ask.

"Not unless the word was 'Fundamental.' I was not prepared to roll over and let some thirty-year-old policy adviser scratch my tummy, not when my people are being hurt."

In fact, with all the turmoil around Toronto, it wasn't long before Shea almost was hurt. Police were called to his home after he received death threats over the telephone. And then there were the teachers.

"I had teachers on my front lawn yelling and screaming," Shea says. "They're carrying a coffin with their children and them, running around my backyard, shining their flashlights through my window and yelling and screaming and hammering on the door at nighttime. It's the kind of thing where your family says, 'What's going on here? How much of this do we have to take?' And you can say that's part of the political process but I don't think it is."

What Shea particularly found upsetting were the thoughts he was thinking in response.

"They raised in me the spectre of saying, 'Gee, maybe I should go out and see if I can get people to want to put on brown shirts or black shirts and go to their house and do the same thing.' And I object to that. I find that offensive."

What got him through those dark times?

"My altar. The Church. For me. It was my own personal special spiritual discipline. And my worship. It's a very precious part of my life."

At age sixty-two, and after four years of tough-as-nails politicking, Shea looked inside his gut and found the fire lacking. He'd had enough. "It was a very tough four years to be a Conservative," he says. "It really did take a lot out of me."

Now that he's out of politics and firmly ensconced solely at the church, does Shea miss public life?

"I don't miss the partisan politics," he says. "I find when I sat and I listened to passionate speeches from NDP or Liberals, in many cases I said, 'Damn right, I'm with you.' And I think many of us could, no matter what party you're in. There were times when I found the partisanship was just nonsense. It was grandstanding just to play to the media. I always felt we were there to perform a service that's at the highest good. I still believe in the philosopher king and *The Republic* and the greatest service. And I regret that sometimes, some practitioners forget that, including the public."

Derwyn Shea may be out of politics, but his days of crusading aren't over. Hundreds of seniors depend on him, as do many more parishioners. He's put in endless hours helping to create an association for former parliamentarians, a kind of self-help group for politicians who've had a hard time finding their bearings after their careers are over. I've known Derwyn Shea for almost twenty years and as we finish our conversation, I can tell there's something about him that's just a bit off. He misses The Life. So I ask him.

"Is your political career over?"

Silence. Long pause.

"Wasn't that an interesting question," he says, stalling for time.

"The pause was far more interesting than the question," I retort.

"Well then, maybe that's where I'll leave it—a pause."

For many, the crusade never ends.

THE HONOURABLE GENTLEMEN

About ten years ago, while roaming the hallways of Queen's Park, I happened upon a large group of high-school students who were getting the official tour of the Ontario legislature. I had a few minutes to kill before the news event I was covering was scheduled to begin, so I began chatting with the students. Truth be told, I interrupted the tour guide's presentation because she got something egregiously wrong. She reported to her utterly bored audience that John Alexander Macdonald was the first premier of Ontario.

"Sandfield," I interrupted, as I walked by.

"Pardon?" the tour guide said.

"The first premier of Ontario was John *Sandfield* Macdonald. John Alexander Macdonald was the first prime minister of Canada. They're two different guys."

"Oh," she said apologetically.

"Yeah, his statue's right underneath the window of the premier's office in front of the building," I added. She must have found me totally contemptible by this point, and I confess, in the retelling of this story, I do come off looking like a bit of a busybody. So, I did what all good conversationalists do when one of the participants is embarrassed. I changed the subject and started schmoozing with the kids.

After I found out what school they went to and who their least favourite teacher was, I wanted to know how many of them wanted to be premier of Ontario some day. Not a hand went up. Okay, how about a member of provincial parliament? We were standing right outside the beautiful double doors that lead onto the floor of the legislature. I was sure someone was entertaining thoughts of marching through those doors one day and continuing our wonderful democratic traditions.

No response.

"Well, does anyone follow politics at all? Even just a little bit?" I finally asked, sounding rather pathetic.

Nothing. Just some embarrassed "deer-caught-in-the-headlights" looks. After a few more questions, it became apparent that these typical Ontario high-school students found politics a gigantic waste of time.

I tell this story because I don't think 'twas ever thus. Unless the memories of my blessedly normal childhood in Hamilton, Ontario, are completely indicative of nothing—and I don't think they are—there was a time when young people in this country grew up thinking politicians were regular, decent folk. They weren't up there with hockey players, but they weren't disreputable bums either.

That view was no doubt shaped by the politicians I became aware of during my early years. One of the teachers at my school, John Smith, became an MPP in 1967, then a cabinet minister in William Davis's government. He was a very fine chap, and even came out of political retirement to run for the PCs in the 2000 federal election. (Alas, he came third, fifteen thousand votes behind the winner.)

But he wasn't the only one. A friend of my parents became an MP representing the west end. Another friend was elected to Hamilton City Council against some tall odds. And I can remember my parents, through a charity auction, purchasing a lunch for my brother and me with the Ontario Liberal leader of the day, Stuart Smith. Having lunch with a couple of school kids couldn't have been top priority for Dr. Smith, yet the memory of his graciousness and intelligence is still with me.

The politicians I knew weren't ruthless, aggressively ambitious egomaniacs determined to stiff their constituents. They actually saw politics as an honourable calling. And in my lifetime, there were two kings on the provincial scene who excelled at, and typified, that calling. They were William Davis and Peter Lougheed.

Much has been written about the rivalry these two men experienced, starting with Davis's desire for cheap gas prices for his millions of Ontario motorists, while Lougheed wanted higher returns for the oil patch. For a time, they were on different sides of the debate over the patriation of the Constitution. And both nearly ended up on opposite sides of the 1983 Progressive Conservative leadership convention.

Notwithstanding all that, these "honourable gentlemen" had a great deal in common. They were both born in July; Lougheed in 1928, Davis in 1929. Both became lawyers. Both were called to the bar the same year, 1955. Both played university football, Davis for the University of Toronto Varsity Blues, Lougheed for the University of Alberta Golden Bears. Lougheed actually has bragging rights in this department, since he played for the CFL's Edmonton Eskimos in 1949–50. He was a defensive half-back and kickoff return man ("I survived, although the knees are feeling it now," he jokes).

They were both Conservative premiers of big, important, rich provinces for fourteen years—the same fourteen years: 1971–85. They both won four elections. They were both intelligent political operators—Davis mastering Ontario's three-party system (a handy skill during the years he wasn't so popular); Lougheed creating a viable PC party in Alberta out of virtually nothing. The party had no seats and had never formed the government. He left a dynasty that's still in place today. And they both thought of themselves as Canadians first, and provincial politicians second. If winning four elections weren't enough, that last statement alone distinguishes them from virtually every other contemporary provincial premier.

Both of these occasional colleagues and rivals have been out of public life for more than a decade and a half now. Until Brian Mulroney came along, each of them had established the highest benchmark in Canada for making the most remarkable transition from first minister to private sector success story. Now in their seventies, they are both just wistful enough about the lure of their former lives to reminisce a bit.

I say "a bit" because anyone who knows the former premier of Ontario knows that trying to get a straight answer out of him about anything remotely controversial is like trying to nail jelly to the wall. Moreover, Davis has been extremely reticent to give interviews about his life. He's an extremely private man who holds so much inside it's a wonder he doesn't burst from all the secrets he's keeping.

In the autumn of 1995, I began pestering Davis with a series of letters and phone calls, asking him to sit down for a lengthy interview about his time in politics. I told him most of the world didn't know it, but the following March 1, 1996, would mark the twenty-fifth anniversary of his swearing-in as premier. I thought it appropriate that he give his first and only post–public life interview to TVOntario, given his indispensable role in the creation of the provincial broadcaster.

For months, he bobbed and weaved around the requests. His schedule, I was told, was too tight. In fact, he did seem to be on a plane every week, jetting off to some board meeting somewhere in North America.

With time running out, I asked the Happy Warrior himself, Hugh Segal, Davis's long-time friend and adviser, to put in a good word for me. I'm told Segal said something like, "Premier, I think you should do this while you still have all your marbles."

Somehow, at the eleventh hour, a block of time appeared and Davis and I sat down for three hours, cameras rolling. The ensuing documentary, *Bill Davis: A Main Street Man*, aired on TVOntario on the night of his twenty-fifth anniversary as premier. Surprisingly, the Ontario Conservative Party itself did nothing to observe the occasion, perhaps because Davis is not much loved by the new, more ideological Common Sense Revolutionaries in the Mike Harris government. (Some of Davis's friends had a small party for him instead.) Contrast that with the extravaganza held at the Palliser Hotel in Calgary in August, 1996, to honour Peter Lougheed's twenty-fifth anniversary. There were 120 invitees to that soiree, and Premier Ralph Klein was notable by his absence.

In any event, I shouldn't complain too much, because when I told Bill Davis I wanted to interview him again, this time for a book, he obliged right away. Although he didn't answer all of my questions ("Now Steven, if I tell you everything I'll have nothing left for my own memoirs . . ."), I believe he spoke more thoughtfully and at greater length "for the record," on issues he's never before discussed.

THE FIRST TIME I INTERVIEWED PETER LOUGHEED was in October, 1986. He'd been out of public life for a year and I wanted to talk to him for a CBC-TV news piece about how the transition to private life was going. At the time, he'd accumulated ten directorships on various corporate boards, while headquartered at the Calgary law firm Bennett, Jones.

Lougheed was warm and open and quite evidently loving his new life. "I'm stimulated without stress," he said. "Higher rewards too!"

Lougheed enjoyed the hectic schedule of public life and wanted it to continue.

"I wanted to be busy, as busy almost without stress as I was when I was premier." And after just a year, he seemed to have found the right mix of corporate boards, consulting, teaching, and community service, such as his honorary chairman's role on the organizing committee of the Calgary Olympic Winter Games.

"You're talking to a very lucky and very happy man," he said.

Now the quintessential politician-turned-businessman has taken on a new project, and it may be his greatest challenge yet. He'd like to convince young people to give politics a whirl, and forego climbing the corporate ladder for just a little while longer.

"I hope I can be a bit of an example to young people who are apprehensive about going into politics, because they're worried about what they can do after a political career," Lougheed said. "I hope I'm a small example of someone who's had a good political career, a lot of stimulation, and who can find a further career later in his life."

William Grenville Davis. Edgar Peter Lougheed. When politicians were more honourable gentlemen.

WILLIAM DAVIS DESCRIBES HIS ENTRY into politics as "environmental." His father, A. Grenville Davis (the "A" was for Albert but never used), was a crown attorney in Brampton, back then a sleepy community an hour northwest of Toronto. The elder Davis "had no politics because of his job, but I knew what his politics were," recalls his son. "Ours was a household where politics was discussed with some regularity." Adding to the political environment were family friendships with the local MP, Gordon Graydon, whose daughter was in the same year at school as Davis; and Tom Kennedy, the local MPP who briefly became premier of Ontario in 1948 after George Drew left the job to try federal politics. In case it needs mentioning, yes, they were all Tories.

By the time he was fourteen years old, Bill Davis found himself going to political meetings all around Ontario. "There was sort of an assumption that at some point in time I would be interested, and that probably I would enter into political life."

Davis's initial interest in politics was at the federal scene, particularly international affairs. During his second year at the University of Toronto he got a scholarship to attend the Institute of World Affairs in Connecticut. Delegates from around the world debated the major issues of the day. Secretly, Davis dreamed of being a future Canadian foreign minister, something to which his chief political mentor, Gordon Graydon, also aspired.

But politics is all about timing, and the next thing Davis knew, Gordon Graydon had died, and the candidate who was going to run provincially ran for Graydon's federal seat instead. And then Tom Kennedy retired, leaving a seat at Queen's Park vacant. Hello opportunity.

Davis grew up in a very proper Methodist home, where his father was also on the local school board, and the local hospital and library boards. His mother, Vera, was president of the Women's Christian Temperance Union and served on the women's auxiliaries at the church and the hospital. "So you grow up in an environment where my parents were all very much of the school that you really have to give something back to the community," he says.

And so, in 1958, at age twenty-eight, with three years of practising law under his belt, Bill Davis decided to stand for office. The decision would not only launch him on a twenty-five-year career in politics, but it would also bring the legal partnership of Davis and Davis to an end. Yes, father and son did law together for two years, occasionally on opposite sides of the same case. Davis insists he never kept score of the almost two dozen times the father tried to put the son's clients in jail.

Fast-forward to summertime in the year 2000. William Davis and I are walking along the peaceful walkways of University College at the University of Toronto. It must be the lovely weather, or the fun we're having reminiscing, or the atmosphere of the place, where he spent many joyous times as a youth, or all of the above, or something else entirely. Because for the first time since I've known him—and that's almost twenty years—Bill Davis is talking, without being prompted, about the most tragic episode in his life.

"My first wife and I met here," he says softly.

I am curious, but at the same time extremely respectful not to ask too much.

"Did you take classes together?" I ask.

"I think she took English and lived here," he says, pointing to one of the student residences. "And I took political science, which..."

I interrupt him. "Which we all know is more art than science, right?" We both chuckle.

The 1960s should have been an exciting time in Davis's political career—his rookie term as an MPP, a probable appointment to Premier John Robarts's cabinet in the offing.

Instead, Davis's wife, Helen, died of cancer. She was thirty-three. They had four children, the oldest of whom, Neil, was only seven. To cope with the tragedy, Davis sent Neil to live with his parents. His two daughters stayed in the family's home with a nanny. And the younger son was sent to Windsor to live with his maternal grandparents.

"It was a very difficult time for all of us," Neil Davis told me five years ago for the TVOntario documentary about his father. "He had to do something in order to deal with it. It was just so tragic to have four young children and lose his wife. He threw himself into politics and tried to deal with it that way."

On January 26, 1963, Davis would marry again, this time to someone he'd known practically from adolescence. Kathleen Louise Mackay was an American whose family spent its summers near the Davis's family cottage on Georgian Bay north of Honey Harbour.

They would also have a child, Davis's fifth. Through it all, the family somehow persevered.

Senator Norman Atkins, Davis's long-time friend and former political organizer, says the loss of his first wife still pains Davis to this day. "I don't think he's ever really gotten over her," he says.

WILLIAM DAVIS'S ROAD TO THE PREMIER'S OFFICE was nothing like Peter Lougheed's. Where Lougheed virtually created the Alberta Conservative Party out of nothing, Davis felt immense pressure to keep alive a dynasty that had ruled Ontario for almost three straight decades. So when Premier John Robarts announced his retirement in December, 1970, Davis found himself thrust into an intense battle to succeed the man they called "The Chairman of the Board." (As an aside, Robarts was probably the only Canadian political figure with the right mixture of gravitas and connection to the business world that would entitle him to share that moniker with Frank Sinatra.)

On February 12, 1971, thousands of Tories gathered at Maple Leaf Gardens for a marathon leadership convention. The event will perhaps forever be remembered for its screw-ups. The convention was run by Alan Eagleson, a one-time Conservative MPP, then the president of the Ontario PC Association. Also memorable were the voting machines. Supposedly "state-of-the-art," they broke down, dragging the delegates kicking and screaming towards midnight, before they could crown a winner.

Finally, Bill Davis defeated caucus-mate Allan Lawrence on the fourth ballot by just forty-four votes.

"It gave me a great sense of accomplishment," Davis recalls, but then adds, laughing, "It also took a day before I realized what I got myself into."

Norman Atkins ran the Lawrence campaign. "Billy Davis never forgave me for it," he says, "for putting him through the agony of surviving the convention. I told him it was the best thing that ever happened to him, but he didn't think so at the time."

On March 1, 1971, forty-one-year-old William Davis was sworn into office as Ontario's eighteenth premier. The outgoing premier,

John Robarts, offered him some parting advice. "He said with a smile, 'I've only left you with a couple of problems,'" Davis recalls. "'Spadina and the separate schools.'"

Describing "Spadina and the separate schools" as "problems" is a bit like that knight in *Monty Python and the Holy Grail* describing the severing of all his limbs in a duel as simple "flesh wounds."

Metropolitan Toronto Council had decided to build the Spadina Expressway through the heart of one of the city's most desirable neighbourhoods in hopes of getting suburban commuters downtown more quickly. It was a debate over public transit versus the car. Cherishing downtown neighbourhoods over transient suburbanites, whose only love for those neighbourhoods was whizzing through them on their way to work. These issues were a huge test for the freshman premier, who represented rural Brampton but wanted to show he understood cities (not to mention wanting their rich number of seats, which could help ensure his re-election.)

And separate school funding—one of the most contentious issues since the founding of Upper Canada in 1791. In Ontario, the public school system had been publicly funded from kindergarten to grade thirteen. The Roman Catholic, or separate, school system only received public funding to grade eight. Catholics thought that discriminatory, that the original deal which brought Canada together promised a fully funded Protestant system in Quebec for the English minority, and a fully funded separate system in Ontario for the Catholic minority. Trouble was, the Constitution only mentioned full funding for "common schools," and Ontario had always interpreted that to mean up to grade eight only.

Liberals and New Democrats traditionally sought extending full funding to the entire separate school system, but Tories didn't. They might add a year or two along the way, but a fully funded Catholic system? No way. Not in Orange Ontario.

At this point, Catholics didn't make up more than half the population of Ontario as they do today. They were a significant minority, but still just a minority. They had hoped the new premier would lend a fresh set of ears to a long-simmering dispute. Both of Davis's chief political opponents of the day thought he'd at least let the issue lie low, if not support full funding outright, lest ethnic tensions be inflamed in the province.

It didn't quite work out that way. Davis became a hero to Toronto's urban dwellers when he blocked the wishes of Metro Toronto Council (dominated by suburban politicians) and stopped the Spadina Expressway. He offered up big dollars to build a third subway line instead, justifiably earning him Transit Man of the Year honours from an American public transit organization.

However, John Robarts's other little problem, the Catholic school funding issue, wasn't resolved with quite so many kudos.

"Bill Davis made a statement that he was not going to extend any additional funding to separate schools," remembers Robert Nixon, the Liberal leader of the time. "And he didn't want it to be an election issue. But by the way, we're going to have an election right away."

The NDP leader, Stephen Lewis, has a similar recollection.

"I'm sure that Bill Davis pulled the plug for political reasons," he says. "We don't live in a world of naïveté and innocence. This was a pretty tough election. It was a very adroit election. Davis knew if he pulled the plug on extension of dollars to the Catholic schools on the one hand, and ran on the Spadina subway on the other, which was also a real *volt face* for the Conservatives, that he would create enough excitement and anticipation that he might ride to victory on it."

For Davis's part, he has always maintained he never promised anyone he'd extend full funding to Catholic schools. In fact, one story illustrates the delicate tightrope Davis tried to walk during that campaign.

Davis was to give the nominating speech at a local high school for Claude Bennett, then deputy mayor of Ottawa and would-be Tory candidate in the upcoming election. As he entered the school, Davis discovered many separate school supporters had jammed the hall, intending to disrupt the nominating meeting.

"There weren't many places we didn't go where there weren't demonstrations," remembers Norm Atkins.

Behind the curtain on stage, several local Tory officials told Davis they wanted to call in the police to clear out the demonstrators, in what would have been a disastrous set of images for the television crews in attendance.

Davis had a different idea. What happened next is a mixture of brilliant political instincts and a fine understanding of show biz.

"That's not how we do things in Ontario," he upbraided them. "They do have a right to express their views."

Davis emerged from behind the curtain to a chorus of boos from the demonstrators. Then the Tory partisans began shouting at the gate-crashers. Davis stood silently at the microphone, waited a few moments for the noise to die down, then made a modest proposal.

He offered to spend an hour listening to the demonstrators' complaints. In exchange, they were to let the Tories then have their nominating meeting, to which they were all cordially invited. Weak applause followed, but Davis took that as a cue to begin. Quite cleverly, he sat on the stage, forcing the demonstrators to sit and put down their placards in order to see him. Davis listened as speaker after speaker urged him to increase public funding to the Catholic school system. Then he told them he understood their frustration and sense of injustice and hoped they understood how tormented he was over the decision ultimately he would have to make.

Hugh Segal was there that day as a University of Ottawa student and a member of PC Youth. Segal remembers Davis telling the crowd he believed fundamentally that at some point before college or work, people from different backgrounds and religions had to study together.

"He told them the Ontario of tomorrow had to both respect religious diversity and also promote a harmony and understanding that came from people who had studied and worked together," Segal recalls.

With that, the premier thanked the demonstrators for their time, promised to carefully consider what they'd said, and assured them his door would remain open to them. Then the meeting was called to order. Half the Catholic school supporters left.

"But more importantly," Segal says, "half of them stayed."

However, Stephen Lewis's prediction turned out to be very prescient. Thanks in large measure to the most sophisticated advertising campaign ever mounted in the province, courtesy of advertising veteran Norman Atkins, William Davis did more than keep the Tory dynasty alive. On October 21, 1971, he improved upon it, winning nine more seats than the Robarts Tories had captured four years previously. Davis's seventy-eight out of 117 seats was good for a majority government, his first time out of the gate. The voters evidently liked the Davis portrayed in Atkins's ads—the family man seen at home, seen at the cottage, but not heard from much on the issues of the day.

But thirteen years later, in what he would call the most difficult decision of his entire political career, Bill Davis shocked everyone. He rose in the Ontario legislature to say the Conservative government *would* extend full public funding to the Catholic school system. Davis was doing something politicians almost never do. Not only was he repudiating the Ontario government's official stance of almost two hundred years, but he was also reversing his own position—a position that helped him win that first election so convincingly.

"I think he always felt a little guilty about the '71 election victory being on the backs of the separate school issue," says Hugh Segal. His fellow Big Blue Machine alumnus, Norman Atkins, agrees. "There was something about his success in that campaign that bothered him," he says, "something he wanted to correct."

Perhaps after years of lobbying from the Catholic Church, Davis, ever the pragmatist, saw an opportunity to marry good policy with good politics. He gave me a much simpler explanation. Davis was cutting the grass at his home on Main Street in Brampton when a few students from the nearby separate school—Cardinal Leger School—walked by.

"Mr. Davis," one of them asked, "we've just been told if we want to go into grade eleven in Cardinal Leger and stay with our teachers and other kids we've come to know, that it's gonna cost our parents a substantial fee. But if we go to Brampton Centennial, which is a few blocks further away from our house, we don't have to pay anything. Can you explain it to us?"

Davis no longer could.

"I think I had come to the conclusion that in terms of equity, in terms of fairness, whatever way you wish to describe it, that it was the right thing to do."

When it came time to vote, only one member of the legislature opposed the plan—Norm Sterling, a minor cabinet minister from eastern Ontario, now the longest-serving MPP in Mike Harris's government. Of him, Davis says: "The thing I always found interesting was that it was a matter of great principle for Norm. But not so much that he would resign from cabinet." There's that smile again. And coming from Bill Davis, that's a put-down of Don Rickles–like proportion.

After that 1971 election, the freshman premier quickly learned these were different times. Watergate was brewing in the United States, and a more aggressive media were uncovering scandals north of the border as well. Davis's poll numbers dropped precipitously. The opposition were having a field day with the slogan "Save Us From Davis." The situation was so dire, Davis gathered his closest advisers at a hotel near Pearson International Airport to consider his options.

"There was some question about whether Bill Davis was thinking about packing it in," says Norman Atkins. "We went around the table, one by one, and only one person said 'Pack it in.' I won't tell you who." The consensus of the room was to persevere.

When Davis went back to the people to renew his mandate on September 18, 1975, things looked bleak. A few days before election day, polls showed the Liberals were on their way to victory. But the 1975 election featured one of the wackiest vote splits in Ontario history. Robert Nixon increased the Liberal vote count significantly and yet came third with thirty-five seats. Stephen Lewis catapulted the New Democrats to official opposition status with thirty-eight seats. And there was Davis, hanging on to the keys to the premier's office with just fifty-one seats—the first Tory minority government in thirty-two years.

Davis's emotions were mixed. On the one hand, he was extremely disappointed at losing his majority. On the other, he was still the premier, which was anything but a sure thing on election night. Larry Grossman, who ran for the first time and barely won that 1975 election, recalls Davis sitting with a group of supporters and simply uttering "Damn."

"It was the closest I ever saw him to thinking about losing his temper," Grossman said. "The place exploded in laughter."

In politics, conventional wisdom holds that the voters prefer minority governments because they keep the premier and his cabinet from getting too arrogant. One false move and the whole house of cards can come tumbling down. The flip side, of course, is that we assume the politicians prefer majority governments, where they can do whatever they want.

Bill Davis's little secret was that he loved the six years he led Ontario in a minority government. Good thing, too, because when he opportunistically called an election just two years into his second mandate, claiming he needed a strong majority government to confront the separatists in Quebec, the voters saw through it. He won just two more seats, and another minority government.

Still, Davis found this period of his political life to be immensely satisfying. His natural inclination for pragmatic solutions rather than ideological confrontation served him extremely well. And beyond that, it was just awfully exciting coming to work every day knowing the government could fall on a moment's notice. That was all the incentive Bill Davis needed to thrive on the job.

It was also at this time that Davis transformed himself into the politician that most Ontarians came not only to respect, but also to like. He took greater control of the government. The cigar disappeared, a pipe taking its place.

The public picked up on the new, more comfortable Davis, and rewarded him with a majority government on March 19, 1981. It was one of the best nights of his political life. His mother was with him at the Bramalea City Centre to watch the returns come in.

Davis was at his best during the first couple of years of his fourth mandate. His control of the PC party was complete. His understanding of government was at its finest. He seemed to enjoy the job, rather than see it as a burden. One day during Question Period, the opposition was attacking Davis. He appeared to be listening to his interrogators through an earphone provided to each MPP because of the bad acoustics in the house. As he rose to answer the question, he handed the earpiece to Larry Grossman. "Here," he said. "Follow this while I answer the question."

Grossman was perplexed, until he realized Davis had just handed him an earphone attached to a Walkman, hidden in his desk. The premier of Ontario was listening to the World Series and didn't want to miss a single at-bat.

PETER LOUGHEED WAS BORN IN CALGARY in 1928 and was similarly destined for politics. After all, his grandfather, Senator Sir James Alexander Lougheed, was Alberta's first federal Conservative cabinet minister. He wasn't elected, but was appointed "the senator from the west" in Prime Minister Robert Borden's cabinet from 1911 to 1921.

"He came west when there were only a hundred people in Calgary. He was in his thirties," Lougheed says. "He died before I was born but his path in public service intrigued me and interested me as a young boy."

But Lougheed's interest in politics ran into a brick wall while he attended Central High School in Calgary. He wanted to be elected head of the students' union. Trouble was, there was no students' union. So Lougheed proposed it, helped create it, then became its first president.

After graduating from Harvard University and being called to the bar, Lougheed spent five years with Mannix Construction, serving as legal trouble-shooter for Fred Mannix. He travelled all over Europe, Asia, and North America as Mannix built dams, powerhouses, and railroads. He spent another five years practising law, then took the plunge into elective politics.

"I could have chosen the federal route, given my family background. But I chose provincial," he says. "As a young person in my early thirties, once I came to the conclusion I wanted to have a political career, I said, you know, Peter, if you could be the leader and maybe premier, you could accomplish so much more than in the nature of federal politics, which is so much a trade-off between regions and jurisdictions. So to me, the decision to go provincial was the real key decision in my life."

At the time, it seemed like a foolhardy move. Preston Manning's father, Ernest, was firmly ensconced as premier and custodian of the Social Credit dynasty. Nevertheless, in March, 1965, thirty-six-year-old Peter Lougheed visited the Alberta legislature to watch the proceedings for the first time. He thought it might be a good idea to check out Question Period first-hand, given that he'd just announced his intention to stand for the leadership of the Alberta Progressive Conservative Party. There may be a stampede in Alberta every year but there wasn't one for this job. It was vacant.

Meanwhile, as the story goes, when Premier Manning saw Lougheed sitting up in the gallery, he sent him a handwritten note saying, "I hope your visit to the assembly doesn't dim your enthusiasm to enter actively into provincial public life. The first twenty-five years are the worst."

In fact, after he got the leader's job, Lougheed says his reaction was simply to say to himself, "God, what am I doing here? I used those words when I was first elected leader with no seats. What am I doing?"

I told Lougheed I'd love to have been a fly on the wall the day he came home and told his wife, Jeanne, that he was leaving behind the law (and its much better salary) to run for a job which had been an exercise in futility for its predecessors.

"We had four children and she had qualms about it," Lougheed admits. "And that was a very real problem in those early years, because to do the job of leader of the opposition meant very limited compensation."

However, Lougheed adds, unlike some spouses who are shocked when their mates enter politics, Jeanne probably wasn't.

"She knew I was the student union president at high school and university," he points out. "She could spot that. She had a hint that was a probability."

What made him think he could take a party that basically didn't exist, and upset an institution?

"I looked at Social Credit over thirty years and believed that in the minds of the public, it had run its course," he says. "Second, I looked at the philosophy of the people of the province and I sensed they were very much in the centre of the road in their philosophy. And if I could marry the words 'Progressive' and 'Conservative,' and could bring together a new group of young people who at that stage were apolitical, I could perhaps build a coalition."

If the journey of a thousand miles begins with the first step, Peter

Lougheed took that step on May 23, 1967. His Tories won six seats, including his own in Calgary West. He wasn't expecting any miracles and he didn't get any.

"I thought it would take three to four elections, but I'd build a coalition that could garner the support of the majority," he says.

Then Lougheed caught some breaks. Ernest Manning retired in 1968, and the PCs won the ensuing by-election. The new Socred premier, Harry Strom, saw the writing on the wall and tried to modernize Alberta by joining the new federal Medicare program, lowering the voting age to eighteen, and loosening up on some of the outdated liquor regulations.

By election day in 1971, the Socreds figured they had preserved the dynasty. And Lougheed agreed. He told friends he thought he'd go down to defeat that night.

Then the polls closed. And the votes were counted. And Peter Lougheed got his miracle. It was the best of many good days Lougheed enjoyed in public life.

"I didn't know I was going to win," he says. "We had ten seats, the Socreds had forty-nine. Journalists and other forecasters didn't think we'd win. So clearly it was an upset. We had polling that indicated it was close, but on the other hand, they were there," Lougheed says, referring to the Socreds. "There's an advantage to incumbency."

Lougheed was also concerned about the vote splits. He worried he could win the total vote, but lose on the seat count because the Socreds' support was thought to be spread much wider across rural Alberta. He needn't have worried. In fact, the only thing Lougheed did need to worry about was where to celebrate.

"On election night, when we looked at the results, we hadn't done too well in Calgary and we'd won every single Edmonton seat. Three or four of us were standing around and we looked at each other and said, 'We've gotta go to Edmonton!' So we chartered an airplane. We saw thousands of people at the Edmonton airport which is clearly focused in my mind."

Lougheed's Progressive Conservatives won forty-nine out of seventy-five seats. The journey he thought might take four elections to achieve took just two.

"There were lots of other days that were exciting and meaningful—standing in the legislature and announcing the Heritage Savings Trust Fund—days like that. But if I'm candid with myself the greatest charge I got was being elected premier, and knowing that I had an opportunity, if I worked at it effectively, to be there for at least a couple of terms and get some things done."

The lure of public life was especially strong for both Bill Davis and Peter Lougheed in the early 1980s because the times called for provincial politicians to assume significant national roles. After his first victory in 1971, Lougheed placed his imprint all over Alberta politics. While Davis was struggling at the polls, Lougheed was digging the foundations of his Tory party deeper and deeper. He won re-election in 1975, gaining a full twenty seats in the process. Four years later, another election, and five more seats. His last election, in 1982, saw him capture yet another seat, bringing the Tories to seventy-five in the Alberta legislature.

To be sure, Lougheed's popularity was aided, in part, by burgeoning energy revenues, thanks to the OPEC oil crisis of the 1970s. Lougheed found he could double the size of government without raising taxes. He also found himself embroiled in a massive confrontation with the government of Pierre Trudeau and central Canada, because of his demand to sell oil and natural gas at market prices, and export it to the United States.

Lougheed tried to respond to the federal government for its National Energy Program by cutting Alberta oil production to central Canada. Almost two decades later, he admits it was one of the most troublesome things he ever did as premier.

"I'm a Canadian before an Albertan, but we had to get out from under the National Energy Program," he says. "And we structured that in the summer of 1980 knowing there'd be a great backlash of antagonism towards us, but knowing we had to do something as dramatic as that to dissuade the federal government. The NEP almost did ruin our province."

Lougheed notes the strategy worked. Prime Minister Trudeau ordered his energy minister, Marc Lalonde, to negotiate with the Alberta government within weeks.

"But at the time," Lougheed recalls, "it was the most difficult decision. It brought into conflict two elements of my being. The Canadian patriot, and my responsibility as premier."

Those elements of Lougheed's being would soon get another workout, courtesy again of Pierre Trudeau.

Trudeau had just returned to the prime minister's office in March, 1980. He reversed his decision to retire and won his fourth election, bringing an end to the Tories' interregnum under Joe Clark after just nine months. Trudeau was determined to set the country on a course to patriate its Constitution from Great Britain, with an amending formula and a Charter of Rights and Freedoms. When Trudeau tried to do all that without the consent of the provinces, Bill Davis and Peter Lougheed found themselves on opposite sides again. Davis and New Brunswick's Richard Hatfield supported the prime minister's efforts, while Lougheed and seven other premiers were opposed. On September 28, 1981, the Supreme Court of Canada rendered one of its most delightfully Canadian decisions. Yes, the federal government could legally patriate the Constitution on its own. But the court also said a "substantial degree" of provincial consent was required before Britain would honour the request.

Despite the ruling, Trudeau was still tempted to go it alone. He held a private meeting at 24 Sussex Drive with Davis, Hugh Segal, and future Senator Michael Kirby, at which he told them he thought further negotiations with the provinces would be a waste of time.

"My own instincts told me another try in public was worth the effort," Davis says, putting oh-so-respectful pressure on Trudeau to reach out to the premiers one more time. In fact, Davis did not favour unilateral patriation by Trudeau. And while he's not the threatening type, he made it clear to the prime minister that Ontario's support might not be so vigorous if Trudeau insisted on flying solo.

As a result, Trudeau convened another First Ministers' Conference on November 2, 1981, during which time Ottawa and nine provinces came to an agreement. The notable exception, of course, was Quebec, where the event has gone down in history as the Night of the Long Knives. Historians will argue forever whether a separatist government led by René Lévesque ever would have or could have signed a document confirming Quebec as a province within Canada, but not a sovereign nation. Certainly, Lévesque's willingness to leap at Trudeau's offer of a referendum by region, not by province, infuriated Lougheed and helped bust up the Gang of Eight, the eight provinces that opposed the PM's repatriation efforts.

In the end, Quebec's demands were unmet, its constitutional place in Canada isolated, and its people, according to the more nationalist interpretation, humiliated. It's also worth noting that seventy-three out of seventy-five Quebec MPs were Liberals who supported the initiative, and they were elected at that point in history with the largest number of votes ever gained by any party in any Quebec election, federal or provincial.

Nevertheless, ten Canadian governments did agree to patriate the Constitution with an amending formula and a charter of rights, while at the same time strengthen provincial control over natural resources. That alone should have made Peter Lougheed ecstatic. Instead, he refers to those November days of 1981 as the worst of his political life.

"I tried to convince René Lévesque to stay and work together on the Constitution. And he walked out the door," Lougheed recalls, with evident regret in his voice. "I knew the magnitude of that. I knew it was a bad moment for Canada. It left me with sadness—the reality that we were in a dangerous situation for our country. It also disturbed me that Mr. Trudeau had put us into a discussion of the Constitution, when there was a separatist government in Quebec."

That night in Ottawa still motivates Peter Lougheed.

"I'm a Canadian patriot. That's why I'm still involved in public life," he says. "Frankly, perhaps as an outgrowth of that very day, I still feel a responsibility as a citizen to become involved, to be constructive."

The conventional lore of this time suggests that the beginnings of the eventual deal were discussed in a hotel kitchenette by three justice ministers: Jean Chrétien representing the federal government, and the two Roys, McMurtry and Romanow, representing Ontario and Saskatchewan, respectively. The trio agreed on some basics, then divvied up the list of first ministers that each would be responsible for "selling" on the plan.

After a full night of shuttle diplomacy between different hotels, there was a deal.

If you want to really tick off Peter Lougheed, just tell him you believe that story lock, stock, and barrel—that, in essence, the deal was struck in a kitchenette at the Chateau Laurier, without Lougheed's signing off on the agreement.

"It's an amazing myth of Canadian politics," Lougheed says, sounding as animated as he ever would be during our conversation. "All the Ottawa journalists were given the bill that Mr. Chrétien and Mr. McMurtry and Mr. Romanow cooked up this deal the night before. If you really want to do something effective in your book, Steve, puncture that myth." These are the words of a proud man, who feels history has slighted his contribution to that first ministers' agreement.

"Peter Lougheed didn't see it until the next morning," says Allan Blakeney, the former Saskatchewan premier who was there. "Knowing the dynamics, if anyone feels there was a deal before Peter Lougheed said there was a deal, they're wrong."

And in case I didn't get the point, Lougheed reiterated it. "Allan Blakeney's the best source you could get on this."

Meanwhile, I can't resist teasing Davis with an anecdote from the autobiography of one of his closest associates over the years—lawyer, Tory fundraiser, political fixer, and all around good guy Eddie Goodman.

Goodman tells the story of how disgusted he was with the federal government on April 17, 1982, the day Queen Elizabeth II came to Parliament Hill to sign the repatriated Constitution into law. Front and centre, of course, were Prime Minister Trudeau and his minister of justice, Jean Chrétien. Goodman said all the provincial politicians watched the ceremony from the political equivalent of steerage. Given Davis's immeasurable assistance to Trudeau on the constitutional file from the get-go, Goodman was more than a little irritated his leader had no formal role in the day's events.

"That bothered Eddie, not me," Davis smiles. "If you're saying all the premiers should have been more front and centre, all right. If Eddie had been in my place, which I'm sure he felt he was for fourteen years, that would have bothered him. It didn't bother me."

Davis's and Lougheed's paths crossed again a year later. At that now-famous Progressive Conservative convention in Winnipeg in January, 1983, Joe Clark determined that two-thirds of the delegates' support wasn't good enough to continue as leader. So he quit and paved the way for a dramatic convention in Ottawa in June.

The main contenders for the Tory crown were all from the federal scene: Joe Clark, Brian Mulroney, John Crosbie, Michael Wilson, and David Crombie. And then, somehow, Bill Davis's name started to emerge. Over and over and over. Pretty soon, it turned into a tidal wave of support, the likes of which he'd never seen before.

"You flirted with the notion of running for the federal Conservative leadership, didn't you?" I ask him.

"I don't like the word 'flirted,'" he laughs.

Egad. The Methodist in him is coming out again. "You considered it?" I try again.

Indeed. Davis was being pushed and pulled by two different groups with, some would say, quite different motives. One side, comprising associates such as Ed Stewart (Davis's own secretary of cabinet), Eddie Goodman, and Clare Westcott, was telling him he'd never been on the opposition side of the house, he didn't speak French, Ottawa was not Pleasantville like Brampton was, the federal Conservative Party had been a deathtrap for every leader, and besides, he was at the top of his game in Ontario. Stay here. Smell the roses. Enjoy yourself a bit.

The other side, featuring the likes of Norman Atkins and Hugh Segal, thought Davis's image as a Canadian patriot, combined with the fact that his time in Ontario was likely coming to an end, argued for a change of scenery. They also, no doubt, were licking their chops at the prospect of a wonderfully dramatic leadership convention with a delightful cast of characters. Ironically, it was a group from Quebec—mostly francophones—that almost convinced Davis to go for it. He met them at the Park Plaza Hotel in downtown Toronto and was blown away by their support.

"It came as a great shock to me because I felt if I were to be interested, Quebec would pose a major problem at the convention," Davis says. "And I was really quite intrigued. I was quite moved by their presentation. I never anticipated this."

Publicly, Davis was telling everyone who was asking—and everyone *was* asking—that he "had no plans" to run for the national Tory leadership. Technically, it may have been true, but it was also a plea for more time to consider the issue. Eventually, the line became such a parody of itself that Davis began saying, "I have no plans to have plans..."

And then there was Peter Lougheed. When the Alberta premier realized those strong winds weren't chinooks, but rather big-time gusts breathing life into a potential Davis campaign, he became concerned.

To this day, Lougheed has never made public whom he supported for the leadership—although I think we can be reasonably sure it wasn't the premier of Ontario.

"Davis supported the National Energy Program and the unilateral patriation of the Constitution," Lougheed says. "They were the two big issues and we were in the opposite corner. We're good friends now, but at that stage it was pretty intense."

Lougheed insists he never tried to mount any opposition to Davis's potential candidacy. But that was certainly not the impression Davis's advisers were getting.

"He didn't have Lougheed's support," says Norman Atkins. "And the threat to work against him was a major factor" for Davis's declining to run. Today, Lougheed claims he was unaware of any role he may have played in the unfolding drama and he never discussed it with Davis at the time. In fact, the Davis camp anticipated Lougheed would be opposed. However, they were devastated when Grant Devine indicated he was also against Davis's candidacy. The proponents had been counting on the Saskatchewan premier's support, but it wasn't to be.

In the end, Davis resisted the urge to inhale the sweet-smelling entreaties for him to run. And he claims never to think about the what ifs.

"I have learned one thing," he says. "Once you make a decision you should accept that decision and not second-guess yourself later on."

"I think he really wanted to run for the leadership of the national party," says former Ontario premier Bob Rae, still a close friend of Davis's. "He didn't because he didn't think he'd win, and because a lot of people told him he wouldn't win. And I think he has some regrets about that. I think he would liked to have been prime minister."

Meanwhile, the premier of Alberta himself was the object of some powerful overtures from a national Draft Lougheed movement. However, Lougheed was approaching twenty years in politics and was ready to move to the private sector. But he did try to influence the contest in a way that infuriated many Tories. He set up a special caucus committee that met all the leadership candidates as they came through Edmonton.

"Dalton Camp was furious," Lougheed recalls of the former Tory president. "He says we were so arrogant to do that."

"Did you think it was arrogant?" I ask.

"I thought it was practical," Lougheed laughs.

Bill Davis would never admit this. In fact he strongly denies it. But there was a definite sense of ennui around Queen's Park after he took a pass on the leadership convention. Davis, himself, only admits to feeling relief once the decision was made and has a theory as to why his fourth mandate seemed to lack gusto.

"There may have been some diminution on the part of some because they felt I should have run, and that I'd missed an opportunity," he says. "I never felt that way. I was never bored. I was always excited by it."

In September, 1984, Davis commissioned a public opinion poll on the popularity of his government and his own premiership. The numbers were stratospheric. Suddenly, rumours shot through Queen's Park that Davis was considering going to the polls to take advantage of his high standing. Then just as quickly, the rumour mill suggested the premier might prefer to put those favourable ratings in his back pocket and simply retire.

Larry Grossman, then Davis's treasurer, told me about the last gathering Davis had with his cabinet colleagues before stating his intentions.

"It was an incredible cabinet meeting," Grossman remembered. "Minister after minister made very emotional statements to the premier, personal statements, which was unheard of in our kind of cabinet. I would summarize them by saying, 'If you need to retire, you have every right to and we all respect that and support you in that. But we desperately need you to stay.'"

After the cabinet meeting, Grossman followed Davis into his office. "Premier," Grossman said, "we really need you to take us through this election."

"You get to a stage of déjà vu," Davis responded. "I've just seen it all and it doesn't stimulate me as it used to, and that's when it's time to go."

For Grossman and many others, that was the spiritual end of the Davis government. Soon after, the premier gathered his family and closest advisers at his cottage during the Thanksgiving holiday weekend. Some advised him to run, win re-election, stay two years, then retire. But it just didn't feel right. Too opportunistic. He knew he'd be asked whether he intended to stay the full term. He knew he didn't want to, but couldn't fudge it.

That weekend was the saddest of all of Norman Atkins's time in public life.

"I was at Robertson's Point at my cottage," he remembers. "Hugh Segal called me and told me we'd lost. I was sick. I didn't sleep a wink that night."

"You know, it was a very personal moment for the family," Davis continues. "There were a few tears and [my son] Neil of course broke that by saying, 'Good heavens, you'll drive your own car now. What will the other drivers of Ontario be faced with?'" Neil's father had enjoyed a government car and driver for more than twenty years.

Davis returned to Queen's Park to hold the most anticipated news conference of the year. With a tear or two, he retired.

"He wouldn't do what just about any other political leader would do," Larry Grossman said, "which is con the public by going for one more, and then not serving out the term."

"He under-stayed his welcome in quite a dramatic way," says Bob Rae. "If he'd run again in '85 he would have wiped the floor with [David] Peterson and me."

No argument from Atkins. "You've gotta believe David Peterson is the luckiest guy alive, because David Peterson bloody well never would have been premier if Davis had run."

Because Davis's retirement was so sudden, many thought he'd have a difficult time adjusting to life outside politics. After all, he'd been in public life since 1959. Leslie Frost was then premier of Ontario.

"There was never any feeling of depression," Davis says. "There was a feeling of relief because a burden was lifted. There was some concern on my part as to what I would do. I had made no plans in advance of my decision. I had talked to no one about any job opportunities."

However, he quickly discovered he needn't have worried. In no time at all, Davis found himself headquartered at the law firm Tory Tory DesLauriers & Binnington (today called Torys—and how appropriate is that name for this guy anyway?). He accepted positions on sixteen corporate boards and turned down many more. He accepted an assignment from Prime Minister Brian Mulroney to be Canada's special envoy on acid rain.

"I told him I couldn't do it for more than a dollar, and there it is," Davis says, pointing to his office wall, where the federal government's cheque for one dollar hangs in a frame.

By any definition, William Davis has made the transition to private life about as seamlessly as one could. And yet, the lure of public life lives on.

"It's not the same," he says of the private sector. "I mean, the tensions, the pressures, the fact that you have to be at Question Period every day at two o'clock, or particularly during minority government, when, in theory, you could be defeated any day at six o'clock. That's not there. Very few people will ever understand the pressure on people in public life.

"I've been in the other world now for fifteen years," Davis continues. "Some of it's exciting. But in terms of the immediacy of issues, the sense of accomplishment, I wouldn't trade my experience at Queen's Park for twenty-five years of running some company. There's nothing quite like the sense of accomplishment, the sense of frustration, the sense you may be playing some limited role in the province or the country, and the little things you can do for people."

Perhaps the thing Davis misses the most is the thing most politicians today seem to enjoy the least—sparring with opponents on the floor of the legislature or scrumming with the media.

I can still see the image of Davis leaning against the front door of the premier's office, smoking his pipe and being totally ignored by the media, who were descending on his replacement, Frank Miller. Davis seemed to be chewing the pipe a little more intensely that day.

For a modest man, he loved the attention. A year after his retirement, he was summoned to appear before a committee of the Ontario legislature to explain his change of heart on Catholic school funding. I've never seen him so much in his glory. He had the committee members eating out of his hand, suggesting his change of heart was a logical progression of his thinking on the issue. The media scrum afterwards was rough and tumble, just the way he liked it. I sneaked in a question about whether he'd really have us believe that he was a "closet separate school supporter all these years." His answer: "Unlike some, I've never really found a lot of activity in the closet."

He kept telling us he wasn't going to do a long scrum, but he did. And after it was over, after the cameramen had all turned their sun-guns off and stopped rolling, he just hung around the elevators, surveying the scene with his wife, Kathy, for just a little longer. He didn't need to say it—the look on his face said it all—he missed it.

"I don't say that being in politics is unique," Davis says today. "But I haven't found anything that's quite comparable to it."

ONE THING I'M CONSTANTLY STRUCK by in my dealings with William Davis and Peter Lougheed is how modestly they describe their accomplishments. Davis's resumé says, "The Honourable William G. Davis was the Premier of Ontario from 1971 until 1985," and that's *all* it says about Davis's time as premier. Getting these guys to boast about any of their achievements is quite a challenge.

Just before we say goodbye, I ask Peter Lougheed whether he has anything else he wants to tell me about his time in public life. And much to my surprise and delight, he offers the following little gem.

"Nobody's ever printed this before," he says. "And I'm not sure anyone can match this record. In three re-elections, we never lost an incumbent seat."

Wow. Now there's a new definition of job security if I've ever heard one—running for office on the coattails of Peter Lougheed—when politics was a more honourable calling.

THE NEXT GENERATION

Some people are late bloomers to politics. John Savage didn't become premier of Nova Scotia until he was sixty. And then there are those who are born into politics. They are, with all appropriate apologies to *Star Trek* fans, the next generation. Politics is in their DNA. Their decision becomes only a matter of "when," not "whether" to enter the fray.

Such was the case for someone born in 1942 by the name of Sharon Connolly, who became one of the country's fastest-rising political stars of the 1980s. At the time of her birth her father, Harold, was minister of industry in the Nova Scotia government. As she says today, "I don't think I was ever aware of a time when there wasn't politics."

Sharon Connolly's earliest political recollections were happy ones. There are vivid memories of being on a platform, electioneering with her father, at the age of six. "I remember singing 'When Irish Eyes Are Smiling' when that wasn't a Conservative song."

Sharon would go to school at the local convent, then spend day after day in the legislature in Halifax. Her brothers and sisters found it pretty strange, but she found it a useful way to get one-on-one quality time with her dad, after his day's business was done.

But Sharon's impressions of politics through rose-coloured glasses came to a crashing halt around the time of her twelfth birthday. After the sudden death of Premier Angus L. Macdonald, the Nova Scotia Liberal caucus unanimously selected her father as the new leader. Harold Connolly agreed to stay on as premier only until party members, province-wide, could ratify his selection at a leadership convention.

Sharon's recollections of the convention are quite bitter. There were five candidates, four Protestants and her father, the lone Catholic. "He was so far ahead on the first ballot, it looked like he couldn't possibly lose. He only needed thirty-five votes to win," she says in a hushed tone. "As each Protestant candidate dropped off, they threw their votes to the next Protestant. My dad didn't win." In fact, he lost a five-ballot marathon to Henry Hicks, who eventually lost the government to Robert Stanfield.

"That was pretty awesome at the time," she says. "I never thought of my religion and my politics being linked together in this way."

Shortly thereafter, Connolly resigned from cabinet. A year later, Prime Minister Louis St. Laurent appointed him to the Senate.

Despite the heartbreaking experience, Sharon Connolly was not turned off politics. In fact, a little more than a decade later, she met a man nine years her senior on a television show featuring young Liberals. That man was John Carstairs. They decided to do politics—and life—together.

John was an oil and gas lawyer. Sharon was a teacher. They got married in 1966 and settled in Alberta, "not exactly a hotbed of Liberal politics." In fact, things looked so bleak for the party, the pair debated whether to move to Ontario to give candidate John a better chance at a political career. But John Carstairs was a child of the Depression. He wanted the security of a good job. So John and Sharon Carstairs immersed themselves hip-deep in Alberta politics. She became president of the Alberta Liberal Party. She and John even wrote Ralph Klein's campaign literature for his first city council run (back in the days when Klein was a Liberal). And Sharon ran for the Grits in the 1976 election. The result—a loss for her personally, and a second consecutive majority government for Peter Lougheed's Conservatives.

Canadians might never have heard of Sharon Carstairs, if not for a change in her husband's fortunes. John came home one night and said he had good news and bad news.

"I'll take the good news first," said Sharon.

"I got a big raise," said John.

"And the bad news?"

"They want me to spend it in Manitoba." And so the couple moved east.

Seven years later, Sharon Carstairs made history by becoming the first ever female leader of Her Majesty's Loyal Opposition anywhere in Canada.

"There was one person more or less designated as the heir apparent," she says. "But I just didn't think he had what it took to be leader of the party. So I did the usual female thing, which you did in the early eighties, which was to go around and try to find a male. And I did try. I spoke to ten men about running. And finally it was John who said, 'Oh for heaven's sake, do it yourself.'"

Sharon Carstairs was embarking on a job whose only guarantee seemed to be political oblivion. The previous handful of leaders had all done the job for two years, then been tossed out. No Liberal leader had won an election in thirty years. "I didn't think I was crazy," she says. "I committed myself to ten years to rebuild the party. I thought, 'I believe in this, I'll do it.' I don't think I thought it was an intelligent thing to do. I thought it was an important thing to do. I really do believe in liberalism."

When Carstairs won her party's leadership on March 4, 1984, there wasn't a single Liberal MLA in the Manitoba Legislative Assembly. Two years later, she won a seat in River Heights and became the one and only.

But on April 26, 1988, Sharon Carstairs experienced one of those thrilling, rare moments in politics—one of those moments that reminds you why you spent all those years in the political wilderness. She took the Liberal Party of Manitoba from one seat to twenty. Gary Filmon's Conservatives formed a minority government that night. But Liberals everywhere delighted in wacky stories of election night victories. Carstairs's favourite was about Ed Mandrake. He spent $2,500, had two campaign workers, put up all the signs himself and won the riding of Assiniboia.

"It was really a family," Carstairs says of her new caucus. "And I was the mom."

Meantime, a new star in Canadian politics was born—ironically, a star who had no idea how historic her achievement really was, until she read the *Maclean's* cover story about herself.

"As a woman, I had shown it could be done," she says. "I suppose that was the most important aspect of my achievement. I was the first. That gave me a real sense of accomplishment. It also put an enormous burden of responsibility on me because I was always terrified I was going to do badly and therefore not just hurt me, but other women who came along."

Most political junkies will remember the 1972 motion picture *The Candidate*. Robert Redford stars as the upstart, anti-establishment candidate who stages a huge upset, then has no idea what to do next. Sharon Carstairs experienced the same moment.

"There's a wonderful CBC clip," she laughs. "There's no audio but you can read my lips. At one point in the evening, we actually were ahead of the Tories for a while. And I turned to John and said, 'What the hell do we do now?'"

She'd have to learn the answer to that, and fast.

LOOK UP THE WORD "CHUTZPAH" IN THE DICTIONARY and you may very well see a picture of Chris Stockwell. Which is kind of funny because Stockwell probably doesn't even know what the word means. It's Yiddish, and Stockwell comes from a pretty Waspy part of west-end Toronto called Etobicoke.

Yiddish words translate rather poorly into English. But "chutzpah" roughly means "unmitigated gall." Kind of like murdering your parents, then throwing yourself at the court's mercy because you're an orphan. Kind of like offering yourself up to the voters year after year as the anti-politician, even though you're actually the second generation in the family to have done it, and you really haven't done anything else for a living—at least, nothing else as effectively.

It's that contradiction which makes Chris Stockwell one of the most interesting and certainly most entertaining politicians to watch.

His father, Winfield Stockwell (everyone calls him Bill), was one of the brashest, most ambitious municipal politicians of his day. He was the master of a good soundbite when most local politicians were duller than dishwater. He also made a lot of enemies, which is why he lost a few campaigns along the way as well. He was just a bit too aggressive for the peaceful burghers of sleepy Etobicoke.

But one thing he did do, apparently by accident, was develop in his son Chris an interest in The Life. Chris was one of five Stockwell children, but the only one who loved—*really* loved—working on his father's campaigns.

"I'd be at city hall at 1:30 in the morning," Bill says of his salad days in elected office, "and I'd look around and there'd be Chris in the stands watching. He was a teenager. Channel 10 [which broadcast the city council meetings] would go off at 11 p.m. and he'd drive down to watch the rest of the meeting in person."

In some respects, politics wasn't that surprising a vocation for the younger Stockwell. He graduated from high school with no intention of going to university. He and his wife, Charlene Thornley, ran a small property-management business. "I don't think he loved it," Bill says.

Apparently not, because at the ripe old age of twenty-five, Chris decided to make his move. His father had just quit politics to become general manager of the Canadian National Exhibition.

"I had no great reason for getting in," Chris says. "My dad was in. I recall the day I said to him, 'I think I might run for your position.' He was neither affirmative nor derogatory."

Succession plans were never made, never even discussed. "Never, never, never ever came up," he says adamantly.

Once Chris's intentions were known, father and son had a heart-to-heart conversation. To this day, they disagree on what was discussed.

In those days, candidates could run either for alderman or board of control. Aldermen ran in one small ward and sat on the local council. Board of control was a better plum. There were only four positions, and controllers ran across all of Etobicoke (population three hundred thousand then), and sat on the larger, more powerful Metropolitan Toronto Council, as well as the Etobicoke executive committee.

As Chris tells the story, he says he wanted to take a run at being an alderman. He says his father suggested he go for controller, on the supposition that some voters would probably think they were voting for the old man, rather than the kid.

Bill Stockwell remembers the conversation somewhat differently.

"I told him he was crazy to run for board of control," he laughs. "I said, run for alderman. You won't win but you'll get good exposure for next time. I told him no one was going to vote for a smart-ass kid."

So what did Chris do? He ran for the big job on the board of control. "He disregarded my advice then," says Bill, "and he's been doing it ever since."

So the Stockwells went out, bought Chris a blue suit, and recycled some of the old man's election signs.

There was still one small problem. Actually, a big problem. "I had a conversation with my wife, who was vehemently opposed because she hates politics," he says with a smile.

"So why'd she marry a politician?" I ask.

"I wasn't when she married me. I never actually gave her an undertaking that I *wouldn't* be a politician, but I never said I would either. It wasn't a subject that came up. I considered my father to be running for a considerable length of time."

Stockwell's first election night was in November, 1982. His father, Bill, was a panelist on one of the broadcasts.

"And I remember watching it and I'd see him on the computer, while everyone else was talking. And I knew full well he was checking the results in my riding. And I remember saying, 'If it's good just go like this [thumbs up].' And he did."

Later that night, father and son got together for a celebratory hug, but no words.

"There wasn't anything else that needed to be said."

Chris Stockwell won the fourth seat on the board of control. Chutzpah.

"I felt sheer exhilaration," he says. "I was a bucket of nerves. All I remember is walking out of city hall at the Etobicoke Civic Centre. They have this stairway down and I jumped from the top to the bottom. Never hit one step. Gotta be ten steps. Couldn't do it today."

And why exactly did he run to fill the void left by his father? And how many politicians do you know who would answer the question this candidly:

"I can't tell you I had some noble cause to represent people," he says. "That'd be a lie. But I thought I had some pretty firm ideas.

There was no epiphany. I thought that I was a bit of a showman, and I had an ability to speak in a public way."

I met Stockwell for the first time during this phase of his political life. He was a constant hellraiser on Metro Toronto Council. He wanted local government to spend less and keep the taxes down. He fancied himself a kind of unofficial scrooge, whose job it was to question every expenditure. And, if you can imagine, he was even a better clip-meister than his father.

"They played Chris down as a snot-nosed kid," says Bill of the powers-that-were on council. "That was a big mistake. He was tenacious."

Some of it may have been jealousy too. Chris loved the media and because he was so newsworthy, the media loved him back. I was the City Hall reporter for CHFI and CFTR Radio. It was my job to keep an eye on Chris Stockwell. How could you not?

"I remember vividly," he starts reminiscing, "driving with my wife very shortly after being elected. We voted in favour of some spending program, and you had it on the radio: 'Even Chris Stockwell from Etobicoke [voted in favour].' And we looked at each other in the car and said, 'People care! Holy smokes! We've made it now!'"

Well, for *now* anyway. Admission to the heartbreak hotel was just around the corner.

IT'S HARD TO IMAGINE A MORE EXTRAORDINARY example of politics being the family business than the Johnsons of Quebec. One father and two sons, representing two different generations, three different political parties, all of whom became premier of Quebec, and all of whom were forced from the job they loved long before they wanted to leave.

The father, Daniel Johnson, Sr., became premier in 1966, representing the Union Nationale, but died in office just two years later. His younger son, Pierre Marc, took over the reins of the Parti Québécois from René Lévesque in October, 1985, but lasted only two and a half months in the premier's office. He was defeated at the polls by Robert Bourassa, who was enjoying a political resurrection after a decade in exile. And it was Daniel Jr. who replaced Bourassa in January, 1994. He remained premier for eight months, until succumbing to the now-traditional flows of Quebec politics, where the sovereignists and federalists take turns governing every second election. Daniel Johnson, Jr., was defeated by Jacques Parizeau.

I meet Pierre Marc Johnson to discuss his family's legacy at the King Edward Hotel in downtown Toronto. Johnson looks exactly like what you'd expect an elegant Montrealer in his early fifties to look like: dressed in an immaculately tailored suit, carrying a bit too much paunch over his belt, a small handbag for his accoutrements, and unfailingly polite, as he offers me a drink and suggests a quiet spot for our talk.

Politics, I discover, was an integral part of Johnson's life since he was five years old. Every weekend, the Johnson parents would schlep their four kids to Saint Pie de Bagot in Daniel Sr.'s riding, about seventy kilometres outside Montreal. In this small village, Johnson Sr. transformed a small garage into his constituency office. He was elected a member of the National Assembly in 1946.

His children frequently spent their weekends watching dozens of people visit their father's office. The children would also come to realize at an early age the demands of public life. Those demands often poison the next generation's interest in politics. Not so for Pierre Marc Johnson. From his teenage years on, he revelled in the public policy discussions he'd have with his father.

But then, on September 26, 1968, the most dramatic event of his life happened, and Johnson's reaction was to resolve never to go into politics. Daniel Johnson, Sr., died suddenly and unexpectedly in his sleep of a heart attack. He was in Manicouagan, about a five-hour drive northeast of Quebec City, where he had gone to preside at the opening ceremonies of a dam.

"On the day my father died," Pierre Marc recalls, "my first reaction was to say, 'My God, he died at fifty-three. So damn young."

A million people passed Johnson Sr.'s casket as it lay in state in the Quebec National Assembly and the Montreal Courts Building for six days.

"It was just unbelievable," his younger son recalls. "People queued for five hours in Montreal to pay their respect. So you can really touch citizens' lives. Because they've got nothing to win by doing that, to go and see you at your grave."

After the funeral, Pierre Marc and his brother Daniel went back to the house and took some of their father's mementos to give to the man who had been his assistant for fifteen years.

"And we realized how much affection had been manifested for our father," Johnson recalls. "So we said, 'Well, he had a heck of an extraordinary life, a very fulfilling one, if short.' And I remember reflecting specifically on that. And six days after his death, as he was buried, my perception and Daniel's had changed. That day, we both realized we might one day go into politics."

The outpouring of emotion for his father had made Johnson reassess his opinion of politics.

"There is something fundamental, there is something true, there is something crucial in the democratic process, which is about the relationship between the members of the house and the people. I saw that the day my father died. The hell with adversity, the hell with the bad press. That's where it really happens. This is where I decided I would one day go into politics."

"I DIDN'T LIKE QUESTION PERIOD AT ALL," says Sharon Carstairs. "It's totally contrary to what I am as a human being. I spent my other life teaching young people to be co-operative, to share, to work together. And now I find myself in the situation where I'm supposed to beat up on the other side all the time. Although I became quite good at it, it was not something I liked at all."

Despite the fact her father was premier for a short while, Carstairs never dreamed of having the top job—never actually saw herself as the premier. Voters may have a hard time believing that. They assume that all politicians crave the most powerful position they can attain. But several politicians have admitted the contrary to me after-the-fact, and it's always perplexing to hear it. One reason they may never reach the mountaintop is that deep in their guts, they don't want to. They don't need to. It's not why they got in.

Sharon Carstairs is one of those politicians. She got into politics to re-establish a place for liberalism in Manitoba's political discourse, not to become premier of the province.

"I think because the Liberal Party had been such a dead-in-the-woods kind of thing, I was realistic enough to think that '88 was just a phenomenon," she says. "I never really thought being premier was going to happen for me."

Then something happened in the winter of 1988 to ensure Carstairs never would get the top job. Premier Gary Filmon pulled the Meech Lake Accord from Manitoba's legislative agenda. His explanation related to events in Quebec. Premier Robert Bourassa had promised to allow the use of English on storefront signs and billboards as a compromise to the Parti Québécois' Bill 101. But the Supreme Court of Canada ruled that Bill 178, Bourassa's French-only sign regulation, violated the Charter of Rights. Bourassa bypassed the Supreme Court's ruling by invoking the "notwithstanding clause" of the Charter of Rights and Freedoms. And Filmon gave a voice to the anti-Quebec sentiment pulsating through English Canada by putting the accord into a deep freeze.

A year and a half later, Sharon Carstairs found herself in Ottawa, ready to oppose Meech. She was part of a three-leader Manitoba delegation. Filmon was one of the "eleven men in suits" inside the secret negotiations. But because he led a minority government, he had Carstairs and the NDP leader, Gary Doer, tag along, if not actually involved in the meetings. Obviously, Filmon's say-so alone wouldn't be enough to get Manitoba's signature on the accord. But that didn't mean Carstairs and Doer were players during the drama. Quite the contrary. During our conversation, almost ten years later, Carstairs still remembers that June in Ottawa with dread.

"Gary Doer and I were there by ourselves," she says. "They kept us basically out of the loop entirely. They accused us of defeating the deal, which we weren't even told of. So for me, it was a really agonizing kind of experience.

"I kept second-guessing myself all the way through it. I lost sleep over it. Every time, I'd say, 'I'm so offside, I'm so different from the rest of them. Is it me?' At one point, I actually said, 'If I am the problem here, then I'll step down. And let them go at it.' I felt I really was the problem. And then I'd step back and say, 'No, I'm not the problem. They've got the problem.'"

Adding to the trauma—her daughter Catherine was graduating

from Harvard University that week and Carstairs couldn't go. "I remember walking around Ottawa the day that she graduated and I kept buying presents for her. I just felt so awful I wasn't with her."

Carstairs also learned you don't have to be paranoid to think people are spying on you. She says she was constantly bullied by staffers in the Prime Minister's Office, particularly chief of staff Norman Specter. Filmon also warned her "to be very careful what you're saying on your cellphone," because her calls were being monitored, presumably by the Prime Minister's Office.

"I felt I was being followed," Carstairs remembers. "I started taking cabs. I got phone calls in the middle of the night. No one was on the other end."

And that wasn't all. Members of the public, lining up behind the barricades outside the talks, jeered at her, saying the country would fall apart without Meech's unanimous ratification. Barbara Frum, host of CBC-TV's *The Journal*, referred to her as the "mother of De-Confederation."

"There was a lot of heavy stuff on me that week," says Carstairs. Finally unable to withstand the constant pressure, the Liberal leader agreed to compromise. Premier Gary Filmon signed the accord for Manitoba.

"I never really forgave myself, which is the reason I fought 'Charlottetown' so hard," Carstairs says in a barely audible whisper. Ten years later, the political wounds still seem very fresh.

"I felt that I had backed off. And the people of Manitoba thought I had backed off," she says. "Of course, all three leaders agreed to the compromise, but people would say to me, 'Yes, but we trusted you. We didn't trust the other two.' That was tough. That was the pivotal moment where I began to think, maybe I don't want to do this any more."

But the worst was still to come. A few days after the first ministers had left Ottawa and returned to their home provinces, Carstairs was in bed, sipping some tea and reading the *Globe and Mail*. She then read a feature on the Meech negotiations by Susan Delacourt and Graham Fraser. She read Brian Mulroney's now-infamous quote about "rolling the dice." (When asked why he chose that weekend in

Ottawa to gather the first ministers, Mulroney said he looked at his calendar, saw the June 23 deadline, counted backwards two weeks, and "rolled the dice" on the weekend in question. Mulroney's critics would point to that turn of phrase to suggest the prime minister gambled with the country's future for his own self-aggrandizement.)

"And I screamed," Carstairs recalls after seeing the quote. Her husband, John, came running in, assuming she'd injured herself.

"The very horror that I'd been played with to that degree. 'I'd rolled the dice,'" she mimics Mulroney saying. "You have no idea how incensed I was."

When she was nine years old, Carstairs was sexually assaulted by a trusted family friend, now deceased, who was a frequent visitor to the Connolly home. Over time, Carstairs learned to cope with the indignity of that history. But those feelings returned to the surface after she read the newspaper article.

"I felt that they'd done it to me again," she says. "So at that point, I was prepared to do anything to make sure that didn't get through the Manitoba legislature."

Almost two weeks after the nightmare in Ottawa, Sharon Carstairs found herself back in the legislative assembly. The joys of politics, first experienced at her father's side nearly four decades earlier, had disappeared. Premier Filmon approached her.

"The prime minister wants to talk to us," he said.

"I don't want to talk to the prime minister," Carstairs answered.

"I don't want to talk to him either," Filmon joked, "but he *is* the prime minister."

Carstairs arrived in Filmon's office later that afternoon. So did Gary Doer. But it wasn't Mulroney on the phone, it was Senator Lowell Murray, whom Carstairs had also known for many years. Murray tried to persuade the Manitoba leaders to change the rules the house operates under, because if the accord weren't passed by 5:30 p.m. the following day, it would be dead. At the moment, NDP member Elijah Harper was conducting a one-man filibuster, preventing Manitoba's vote, because the accord was silent on native issues.

Carstairs had had it with the PMO's game plan. "There's no goddamned way, Murray!" she screamed into the speakerphone.

Carstairs returned home to find Newfoundland Premier Clyde Wells on the phone. Wells wanted to know whether Manitoba intended to pass the accord by the deadline. Carstairs assured him it wouldn't. Wells told Carstairs he'd just come out of a meeting with the prime minister, who told him Manitoba did intend to pass it tomorrow. Carstairs repeated her pledge. Wells, who headed Canada's only other anti-Meech contingent, wondered how he'd know for sure that Manitoba was holding firm.

Carstairs proposed a solution. Both Liberal leaders' offices would keep a phone line open between her executive assistant and Wells's executive assistant the entire time the Manitoba legislature was in session. With her assistant providing occasional play-by-play over the phone to Newfoundland, Carstairs kept her promise not to change the house rules and to prevent the Meech Lake Accord from passing.

"We didn't pass it. They didn't pass it," she says.

Carstairs had put her own personal integrity through the wringer over Meech Lake. Her own Liberal MLAs were badly split on the issue. She expressed her concerns to Premier Filmon in a private meeting.

"Look, Gary," she told him, "this isn't going over particularly well with my caucus that I've compromised on this. So I need to be able to go to them and say there will not be an election this summer."

"I promise you," Filmon said, "there will not be an election this summer."

Guess who called an election for August 7?

I ask Carstairs, "Wasn't there a temptation the next time you saw the premier to say, 'Gary, you bastard, you lied to me'?" She insists not.

"Maybe that's the difference between men and women," she says.

"You expect men to be bastards?" I ask.

"Yeah!" she offers with a hearty laugh. "I wasn't shocked when he called it. What could I do? I lost the election in 1990 and I take full blame and responsibility for that. Because the spirit and fire I had in '86 and in '88, I didn't have in '90. I was emotionally and physically exhausted." The Liberals, who had skyrocketed from one seat to twenty, crumbled to just seven.

Ten years later, Sharon Carstairs admits she still suffers from the role she played in that national melodrama known as the Meech Lake constitutional negotiations. However, two years after the death of Meech, Carstairs got a chance to atone for her "sin." The federal government's next effort at making constitutional peace, the Charlottetown Accord, was on the national agenda.

"When 'Charlottetown' was as botched as I considered 'Charlottetown' to be, I thought here's my time to expiate my sins," she says. She got on the media circuit, and campaigned hard against the agreement. Manitobans voted No by the second-highest percentage in the country—62 percent against.

"As soon as 'Charlottetown' failed," she says, "I resigned. It worked."

But Carstairs wasn't done with politics. In fact, she would emulate her father's career in yet another way. Prime Minister Chrétien called her in February, 1994.

"I hear you don't want to come to the Senate," he kibitzed with her on the phone. In fact, Carstairs wasn't thrilled with the idea. "I don't know, Jean (yes, she calls him by his first name—always has). My living in one city and my husband in another ... I'll have to talk to John."

John Carstairs, ever the supportive husband, said of course she should take it.

So Carstairs called back and said yes, she would accept the appointment. Chrétien answered, "Well, I haven't offered it. I was just trying to find out if you would." And she didn't hear another thing about it for seven months.

Eventually, in September, the call came. Of course, maybe with the sole exception of Frank Mahovlich, no one gets appointed to the Senate by Jean Chrétien without some controversy. Carstairs faced the charges head on. That night on CBC-TV, she was asked bluntly whether the appointment was out-and-out patronage. Her response was equally candid.

"Well, of course it is," she said. Then, after pausing a beat, she added, "The people of Manitoba have to decide whether I will serve them well or I won't." And that pretty much ended the controversy. Whenever school groups tour the Parliament buildings, Carstairs can rest assured the first question will be "How did you get your job?"

"And I say, 'Because I'm a friend of the prime minister's.' But then I say, 'I'd also like to think I'm here because of the things I've done.'"

The Senate appointment also meant Carstairs got to follow in the footsteps of the only politician she has really ever considered her mentor—her father.

"He was a former premier so he sat in the front row [of the Senate]," she recalls proudly. Carstairs was thirteen when her father was appointed to the upper chamber. "I sat in the front row when I was deputy leader—six seats away from where he was. When I was sworn into the Senate that was really kind of a special moment."

They share the same interests. They both wrote their own speeches. And yes, in case you're wondering, "that's where my funny voice comes from."

These days, there's not too much about politics that haunts Sharon Carstairs. But there are the anxious doubts that perhaps she spent her life in the wrong pursuit.

"There's another side of me that says, maybe you did more good as a teacher. Maybe you inspired more young people to make the best of themselves. I always thought if I could take a kid and by the end of June have their ego be just a little bit better than it was at the beginning of September—and I'm not talking about bravado, I'm talking about genuine self-esteem—then I had accomplished my job as a teacher. Sometimes I do step back and say maybe I would have done better with those ten years if I had stayed in the classroom."

She hasn't taught a class in seventeen years, but Sharon Carstairs still gets Christmas cards and birth announcements, and still gets stopped in the grocery story by former students.

And then there are days such as the following one, which may have made politics the right choice after all.

"I still think the best day of my life in politics was when I was sitting as the lone member," she says.

A woman had come to her saying the authorities were trying to kick her out of public housing because she'd cashed an RRSP. The bureaucrat had interpreted the money as yearly income, when in fact, it was a one-time bonus. It was only $1,000 but it made the woman ineligible for social housing. Carstairs got involved and straightened out the misunderstanding. The woman got to keep her home.

"She came to my office and knocked on the door," she recalls. "She had a single flower. And she gave it to me."

The toughest lady in Manitoba politics is tearing up as she remembers the story.

"And I still think that was the very best day of my life in politics. You don't do it for the glory. You know how fleeting glory is."

Carstairs remembers when her father was in politics, he always got lots of presents from constituents. Cigars. Chocolates. Liquor.

"Every Christmas, we'd spend hours opening them," she says. "After he lost, the presents all disappeared. I knew from the beginning, the fame was fleeting, that you had to take your pleasures from other things."

CHRIS STOCKWELL'S SECOND ELECTION IN 1985 was bittersweet. Father and son together. They called themselves "The Taxpayers' Team"—Bill for mayor, and Chris for re-election to the board of control. When the votes were counted, both had lost.

But luckily for the younger Stockwell, there were vote-counting irregularities aplenty that night. He asked for a recount, and his forty-vote defeat became a one-hundred-vote victory—quite a swing.

Stockwell won another municipal election, his third, then decided he was ready to move up. His timing couldn't have been worse. David Peterson's Liberals had won every seat in Toronto in the previous election in 1987 and appeared to be impervious leading up to the 1990 campaign. Even his chief adviser, his father, told him to take a pass.

Stockwell didn't care. He ran. The Liberals tanked. Stockwell won. The brashest voice in Toronto politics was taking his act to Queen's Park. The Conservatives under Mike Harris were in third place and looked to be going nowhere fast. But Stockwell only enhanced his reputation on the opposition benches.

Five years later, Mike Harris's Tories performed a shocking upset by becoming the first party in seventy years to move from third place all the way to government. But what should have been the happiest day of Chris Stockwell's political life instead launched him into a year-long depression. Harris was making phone calls—the ones where you're told by a nice-sounding operator to "hold for the premier," because he's about to invite you to come to his office to join the first Ontario Tory cabinet in ten years. The kind of call that says we actually want you to run a department, not just be a troublemaker for another four or five years.

Stockwell got the call, and it was Mike Harris asking for a meeting. But the rest didn't quite go according to script.

"He called me down and just basically said I wasn't going into cabinet," he says. "He had a series of reasons but I was in a blind rage at that point. I couldn't even hear him. And I just blew a gasket. 'Fuck you. Fuck this party. Fuck this place. Fuck off.'"

This is what's known in politics as a career-limiting move. In case you hadn't noticed, Chris likes the F-word.

"He gets that from his mother," says his father, Bill, with a straight face. Okay, maybe a little tongue-in-cheek.

"I'd felt in all honesty I'd earned it," Chris continues. "I didn't need anyone to validate my position any more. I didn't need anyone to tell me I should have been there. I looked at the cabinet and looked at who got sworn in. I know them better today than I did then, and they're all nice people and good people and I respect them. But there was no reason they were there and I wasn't. There wasn't a reason on God's earth.

"The worst day of my political life was Mike phoning me and telling me I wasn't going into cabinet. I went into a funk for a year. I was really, really depressed," he says.

Stockwell thought his political career was over. Washed up at thirty-eight years old.

"I thought I was fundamentally unemployable," he says without a trace of false modesty. To know Chris is to know deep down he'd be miserable in the private sector, even though, like most Tories, his praise for it borders on religiosity. Private business may be a wonderful thing to praise, but in his heart Chris Stockwell knows he'll never find happiness there.

"I didn't think there was a call out there for a politician who'd been on local council and spent a few years in opposition. My wife suggested I look for a job, but I didn't think anyone would hire me. So I really didn't look for a job."

Stockwell found his solace in his family. Charlene had a job, so he stayed at home for a year. He'd get the kids to school, clean up the house, then check in for another dreary Question Period at 1:30 p.m. No answering tough questions as a minister of the crown. No asking tough questions as an opposition critic. Just a bored, depressed backbencher.

"Chris loved the parry and thrust of the floor," says his dad.

Instead, he'd watch some of his Conservative colleagues strike out on the easiest soft balls. It galled him that he was being denied a chance to strut his stuff in a forum tailor-made to his rhetorical abilities. After Question Period, he'd pick the kids up from school, bring them home, and be Dad again. Then he'd go to his constituency meetings at night.

"It stabilized my life," he says. "There's no greater equalizer than making lunches and picking kids up. And kids are kids. There's no effect on them that I was in that state of mind. I had to look after them, which was a great experience for me. It allowed me to develop huge relationships with them. In hindsight, I can't tell you I was happy about not making cabinet, but there was one silver lining. It created an opportunity for me to be an at-home parent."

Even though his relationship with Mike Harris had hit rock-bottom, Stockwell couldn't give up the dream of one day sitting at the cabinet table. So he did something he swore he'd never do in politics: he kissed his boss's butt—figuratively of course.

The issue was the government's massive Omnibus Bill 26. The printers must have killed an entire forest to make the paper for the bill, it was so thick. It was one of those "everything-but-the-kitchen-sink" bills, designed to alter dozens of files radically and in one fell swoop. In his heart, Stockwell felt the law was anti-democratic, that the issues deserved more intense scrutiny, that at the very least, the bill ought to be broken up. And yet, he voted in favour of it.

"I was in the can having a leak just before the vote," Stockwell recalls. He saw his fellow Tory caucus mate and another maverick MPP, Gary Carr, there as well.

"I'm voting against it, Gary," Stockwell said to him.

"Don't vote against it, Chris," Carr advised. "Don't vote against it. They'll kill ya. You'll be dead."

At the last second, Stockwell reconsidered. "I'd gone to the bathroom confident I was going to vote against the bill and he talked me into it. That was sad."

I suggest to Stockwell that, in the end, the bill would have passed anyway, even without his vote.

"Exactly. But I would have felt better about myself."

Then came the saga of Al McLean.

McLean was a millionaire pig farmer from Simcoe County, an hour and change north of Toronto. He was also the Speaker of the Ontario legislature. Not the sharpest knife in the drawer but not a bad guy either—at least that's what everyone thought. Until one of his employees accused him of sexually assaulting her.

It was actually the third time McLean had faced those kinds of allegations in his political career. On the prior occasions, the cases were settled quietly. But not this time. McLean's fellow MPPs decided three strikes were enough. He was ousted as Speaker.

Ironically, one of his staunchest defenders during confidential discussions in the Tory caucus was Chris Stockwell, who didn't like the idea of firing someone before he'd had his day in court. But when legislators were looking to replace McLean with an independent-minded MPP who wouldn't take any crap from the government, Stockwell's selection made a lot of sense. His political career was resurrected from the dead when he was elected the new Speaker by the majority of his fellow MPPs.

"I was in the wilderness for a long time," Stockwell says. "I would have been in it longer, had Al McLean not slipped."

By all accounts, Stockwell was an excellent Speaker. Where most previous Speakers were older members just about ready to be put out to political pasture, Stockwell brought his typical brand of humour and brashness to the position. And he was fair. He ruled his own Conservative government "in contempt of the legislature" on one occasion—an unprecedented ruling, and an indication that there was a new, less partisan sheriff in town.

But Stockwell still burned to run a department, a real honest-to-goodness ministry. Even though the Speaker's job carried prestige and responsibility for overseeing a one-hundred-million-dollar budget, it wasn't the same.

The Speaker is the referee. Chris Stockwell has always been a player. Ask anyone who's played hockey against him. I have. I know. He's the kind of guy who likes to muck it up in a non-contact game. He'll try to sneak that slapshot in, when the rules clearly say no slapshots. He plays politics the way he plays hockey—elbows up. And unfortunately, the Speaker is required to keep his elbows down.

"Nobody's going to put their name on the line and run for election in the most public competition of all unless they're a competitive person," he says. "It's like playing a pickup game of hockey. If you want to play a pickup game of hockey with a bunch of politicians, it's different than playing a pickup game of hockey in the neighbourhood. Because it may start out as a pickup game of hockey, but ends up as a FUCKING GAME OF HOCKEY 'cause they are so competitive."

And then a funny thing happened on the way to Mike Harris's second term in government. The PCs went from eighty-two seats in 1995 to just fifty-nine in 1999. Despite the drop, it still represented a solid majority, since there were fewer seats up for grabs. (The Tories eliminated twenty-seven MPP jobs when they disbanded the provincial boundaries and adopted the federal ones.) However, only eight Conservatives survived in Toronto.

One has to remember that at this point, Mike Harris and Chris Stockwell are barely speaking. They might say "hi" and "bye" to each other in the hallways, but for four years, the conversation never got any deeper than that.

And then, out of the blue, Harris sent Stockwell a note during Question Period, congratulating the Speaker on winning a tough nomination fight over fellow MPP Doug Ford. (With fewer seats up for grabs, many Tory MPPs had to face off against one another in bitterly contested nomination fights.) It was the first tangible sign that Harris was trying to mend fences with Stockwell. It was also, to use an overworked phrase in Ontario these last six years, good common sense. With a re-election battle in the offing and Tory fortunes in

Toronto looking pretty terrible at the time, Harris couldn't afford to write off any seats—even his worst enemy's.

June 3, 1999. Ontarians decide the Common Sense Revolution should continue. And voters in Etobicoke Centre decide they want Chris Stockwell back too—big time. Stockwell wins the largest majority of any PC candidate in Toronto. He has more votes cast for him—25,512—than any other candidate of any political stripe in the city.

"There are some cold days in this job," Stockwell says, "where you think, 'Oh Christ, am I doing the right thing?' You don't know. And particularly in those four years where it was hard to find friends, in my own caucus especially. Then you go back to the people and they give you an endorsement like that."

After the election, Harris called again. This time, it was to invite Stockwell to hang up the referee's robe and become a player. He was offering the Ministry of Labour.

"Harris probably looked at the results and said, 'Jesus Christ, we can't ignore this guy any more. They're just going to keep sending him here,'" Stockwell smiles.

And what kind of cabinet minister has Chris Stockwell become? Has he let the job he's coveted for so long go to his head? Doesn't seem so. As we sit in his office on the fourteenth floor of the Zurich Building on University Avenue, just down the street from the Ontario legislature, I see no pictures on the wall of the minister shaking hands with anybody famous. His staffers are virtually all the same ones who've been with him since the beginning of his political career.

"There's nobody in this place that calls me 'Minister,'" he says.

"What do they call you," I ask.

"Chris!" he says. "Fuckin' right. I insist."

I always wondered whether Chris Stockwell would change the job, or whether the job would change Chris Stockwell. Up until his elevation to cabinet, he always had the luxury of being able to say whatever was on his mind, whenever he wanted. After all, how bad could the consequences be? He was already living on the political equivalent of Pluto.

If ascending to cabinet has caused Stockwell to temper his remarks, let me suggest that I sure haven't noticed.

"Amongst my friends outside of this world—that we play hockey with or hang with or go to the cottage with—I have a huge ego," he admits. "The biggest of them all. When I come here to Queen's Park, I have one of the smallest egos in politicians compared to my caucus mates. My wife says, 'How do they stand you, you've got such a big ego?' I say, 'Yeah, but, Charlene, it's not big down there. It's all relative."

Chris Stockwell's success in politics these days doesn't stop at the door to the Ministry of Labour. He's become a trusted adviser for many Tory MPPs who like his down-to-earth approach. He has friends on the opposition benches—no mean feat in today's Ontario, where politics hasn't been this polarized in half a century.

"He's earned his spurs the hard way," says his father, Bill. "People respect him for that. He's been his own guy. He hasn't been a toady."

He thought about challenging Mike Harris for the leadership eleven years ago, but ultimately didn't because he knew he couldn't win.

"Winnability is important," says the man who's won six straight elections and never lost. "I won't get into a fight I can't win."

"If there's a convention in the next couple of years?" I ask.

"Oh I'd run. I'm almost convinced. If I could win. I think I could win. You look around the cabinet and say, who's better than me? That's arrogant, but that's me. When you work with these people you begin to realize they've got nothing on me. I'm a bit of a fatalist too. I believe a lot of this stuff is predestined. Timing is everything. You could be the brightest guy in the world but if you've got bad timing, you're digging ditches. There's a million people who could do this job in this province. It just happens to be me."

And just so you don't miss the point, Stockwell doesn't begrudge any of his colleagues—some of whom will be future leadership challengers—any of the ego that comes with the job.

"You've gotta have thick skin that creates the big ego," he insists. "You've gotta be prepared to have people call you whatever they feel like calling you. You couldn't survive without a big ego in this business because you'd be crying all the time. If you took every assault personally, you'd be dead. Dead. DEAD! You have to have it to survive. Because you're being constantly examined, dissected, and criticized. You go into the legislature, no one stands up and says, 'You are doing a wonderful job.' Never happens."

Politics has been and may continue to be the family business. Stockwell's son Kale is only fourteen, but is already showing signs of having been bitten by the political bug. "It's chewing him up," says Chris, who remembers, during his days as Speaker, that Kale acted as if he were the "deputy speaker," when father and son went to a political convention overseas.

"Would I advise him to [run]?" he asks. "I'd tell him this, which is what my father told me and I didn't listen. Get a good education. Get yourself set. Don't go into this business at twenty-four, because you've got nothing after it's done. There's no respect out there from the public any more. I'm not an old man, but when I got into this business in '82, there was so much more respect for politicians then. Today, I don't know a profession that has a worse reputation than politics. And we deserve it. That's the one thing that makes me so mad. Because we're a bunch of liars a lot of times. We've done it to ourselves. But I know full well he is who he is and if this is what he chooses to do, then God bless him, I'm behind him one hundred per cent."

It would be easy to dismiss Stockwell as a superficial, mouthy, bit-too-vulgar flash in the pan, except for the fact that he genuinely seems to have life figured out. For almost twenty years, he's battled colitis. Despite his youthful exuberance, he can look ten years older on days when his condition kicks in. Once, while on Metro Toronto Council, he lost twenty-five pounds and missed more than a month on the job because of his health. He used to pop sixteen pills a day to get through it.

"That was devastating," says his father. "We thought he had cancer."

Chris Stockwell loves politics, would hate to give it up, but it's not his life. And he knows it.

"We're on a ride," he says. "We got on, we got a ticket, and we're not sure when they're going to tell us to get off. So we just keep riding. That's what I believe."

In fact, after he retired as Speaker, the clerks gave him a souvenir gavel inscribed with the following: To Speaker Stockwell—Thanks for the Ride.

"It's a great, great life," Stockwell continues. "And I want as many people as possible that I know to experience this, because it's the greatest thing in democracy we're doing here. Serve the public through elected capacity and effect good honest change. I find when people experience it, they're bitten. It's a tsetse fly. They can't get out. There's no explanation."

Things can sometimes get a little sticky, when the next generation surpasses the record of the prior one. If Bill Stockwell is even a little jealous of what his son has achieved, he certainly isn't letting on.

"I think it's wonderful," he says, with genuine sincerity in his voice.

"We've grown to the point where he is the adviser, but I absolutely am the decision maker," the younger Stockwell says. "He absolutely, absolutely bends to my view at the end of the day. You can sense with him he still wants to be 'the guy' out there. And he's not. People still recognize him, but not to the same degree they recognize me now. I got elected on his coattails and that was hung on me for some time. Well, nobody has said that in so long it's not even worth repeating."

PIERRE MARC JOHNSON IS ONE OF THOSE TRULY rare talents in our country, a kind of Bo Jackson of the arts and sciences. Jackson played professional baseball and professional football at the same time. He was a track and field star too, and no doubt could have played on a line with Wayne Gretzky if he'd wanted to—he was that good at everything.

Pierre Marc Johnson hits a similar trifecta—lawyer, doctor, and politician. And it wasn't long into his political career that he discovered the same highs his father experienced.

"Practising medicine for me in the emergency rooms for a year and a half, I felt pretty comfortable every morning in front of the mirror as I brushed my teeth, because I knew I'd done what I could the night before," he says.

"In politics you have the same kind of feeling, except you're not dealing with individuals, you're dealing mostly with collective issues. But fundamentally you deal with public concern and public good every day. It can be an enormous portion of a week, where you work hours until late at night to get some kind of legislation through, to finish a consultative process with organized groups in society or whatever. But ultimately you wake up in the morning and you say, 'I did something right yesterday.' You can say that in politics most of the time. So the substance is very rich and I think that's what attracts a lot of people to politics."

It was the main attraction for Pierre Marc Johnson. While he despised the endless political wrangling within the Parti Québécois over how hard the party should push the sovereignist agenda, he loved the issues that affected the daily lives of Quebecers.

For example, when he was René Lévesque's minister of labour in the late 1970s, Johnson wanted a dramatic overhaul to legislation governing the workplace. The law in question hadn't had a facelift since 1946. Johnson wanted improvements in the minimum wage, maternity leave, parental leave in the event a child was sick, rights for workers with more than five years on the same job, protection from arbitrary dismissal, and overtime provisions, to name just a few elements in the bill.

"And I did a complete overhaul of that law," he says with apparent pride, more than twenty years after the fact. "That covered two million workers in Quebec. And to get to there, it took almost a full year of work. I'd say half of my time in that ministry was spent on driving three legislative committees, driving the consultations. Unions were against it because they said if you pass a law like that, people will not want unions, which I found to be pretty horrendous. And then, of course, business was largely against it because they felt it was too much."

Johnson remembers five different meetings with the head of the CNTU, Quebec's powerful Confederation of National Trade Unions, over that one issue. Their talks were pretty tough.

"I'd say to him, 'Come on, let's be blunt and frank about this. You'd like people to be in deep trouble—deep shit—so you can justify whatever unionization efforts you can make and take a piece of power. But we're going to protect people better than that. And they might find out that the government can protect them fairly well, and if they decide they won't have unions it's their choice. Some union leaders, particularly at the CNTU, tried everything in terms of lobbying within the government for that law not to pass."

Eventually, the bill passed the Quebec National Assembly and received royal assent from the lieutenant-governor at two o'clock in the morning. One of Johnson's aides, who was with him at the signing, broke the solemnity of the moment.

"He looked at him and he said, 'Excellency, I hope you realize that what's contained in this bill allows you to have double pay for tonight, considering the hour.' It was pretty arrogant, but it was funny."

Perhaps the best day in Johnson family history took place January 11, 1994—the day Pierre Marc's brother, Daniel Johnson, a Liberal, was sworn in as premier of Quebec to replace Robert Bourassa, who was retiring from his second go-round as Quebec's first minister. It meant, of course, that both brothers had followed in their father's footsteps.

"Oh it was quite emotional," says Pierre Marc. "I was very proud of my brother and I'm still very happy [I did it]. I spent eleven and a half years—amongst the best of my life—in politics."

While it's true that the three Johnsons got to the top of Quebec's political mountain, it's also fair to say that the ride was often brutal. Daniel Johnson, Sr., faced constant put-downs from the intelligentsia of Quebec society. The stress of the job doubtlessly contributed to the massive and fatal heart attack he experienced while in office. Daniel Johnson, Jr., came within half a percentage point of matching Jacques Parizeau's total vote count in the 1994 election, but because of the way the votes split, the PQ won a large majority government. He was then forced to endure three years of almost non-stop frontal assault on his leadership from Liberal Party members who thought the party could do better. Eventually, Johnson Jr. resigned, Jean Charest quit federal politics to win acclamation as the new Liberal leader, and suffered the same fate Daniel Johnson, Jr., no doubt would have faced had he stuck around. Charest lost the 1998 election to Lucien Bouchard.

Endless harassment had become a regular feature in the political life of all three Johnsons. The militant minority within the Parti Québécois thought Pierre Marc Johnson wasn't hard-line enough on sovereignty. While he relished the thought of a rematch with Bourassa, he thought the price of keeping the leadership was too high.

"I knew that they'd keep me busy with internal squabbling within the party and it would be impossible for me to face Bourassa during the election," he says. "I'd be weakened because of that. Then I'd be beaten again by Bourassa. I'd been beaten [before] but everybody sort of understood that when I replaced Lévesque I had three months. That was it. End of a second mandate."

Johnson fell victim to the "two-terms-and-out" pattern of Quebec politics—the same pattern that defeated Jean Charest, despite the tidal wave of enthusiasm that greeted his arrival into Quebec provincial politics.

"We didn't expect to win [in 1985]," Johnson says. "So I said two years before the [ensuing] election, 'You want it, take it. I'm not going to go to the slaughterhouse with people from my own party making it difficult to win against Bourassa that time around.' So I decided I would go."

Johnson may have had it with the slings and arrows of Quebec provincial politics, but he also had a rather large dilemma staring him in the face. He was forty-two years old. He'd had the best job The Life had to offer in Quebec. And now his political career was over.

"The day I decided [to resign] I didn't have the vaguest idea, not a clue about what I'd be doing," he says. "Not one clue. And then there's a period which lasts about a couple of months where you sort of unwind all this adrenaline that you've got up for ten years, fifteen years. So I wrote a lot." Some day, Johnson hopes to publish what he wrote during that time of decompressing from politics.

"For the first six months. I really didn't know where I was going," he says.

So he taught. Louise Arbour, a long-time friend of Johnson's from law school, now a justice on the Supreme Court of Canada, brought him to York University in Toronto to teach constitutional law one day a week. It seemed a good fit for a former minister of intergovernmental affairs and justice.

Then McGill University came calling and signed him up as a

full-time law professor, after which he came to realize he missed contact with decision makers. Participating in meaningful issues.

Prime Minister Brian Mulroney's office put out some feelers to see whether Johnson would be interested in being ambassador to Great Britain or France. He declined.

"I felt too young, too young," he says. "I mean five years later you wind up with what? They offer you a post as vice-consul in southern Romania or something because there's been a change of government. No."

So Johnson essentially reinvented himself. He broke open a copy of former Norwegian Prime Minister Gro Harlem Bruntland's famed report for the United Nations on sustainable development. He published half a dozen academic papers on the links between the environment and the economy. He became vice-chair of Canada's National Roundtable on the Environment and the Economy. Now, he advises governments here and abroad on international environmental issues.

"I don't touch national unity," he says with a smile.

Johnson is also full-time senior counsel at the Montreal law firm Heenan Blaikie. He doesn't litigate. He doesn't write contracts. He puts people together into strategic partnerships. He's discovered there is life after politics, but hasn't completely shut the door on a comeback.

"If I went back, I'd probably tell myself, 'I'm going to go in for five years. I'll do what I want and I don't give a damn about those who are unaccounted for," he laughs, referring to the Quebec media and the vocal minority within his former party, who hounded him out of public life almost a decade and a half ago.

And then Pierre Marc Johnson gets a little twinkle in his eye as he looks off in the distance and really thinks about politics. He enjoys what he does. It satisfies him. He advises some of the heavy-hitters in the corporate sector. But he's not "the decision maker" any more and he knows it.

CLEARLY, THE BEST EXAMPLES OF THE NEXT generation grabbing the torch of political leadership are in the United States. George Bush was America's forty-first president. His son, George W. Bush, is its forty-third. Another son, Jeb, is Florida's governor. The Kennedy clan is now in its third generation in American political affairs. Jesse Jackson's son is a congressman.

We have our own examples in Canada. William Lyon Mackenzie was a great nineteenth-century rabble-rouser. His grandson William Lyon Mackenzie King became Canada's tenth prime minister. Michael Meighen sits in the Senate, his grandfather having lost an election to Mackenzie King. Elmer McKay was a PC cabinet minister. His son Peter is a Tory MP from Nova Scotia, thought by many to be the best choice to lead a potential merger of the PC and Alliance parties. And we have our own three-generation family in the Nixons of Ontario: Harry a one-time premier, his son Robert a one-time treasurer, and his granddaughter Jane Stewart in Jean Chrétien's cabinet. Initially, her instinct was to avoid politics and seek her own path. Ultimately, she couldn't resist the tug of making her contribution, although in her own way (federally, not provincially, and running on her married name rather than exploiting her family name).

Ironically, where Harry and Robert Nixon adored public life, Jane Stewart told me she hates it. And she told me this before she became the target of a vicious witch hunt at the human resources development ministry.

"I don't enjoy public life," she said. "I hate it. I didn't realize how much I wouldn't like it. I like the issues and I really enjoy and want to do the work of being a minister. But do I like the *public* life? No. I hate it."

But she does it, because despite all the opposition attacks, the unemployment rate did go down in Brantford on her watch, and she's proud of having had something to do with that.

She hates politics. She loves making decisions which improve people's lives.

As Pierre Marc Johnson says, "You listen, you're accountable for these decisions, but *you* decide, period. And once you've decided, normally nothing is going to stop. There's nothing like deciding. There's nothing like that."

THE TRAILBLAZERS

When Sharon Carstairs became leader of the Liberal Party of Manitoba, it was an historic moment in the political life of Canada. And Carstairs didn't even know it. Still, she was happy to have the honour. But it was certainly not a life-long, abiding passion to achieve it.

Based on dozens of interviews I've done with politicians who have experienced other "firsts" in the life of our country, I'm struck by how little achieving their place in history appears to have motivated them. Part of it can be written off to modesty, both false and genuine. Most Canadians generally are loath to boast about achievements of an historic nature. They certainly want us to know about those achievements and are proud of them. But bragging about them is unseemly. Some politicians experience quite the opposite reaction—the added pressure of being "the first" can be oppressive. In the end, like most politicians in general, they prefer to be remembered for the issues they championed and the things they accomplished.

Having said that, there was a time in Canada when you had to be a man to be a politician. Then women were admitted to the club. Then so-called hyphenated Canadians worked to establish their place on the political landscape. Even in a country as modern as Canada, there are still too many people who have not been accepted as full-fledged players in our political system. But in this chapter, you'll meet people who have blazed unique political trails, some through sheer determination, others by having the good fortune to be in the right place at the right time.

"I WAS NEVER UNDER THE ILLUSION THAT I was likely going to change the world."

Maybe not, but Audrey McLaughlin did. Not by winning general elections or introducing significant legislation. But simply by becoming the first woman to lead a major political party in North American history. She may downplay it (and she did during our conversation). But the reality is, an entire generation of female politicians will find it easier to win their party's leadership because Audrey McLaughlin did it first.

Apparently, it ran in the family. When she was in her early teens, McLaughlin (born Audrey Brown in Dutton, Ontario) watched her mother, Margaret, become the first woman ever to win a seat on Essex town council in southwestern Ontario.

If one were to draw a roadmap of the most direct route to leading a national political party, that map would look nothing like Audrey McLaughlin's life. Her entry into politics was circuitous, to say the least. After completing her undergraduate degree from the University of Western Ontario in 1964, McLaughlin, her husband, and two kids went on one of those extraordinary family adventures. From 1964–67, the family lived in Ghana in West Africa, ostensibly because her husband got a job teaching at Adisadel College in Cape Coast. After the McLaughlins arrived, the locals decided they wanted Audrey to teach too, which she did.

"We went mostly for the change and adventure and hopefully to contribute something," she says.

When she got back from Africa, she attended the University of Toronto's School of Social Work, graduated in 1970, then started working for the Children's Aid Society. "I certainly could see that much of what social work was doing was kind of a mop-up for a lot of structural changes that could make people's lives a little better," she says. She naturally gravitated to the NDP.

McLaughlin moved to Yukon Territory in 1979, another unlikely locale from which to launch a national leadership run. The North had always held a certain fascination for McLaughlin ("Sergeant Preston movies, no doubt"). Just as the trip to Africa was part adventure, part crusade, so too was the move to the Yukon. McLaughlin's marriage had broken up, her kids were off doing their own thing, so she took out a map of Canada, looked up, way up, and vowed to start again in one of the two northern territories. She saw the Yukon had more mountains and that was that. She quit her job, packed up, and promised herself she'd give the adventure six months.

When old Velcro Lips, Yukon MP Erik Nielsen, resigned, the arm-twisters got into action. McLaughlin had worked on various projects such as improving child-welfare legislation, conducted research on land claims and aboriginal self-government, and was active in local NDP election campaigns. She was turning heads.

McLaughlin had just finished a volunteering stint with Canadian Crossroads International, a group which puts people into foreign countries, living with local families in an effort to foster better international understanding. She then took three months to travel around Latin America. She had just returned, was pretty much broke, and hadn't yet got a job. So when local NDP officials suggested she go for the nomination, she thought, why not?

Easier said than done. McLaughlin had to fight three other candidates for the nomination and, ironically, she wasn't the party's preferred choice. She won a nasty tussle by twelve votes. Compared to that, by-election night, July 20, 1987, was a breeze. Well, maybe not a breeze. She did win by only 332 votes.

Representing the Yukon might be the toughest job in national politics. There's no riding in the country that's farther from the capital, both geographically and spiritually. (When McLaughlin's political career began, it took her two days to get from Ottawa back to Whitehorse. "You couldn't nip home every weekend, that's for sure.") Yukon issues are as harsh as the weather in winter—youth unemployment, First Nations, poverty, lack of public services. For McLaughlin, it was a once-in-a-lifetime chance to bring some local causes to a national stage.

A year later, she went back to the polls in the 1988 general election and proved her by-election win was no fluke by capturing more than half the votes cast. Soon, she became chair of Ed Broadbent's NDP caucus (again, the first woman in Canadian history so honoured), a clear sign that her star was rising on Parliament Hill. When

Broadbent announced his retirement from politics a year after that election, McLaughlin ran for the leadership, despite having had just two years of experience as an MP.

Right from the outset, she realized the historic nature of her efforts. Never before in the history of either Canada or the United States had any woman led a major national political party, although McLaughlin was not the first to contest a party's leadership. Rosemary Brown had challenged Broadbent in 1975. And in perhaps Canada's most famous leadership run by a woman, Flora MacDonald came sixth in 1976 at the PC convention that chose Joe Clark.

In any event, if McLaughlin ever forgot for a moment that she was the first woman with a real shot at winning, reporters happily reminded her daily.

"Certainly during that period everything tended to focus on, 'How does it feel to be a woman doing blank, blank, blank,'" she says. "I began to really realize what a shift in the power paradigm that could mean to some people."

Many New Democrats championed McLaughlin's quest. Others were quite threatened by it. That part of the debate McLaughlin could handle. What irritated her were the typical comments about her clothes or her hair—issues no male leadership candidate would have to confront.

"So that, obviously, is when it hits home that you're on a different score card and playing field here, to use a jock analogy," she says. However, McLaughlin had to walk a bit of a delicate balance. Part of the game of politics is proving you can take a punch, figuratively speaking, then get up off the mat and engage in an issue again. ("It doesn't matter if you have passion or information. If you don't look tough, you really haven't got it," she once said.) McLaughlin wanted to prove she belonged, so she avoided playing the victim card.

"I really had to try very hard," she says, "not to do that kind of 'poor me, look at what they are doing,' and just say 'screw it.' Just go ahead and do what you can. If you're going to carry the baggage of all the travails of the day, I mean, you'd drive yourself nuts."

On December 2, 1989, McLaughlin was elected leader of the party in an exciting three-ballot nail-biter over fellow MPs Dave

Barrett and Steven Langdon, in Winnipeg. Barrett, a former premier of British Columbia, was a much better stump speaker than McLaughlin. But the majority of delegates fancied the idea of making a little history, and taking a chance on someone they thought had tremendous growth potential. McLaughlin may not have been impressive at the show biz of politics, but she was deeply committed to the issues the NDP championed and exhibited warm interpersonal skills. She had the ability to lead without being overbearing or demonstrating too much ego.

However, if she thought her previous experiences in life—world travel, significant expertise in social policy, not to mention divorce and single motherhood of two children—would prepare her for the learning curve that is the national spotlight, she was mistaken.

"In the end you're alone," she says. "It's a cliché but it's like death. No one does it for you." What got McLaughlin through the circus was constantly reminding herself why she was in politics. She also had the advantage of being, in her words, a more mature woman who had a good perspective of what was important in life.

One of the best things she had going for her was the fact that the NDP had to be taken seriously as a player on Parliament Hill. Broadbent's 1988 election showing was an all-time best for the NDP—forty-three MPs. The party was shut out in Quebec and Atlantic Canada, but won more seats than anyone else in British Columbia and Saskatchewan, showed decent strength with ten seats in Ontario, and actually captured one seat in Alberta for the first time in its history.

Audrey McLaughlin would enjoy many fine days leading up to the 1993 federal election. And then she would experience something that still haunts her, nearly a decade later.

It was, perhaps, the most frightening time of the past fifty years in Canada. The British high commissioner in Montreal, James Cross, had been kidnapped by the Front de Libération du Québec, a self-proclaimed group of freedom fighters whose aim was independence for Quebec. Shortly after the kidnapping, the provincial labour minister, Pierre Laporte, was also abducted, then found murdered in the trunk of a car.

As far as Prime Minister Pierre Trudeau was concerned, the FLQ was not a group of freedom fighters, engaged in some romantic quest. They were now terrorists, pure and simple. Ostensibly at the request of Quebec's premier, Robert Bourassa, Trudeau imposed the War Measures Act in October, 1970. Armed soldiers and battle tanks became familiar sights on the streets of Montreal, as the federal government tried to restore order. English Canada responded with tremendous support for the prime minister. However, some French Canadians were more concerned about the hundreds of innocent Quebecers, arrested and put in jail, without any charges ever being laid or any legitimate explanation for their arrest given.

In the midst of the October Crisis, a thirteen-year-old boy watched his first ever political speech on television in his parents' living room in Montreal. It wasn't the prime minister's strength under fire that captured his attention. Rather, it was the leader of the federal New Democratic Party, whose words somehow resonated.

Tommy Douglas was at his oratorical finest, admonishing Trudeau about the need to safeguard democratic rights in a civilized society. It was a speech remarkably absent of pragmatic politics. Douglas's NDP base in Western Canada thought the War Measures Act was completely justifiable. And Douglas could hardly be accused of trying to suck up to the Quebec electorate. The NDP hadn't elected any members of Parliament there, and weren't about to either.

Glen Murray, who was born, raised, and educated in Montreal, found all of this terribly impressive.

"It was such a visible, principled, honest, and courageous position to take," he says. "And I thought, that's what leadership is all about."

Somehow, Douglas's speech got Murray thinking about the sorts of things most thirteen-year-olds don't think about: the power of politics, ideas, and contributing something to the public discourse.

Who knew that a quarter of a century later, Glen Murray would make his mark in all those areas, in a way no Canadian ever had before, just by being gay?

AS FANTASTICALLY MULTICULTURAL A PROVINCE as Ontario became over the latter part of the twentieth century, the fact remained that

Canada's largest province had never seen a black face sit at the cabinet table until 1985. Part of the reason was that from 1943 to 1985, the Progressive Conservative Party created a dynasty almost unique in Western democracies, and the party had never really made much of an effort to grow beyond its white, Anglo-Saxon, suburban and rural base. Until the 1980s, Caribbean communities had made up a small fraction of the population, and it's probably fair to say the vast majority had as much interest in penetrating the ranks of the political class as that class had in wanting to admit them.

This was the political climate Alvin Frederick Curling found himself in, in the early 1980s. Curling had come to Toronto from Kingston, Jamaica, in 1966, looking for a fresh start to life. He was the sixth of nine siblings. His dream was to earn one hundred dollars a week, and within a year that dream came true. He was hired by GO Transit to work behind the counter in the parts shop at the main depot.

By 1984, Curling had transformed himself into an education administrator. He was in charge of all orientation and convocation services at Seneca College of Applied Arts and Technology in Toronto. He'd speak to two thousand students, class by class. By the time their three-year term was up, he knew them all.

Trying to run Seneca was like trying to run a small town in the middle of a big city. Housing and social problems were rampant and Curling was consistently being called upon to find solutions. His politics were always liberal. But as the 1984 federal election approached, he thought he might give big-L Liberal politics a try as well. Curling had some vacation time banked and thought this might be "a great adventure." There was an open seat in York–Scarborough, the riding right next to where Seneca was located. And Curling was just naïve enough to think these nomination fights were open, democratic contests. Not quite. Former cabinet minister David Smith, who was now running the candidate search unit for the new Liberal leader, already had a candidate in mind for that riding and it wasn't Alvin Curling. Smith and Curling met.

"John Turner sent me to say that we'd rather you came out [of the nomination race]," Smith told him. "We want June Rowlands."

That wasn't too tough to understand. Rowlands was a high-profile, experienced, and respected municipal politician, who'd eventually go on to become mayor of Toronto in the early 1990s. She was, however, a Toronto politician seeking a nomination in Scarborough. If you're from outside Canada's biggest city, that nuance may not mean much. But inside the city, a Torontonian seeking votes in Scarborough was as appropriate as someone from Idaho running, claiming he was still reasonably local. Curling just didn't buy it, didn't figure the voters would, and wasn't impressed with the message Smith was delivering.

The more Smith pressured him to step aside and wait his turn, the more Curling was determined to contest the nomination and let the chips fall where they may.

Alvin Curling did not win his first political encounter. The organizational power of Turner's minions carried the day for June Rowlands. But not by much. She won the nomination by five votes. In the end, it didn't matter. Despite her credentials and profile, Rowlands was swamped on election day, as so many other Liberals were, by a PC landslide.

What was Curling's reaction to his defeat? "Wow, that was a wonderful ride," he smiles.

How could it have been wonderful when the party establishment was against him, and probably would be in future too, given what he'd put them through?

"Because to me, liberalism wasn't owned by any of those guys," Curling says. "You think John Turner owns this thing? I thought it was rather funny for them to say, 'no,' therefore, I can't be a Liberal."

(Ironically, Curling fared better than two others who contested that nomination: Tony Ianno and Derek Lee, both of whom would go on to become Liberal MPs.)

Curling went back to Seneca College, this time as director of student services, figuring his political career was over. He thoroughly enjoyed the nomination skirmish but still thought that was it. Then Hershell Ezrin called. Ezrin, who was chief of staff to opposition leader David Peterson, was looking for candidates to run for the Liberals in the upcoming Ontario election. He remembered Curling's moxy in challenging Rowlands.

"Would you consider running for us?" Ezrin asked him.

"I'm done with it," Curling insisted.

But this situation was different. This was provincial politics, where Liberals always lost, not federal politics, where Liberals almost always won. There weren't long lineups of star candidates hoping to run for Peterson as there were for John Turner. In fact, nobody else wanted to run in the riding Ezrin was recommending—the largest constituency in the country—Scarborough North, population 220,000. Not only that, the riding was the home base for Tom Wells, a significant player in William Davis's government and a fixture on the scene for more than two decades. In fact, in the previous election, Wells had won 413 polls. His opponent won one. All in all, it seemed as if Ezrin was offering Curling the political equivalent of a kamikaze mission. But the more he thought about it, the more attractive the challenge sounded. Curling reconsidered and said yes.

"So here's this sacrificial lamb going ahead not even knowing what the hell he was doing," Curling says of himself. "It was like someone threw me into the Niagara River and said, 'Swim for it.'"

And then a strange thing happened. Two months before the 1985 election, Tom Wells threw Alvin Curling a life raft. He announced that, like his friend Premier Davis, he too was retiring from politics. Suddenly, Scarborough North seemed a little less fortress-like.

Having said that, Curling still had no idea what to do during an election campaign. The only thing that came to mind was something he'd seen on television ten years earlier. He recalled watching a southern governor in the United States going door to door, saying, "I'm Jimmy Carter and I'm running for president." Curling remembers thinking Carter was nuts running that way, but come to think of it, the impact was enormous and the guy won.

"So I thought, that's the only strategy you need," Curling says. "We went out and knocked on doors for eighteen hours a day with my ragtag team because we had no strategy. And no money. I knew I would run as hard as possible and let the result take care of itself."

Election night was one for the ages. Curling was so exhausted from his constant canvassing, he went home, had a bath, and cleared his head, while the election returns came in. Later, as he walked back to his campaign headquarters, he was listening to election coverage on a Walkman radio, still exhausted and not quite with it. Then the announcer on the radio said, "There's a guy named Alvin Curling who's won Scarborough North tonight. Most of the polls are reporting in, and he's going to win big." The funny thing was, Curling didn't react. He was still in the twilight zone and the news simply didn't register.

But it did when he arrived at campaign headquarters. People were screaming. Curling was paralyzed. He was like a rock star in the middle of a crowd of teenagers. They tried to rip his clothes off. One staffer yelled at another, "Get him outta here!"—so palpable was the fear that Curling's supporters were going to crush him with their exuberance.

All Curling could think was, "What the hell have I done?" Tears started to stream down his face and he couldn't understand why. He looked at the crowd and saw a sea of black faces. He looked into their eyes, eyes that understood the significance of Curling's victory, even though he didn't yet. It was one of the most powerful moments of his life.

The extent to which Ontario had changed was manifested no more clearly than in Scarborough North that night. This traditional Tory territory voted so overwhelmingly for Alvin Curling that the candidate discovered he'd won more votes than any candidate in any parliamentary election at any time in Canadian history.

Curling's high, while awe-inspiring, was also a curse that would dog this trailblazer for the next five years of his life.

HAS THERE EVER BEEN A MORE DRAMATIC story of blazing trails in public life than that of Kim Campbell?

Canada's first female prime minister. The first prime minister from British Columbia. The first baby boomer prime minister. The first divorcee (not once but twice) to be prime minister. A meteoric rise. A fall of historic proportions.

Campbell's background is well known. She was born Avril Phaedra Douglas Campbell on March 10, 1947, in Port Alberni. When she was twelve, she changed her name to Kim after her parents split up. She didn't see her mother for another ten years. She knew from an early age that politics was her calling, as evidenced by her winning the presidency of her high-school student council, and the freshman council at the University of British Columbia (the first woman to do that too).

Years later, when Campbell became a professor at UBC, one of her students offered her perhaps the best political advice she'd ever receive. His name was Andy Stark and he was national president of the Young Progressive Conservatives. When Campbell told him she might go into politics some day, Stark gave Campbell some of Robert Stanfield's speeches to read and urged her not to enter politics by working her way up through the traditional party ranks. "Become a star," he told her.

A quarter-century after receiving that advice, Kim Campbell still thinks those are words to live by.

"With women in particular, working your way up through the ranks isn't particularly rewarded," she says. "What he was saying was, you need to have that kind of critical capital that makes a party want you to be a candidate."

Campbell took the advice to heart and started her road to stardom by winning election to the school board on a non-partisan ticket. She had a knack for getting headlines, thanks to her plain-spoken bluntness, intelligence, and sense of humour. In 1983, she came to the attention of the Social Credit government, which recruited her to run in the provincial election. Premier Bill Bennett's party was re-elected, but Campbell refers to the campaign as her "kamikaze run." She got trounced.

Still, she must have shown the Socreds something, because by the summer of 1985 she found herself working as the executive director in Premier Bennett's office.

Campbell's career has been punctuated by moments of incredible chutzpah, and the next one occurred within a year of her taking the job in the premier's office. She resolved to run for the leadership of the Social Credit Party. At first blush, it seemed an act of ridiculous hubris. Then again, more than a dozen candidates had their eyes on that prize, so there may have been plenty of hubris to go around. William Vander Zalm won the convention.

Campbell collected just fourteen votes on the first ballot. But she also had the most memorable line of the weekend. During her speech, she warned delegates in a not so thinly veiled reference to the eventual winner, that "charisma without substance is a dangerous thing. It creates expectations that cannot be satisfied. Then come bitterness and disillusionment that destroy not only the leader but the party." Campbell's prescience earned her Vander Zalm's ire and a standing ovation.

Nevertheless, she contested the next election on October 22, 1986, this time winning a seat in Vancouver–Point Grey. However, thanks to her convention speech, a trip to the cabinet was not in the offing. Campbell and Vander Zalm simply disagreed with each other on too many issues, particularly abortion. Fifteen years after they shared that election-night triumph, there's still not much love lost.

"For all the years I was in politics, I met many, many more intelligent people than I met smart people," Vander Zalm tells me carefully. "And I guess she was more the intelligent type."

For her part, Campbell is no more complimentary.

"What motivates him is beyond me," she says. "The guy has an extraordinary ego. And I think the kind of rush he gets from it is very different from the kind of rush that I got from politics. That may sound self-serving. But I think the attention is something that he just loves. The kind of quiet, interesting work that you do behind the scenes is not the sort of thing that turns his crank. But he has a following. Boggles the mind but you know, there it is. That's the nature of democracy."

Campbell hung around Vander Zalm's world of provincial politics just long enough to keep her star rising. She resigned as a Social Credit MLA two years to the day after winning the job, and opted for federal politics. Less than a month later, she joined the Progressive Conservatives' second consecutive majority government, but just barely. At four o'clock in the morning, she got a call telling her she'd taken Vancouver Centre by a whisker. It was so close, there was a recount, after which Campbell actually lost ten votes. She was on her way to Parliament having won by 269 votes.

But a win is a win and Kim Campbell was about to find herself on the fast track to the stars. She was also about to get involved in an alternately wonderful and disturbing relationship with a man named Brian Mulroney.

IT SEEMS THAT ONE OF THE MOST SIGNIFICANT differences between New Democrats and other politicians is that New Democrats almost never say their best day in politics was winning an election. Maybe it's because the moral victory has always seemed more important for the social democratic movement. There's an acknowledgement that if you're going to run for the NDP, you're going to spend more time losing than winning and you'd better get used to it.

Audrey McLaughlin is no different. She enjoyed three personal election victories in just six years of federal politics, and none of those nights hits number one on her hit parade.

McLaughlin preferred those occasions when she supported an important principle, particularly when doing so flew in the face of public opinion. Her New Democrats became the first major party in North America to question the wisdom of the Gulf War against Iraq in 1991. The NDP's polling numbers, already precariously low, dipped even further. But McLaughlin and her foreign affairs critic, Svend Robinson, stood by their principles, political costs be damned. Prime Minister Mulroney also showed her respect by swearing McLaughlin in to the Privy Council, so she could receive confidential security briefings on the war's progress.

She made another politically unwise decision to support the Charlottetown Accord. The constitutional agreement, negotiated by Prime Minister Brian Mulroney and the first ministers, went down in flames across the country. But McLaughlin liked many of the things in the accord that spoke to northerners and First Nations people, so again, she went to bat for a cause, political consequences be damned.

"I had many people advising me that politically it was totally stupid to support it [the accord]," she says. "They were, of course, correct." "Charlottetown" became a referendum on Mulroney, rather than a debate about the merits of the agreement. "It was sort of like, 'If he likes it, then I hate it,'" McLaughlin says. Perhaps the minor miracle, unnoticed by most, was that McLaughlin kept her caucus intact despite intense differences on the agreement. The NDP supported Charlottetown unanimously.

But McLaughlin paid a price for her principles. As Canadians were preparing to render their judgement on Brian Mulroney's government and Kim Campbell's attempts to revive it, the numbers for the NDP just kept dropping. The leaders' debate offered McLaughlin a last chance to show Canadians the qualities her fellow New Democrats saw in her when they chose her as leader four years earlier. She acquitted herself well, getting off some good lines and amusing the scribes afterwards with her assessment of the event.

"It is kind of a demolition derby of politics," she told the *Ottawa Sun* years later. "Who's going to crash? So there's a certain fascination, I suppose."

On October 25, 1993, as Canadians tried to wage war on the Conservatives, plenty of New Democrats got caught in the crossfire. Because the Tory situation was so horrendous, the story of the NDP demise was almost lost in the shuffle. But a demise it was. The most telling blow was a complete wipeout in Ontario, no doubt contributed to by the low popularity of Bob Rae's provincial government. British Columbia was almost as bad, going from nineteen seats to two. Even in Saskatchewan, the NDP lost half its seats. Add it all up from coast to coast to coast, and all the NDP faithful could find were nine seats, and that flattered the party, which captured less than 7 per cent of the total votes cast. The Tories only won two seats, but actually received more than twice as many votes as the NDP.

"There is just no good face you can put on it," McLaughlin says.

The New Democrat leader took the loss very personally. Almost three hundred NDP candidates—including a record high number of women—put their hopes in her ability to show the electorate something they could grab onto. She couldn't, and she felt responsible.

"Did you resist the temptation to beat yourself up over that night?" I ask her.

"No," McLaughlin responds bluntly.

"Do you still feel lousy about it?"

"I do," she says.

"It's almost a decade later," I remind her.

"I know."

"You know, you did beat the sitting government," I remind her.

"Yeah, well, another first, right?" she says. "The only time the NDP has ever beat the Tories."

McLaughlin became quite depressed after that election. Not so much that she couldn't get out of bed in the morning. But it was debilitating enough. She wasn't a drinker ("and I'm too old to have been in the drug culture"). So she did what she's done during other challenging times in her life. She rolled up her sleeves and tried to remember why the voters of Yukon sent her to Ottawa (and incidentally, they clearly still wanted her in Ottawa, rewarding McLaughlin with a two-to-one margin of victory over her closest challenger).

So she began touring the country, meeting with the party faithful, trying to figure out what went wrong and how the rebuilding could commence. She did that for two years, fighting the devil of depression the whole time.

"Yes, I was depressed," she says. "Absolutely ridiculous to say I wasn't. I'm still depressed about it. I feel it very much as a personal failure."

And then there was the "woman thing."

"You kind of feel you let the side down too," McLaughlin says. "It is failure. In politics not winning is a failure whether you want to put a nice face on it or not."

Half a year after losing official party status in the '93 election, Audrey McLaughlin felt her time had come. She announced she would serve out her term as an MP, but resign the leadership. She actually stayed on in an interim capacity for another year and a half. The party was in rough financial and emotional shape and in no condition for a quick convention. When the party chose another woman with the initials A.M. to replace her (Alexa MacDonough), McLaughlin's political career was effectively over. It had all started so improbably, so far away from the nation's capital. Now, she was a year away from her sixtieth birthday, facing one of the hardest challenges every former politician encounters—finding a meaningful life after politics.

She continues to speak out on issues she cares about and frequently hears compliments—from young women in particular—on how she inspired them to consider public life.

"That's great," McLaughlin admits. "If that's true and not just a social nicety, that's lovely. And if it's a social nicety, hey, I'll take flattery any time."

That aside, life is pretty good for the former NDP leader. Her house and her car in Whitehorse are both paid for. She flies all over the world—a dozen international trips last year alone.

She was president of the well-known worldwide organization Socialist International Women, travelling from Sarajevo to Latin America for that one-hundred-year-old organization. She went to Zimbabwe for the National Democratic Institute of Washington (and collected a whack of Air Miles to help pay for other trips).

In September, 2000, she spent three weeks in Kosovo, offering campaign training for women candidates, in anticipation of the pending fall municipal elections.

Like most politicians, Audrey McLaughlin is not getting rich in post-political life. Her MP's pension pays her $2,500 a month and it's fair to say she doesn't make much more than that from other sources. She will turn sixty-five in a couple of months, so other seniors' benefits are just on the horizon. She has learned to live very frugally, very far away from the rest of Canada's population.

She knows it sounds corny, but she still feels she was privileged to have experienced The Life, if only for a decade.

"What I did hope was to do things responsibly, to do it ethically, to be able to exercise some of the things I believed in, in the interest of the people whom I represented," she says. "I know that sounds very political, but sorry, that's really why I did it."

HAVING BEEN IMPRESSED BY HIS BOYHOOD idol Tommy Douglas, Glen Murray didn't wait long to test the political waters. As a student at Concordia University, he ostensibly majored in communications. However, as a member of the student body for four years (and president for one), he no doubt spent as much time thinking about politics as he did in pursuit of a degree.

Murray first went to Ottawa to work for the Canadian Labour Congress, only to find his job disappear shortly after he got there.

Then someone he knew at Canada Post suggested he come work as a summer replacement in their special events branch. Murray was evidently good enough at the job that he parlayed it into a full-time job in corporate communications.

The nation's postal service may seem an unlikely place from which to launch a political career. But had Murray not taken that job, there's no question his life would have turned out to be completely different. Not that the work at Canada Post was so fascinating. In fact, it wasn't at all what Murray had hoped for in his career. However, what the Crown corporation did that inalterably changed Murray's life was send him on an assignment to Winnipeg. And that's where it all began to unfold politically.

Murray fell in love with Winnipeg. He loved the diversity of the people. He loved the vibrant arts scene. He loved the neighbourhoods. His arrival in Winnipeg also coincided with the public's becoming increasingly aware of one of the worst health scourges of the late twentieth century: the AIDS crisis. While still working for Canada Post, Murray got into the habit of visiting one particular AIDS sufferer named Jim Farley every Wednesday and cooking him dinner. One evening, the two had a heart-to-heart talk.

"What are you doing with your life and what do you really want to do?" Farley said to him.

Murray said there were five things he really wanted to accomplish in Winnipeg. He wanted to become a parent. He wanted to see a Gay Pride Day proclaimed. He wanted a new, more effective law protecting gays and lesbians from discrimination. He wanted to run for office. And he wanted the community to come together to defeat AIDS. He'd already seen more than forty of his friends killed by the disease.

"Working through the AIDS crisis was a huge turning point in my life, in understanding myself and understanding the limitations of life, and my own mortality," Murray says.

Farley was blunt. "Well, why aren't you doing any of those things?"

The answer distressed him. There were no openly gay politicians in Canada at this time. (Svend Robinson was still officially in the closet.) "And no one's going to allow me to be a parent," Murray retorted, presuming his sexual orientation would disqualify him. He had done a lot of work volunteering to help street kids and thought he'd be a good parent to some troubled kid who needed a home. But he convinced himself his homosexuality was an impenetrable barrier to parenthood.

Again, Farley had some advice. "You know, the world isn't just going to change by itself," he told him. "If you want to do these things, go out and change the world."

And that's just what Glen Murray did. He joined forces with other AIDS activists to form the Village Clinic, at the time the only volunteer medical program being run in Manitoba. The doctors and nurses all volunteered their time. One down.

He worked with a street kid named Michael, who asked Murray to be his father. After jumping through a million bureaucratic hoops, Murray did become a foster father to Michael. Two down.

Then Murray and friends had a meeting in Jim Farley's basement to plot strategy for bringing a Gay Pride Day to Winnipeg. That, too, was eventually successful. Three down.

They also lobbied the province for new human rights legislation, protecting gays against discrimination as it related to housing or employment. And they got it. Four down.

Then, finally, in 1989, Murray ran for a spot on city council against two much better-known and much better-financed candidates. No one gave him much of a chance. So, of course, he won. He was the councillor for Fort Rouge. Five down. Slam dunk. List achieved.

Just as he'd suspected, Murray discovered he loved politics, and civic politics in particular. He was fascinated with how neighbourhoods thrived, how people from different ethnic groups lived together, how cities looked and the role good architecture plays in that, how arts groups added to the vibrancy of city life. He also liked the fact that city politics was individual politics. Parties didn't whip him to vote or speak a certain way. Issues got decided more on the merits, rather than out of blind party loyalty. Murray liked all these things about municipal politics, and the system truly allowed him to speak his mind.

Murray discovered that politics gave him a richer, better-lived life.

After three terms as a city councillor, Murray decided to throw his money on a real long shot—winning the mayoralty. It seemed an almost impossible dream. As a mid-western city, Winnipeg is fairly socially conservative. There are tens of thousands of Mennonites and devoutly Catholic Filipinos, who might not be inclined to vote for an openly gay candidate. Even if you took the issue of Murray's sexual orientation out of the mix, there's still the fact that Winnipeg's mayors, as far back as anyone can remember, were born and raised there, and no candidate from the left wing of the political spectrum had won since World War II.

So against all odds, Glen Murray blazed his own trail into the mayor's office on October 28, 1998. He became Winnipeg's forty-first mayor, in a remarkably polarized election. With almost 222,000 votes cast, Murray won by fewer than eleven thousand. He took 50.5 per cent of the vote. But more important, he became Canada's first ever openly gay mayor. He was forty years old.

"It seemed so beyond the pale," he says. "It was one of those moments when you realize attitudes about gay people and minorities in the city had changed, that the mayor's chair was no longer guaranteed to the old, right [wing] coalition that had run the city for more than half a century."

Being the mayor of a large Canadian city is a unique job in politics. Prime ministers and premiers have a handle on the politics of their jobs. Governors general and lieutenant-governors are responsible for the ceremonial aspects of public life. Mayors do both. They are the political and ceremonial leaders of their cities.

Some may mock the ceremonial aspects of the job—who can stomach yet another ribbon-cutting—but Murray eats it up. "The ceremonial stuff is important to the community. I believe in ceremony and tradition," he says. So it's not unusual to see the mayor flipping pancakes at the teddy bear picnic on a Sunday morning to raise money for the Children's Hospital. Or speaking to war veterans to thank them for their sacrifice. And Murray does it with a sincerity not often seen in politics.

"People gave up their lives for the kinds of freedoms and democratic rights and responsibilities that this building called City Hall here in Winnipeg represents," he says.

Having said all that, succeeding at The Life has its price and Murray has had to pay his.

"What I find very hard to live with is a complete loss of personal freedom. It is really a scheduling straitjacket," he says. Spontaneity? Forget it. It's gone. Call up a friend and say let's hit a movie tonight? Rarely happens any more. What's he doing on June 5, 2002, at four-thirty in the afternoon? His staff can probably tell you. The irony of winning is that all the close friends and family who helped you get elected are the people you will see the least once you're successfully ensconced in office. It's the nature of The Life. In the midst of a particularly busy time, Murray confessed to himself, yes, he got his list of five things done but, "At some point I want a life again."

As for governing itself, Murray rolled up his sleeves and started to make a difference from the get-go. After all, he says, it's the political and legislative record on which you're judged. He moved Winnipeg to a three-year budgeting cycle so the city could plan its future better, then brought in a 2 per cent tax cut in each of those years. The plan passed council by a fifteen-to-one vote.

There were other initiatives. Murray spent a year helping to create a downtown development corporation to improve Winnipeg's troubled inner city. Fixing up housing, keeping an eye on expenditures, making the streets safer, and enhancing the cultural life of the city were all on the agenda.

Murray has also changed the style of the mayor's job. The car and driver are gone. The mayor gets himself from event to event driving a Ford Explorer that can handle Winnipeg's brutal winters. He hates cellphones but keeps one in his SUV, one of the personal compromises he's had to make because he's the mayor.

Murray's best day in politics started with a phone call from Lloyd Axworthy. His staff knew the call was coming, but Murray didn't. They wanted to surprise him. Even though Axworthy was minister of foreign affairs, he was also the man whose tentacles were on every single project in Manitoba in which the federal government was involved. Murray had spent a year trying to get both the federal and provincial governments to join Winnipeg in creating a forty-million-dollar affordable housing plan, but couldn't seem to find any takers. Certainly, Gary Filmon's provincial government wasn't interested.

But then some things changed. Nine months after Murray became the mayor, Filmon was defeated by Gary Doer's New Democrats, who *were* interested in cutting a housing deal. And then Axworthy called.

"We've read your stuff and we're very committed to it," Axworthy told the mayor. "The federal government's going to get back into housing. We're really going to put some money into it." The minister offered to write a twelve-million-dollar cheque right there.

"Can I buy you lunch anywhere you want to celebrate?" Murray replied.

Within a week, Gary Doer called offering eight million dollars. "And we're going to build on that as well," he promised.

"We went from having had a decade of absolutely nothing, to rebuilding housing," Murray says. He acknowledges his good fortune in becoming mayor at a time when senior levels of government shared his vision for his city.

Murray's political star would continue to shine. Last autumn, despite his having been mayor for less than two years, he was the target of a draft campaign by local Liberals, who wanted him to run for the nomination in Lloyd Axworthy's old riding, Winnipeg South Centre. There were some other solid names expressing interest, but the nod was probably Murray's for the taking if he'd wanted it. He thought long and hard about it, but ultimately took a pass. There were still too many things to do as mayor. His views of Jean Chrétien may have played a role in the decision as well. Several months before the speculation about his political career arose, Murray described the prime minister this way: "I would have trouble defining him as a visionary nation-builder. He's more a contented, status-quo, try-to-maintain-consensus-in-the-country type. There is a leadership crisis in the country right now."

Murray's political life was endlessly interesting. His personal life was a different story. Relationships and politics are a tricky mix at the best of times. Try adding the wild card of being gay into the mix.

Murray and his significant other, Rick, have been together for seven years now. They deal with many of the typical stresses and crises that any relationship encounters. And then, of course, there's the issue of the couple's homosexuality. For the vast majority of Winnipeggers, it seems not to be an issue. So many people in Winnipeg identify themselves as some kind of hyphenated Canadian that seeing the mayor representing another minority group isn't a big deal. But the couple themselves are still working through a few things. Rick, it seems, isn't crazy about tagging along to all the events the mayor has to attend. Where Murray loves crowds, his partner prefers the solitude of reading a book or renting a movie. Rick is an operating-room nurse, prompting Murray to suggest, "He's used to going into a small room where everyone is gagged or has been put under. He doesn't have to deal with many active talking human beings."

Murray also wonders how visible the two of them should be. "Do we want to be the poster gay couple?" he asks rhetorically. "You have to be extra good at everything because you're the first in this kind of office at that level from a minority community. That creates stress."

Personal issues aside, Glen Murray admits he loves The Life.

"I think I do get back so much more than I give," he says. "When I go to bed at night, I feel better about the life I have than I would if I were doing something else. I don't find any other pursuit as interesting or as challenging."

ALVIN CURLING'S INTRODUCTION TO ELECTIVE politics coincided with a unique moment in Ontario history. In 1985 the Conservatives, under Frank Miller, had been knocked down to minority government status, only four seats ahead of the Liberals, who actually garnered more votes. Both the Tories and Liberals entered into negotiations with the NDP, who held the balance of power. What emerged was a bold new political accommodation. The third-place NDP would join the second-place Liberals to end the Tory dynasty. Then the Liberals would assume power.

It was into this historic ascension to power that Alvin Curling marched. He was one of forty-eight Liberal MPPs, almost none of whom had any governing experience. The extent of Curling's legislative experience was having seen Question Period twice.

The Liberals were looking to make a splashy, clean break with old Tory Ontario. The new premier, David Peterson, had his cabinet sworn in on a beautiful June day on the front lawn of the legislature. That was a first. He opened up the building and invited thousands of members of the public to take a tour. When they accepted the invitation en masse, the floor of the second storey of the legislature gave an audible groan. (Later, that floor would undergo a serious renovation. Rumour has it, it almost collapsed under the weight of an unprecedented number of visitors.)

The day before the swearing-in of the first Liberal government in forty-two years, Peterson invited Alvin Curling to his office. Because it took almost two months to defeat the Tories in the house, then transfer power to the incoming Liberals, there was ample time for the media to speculate on who'd get what in the new government. Every observer expected Curling, despite his inexperience, to win some kind of cabinet job. The temptation to appoint the first black cabinet minister in the more than two hundred years since settlers first arrived in Ontario seemed irresistible.

To get to Peterson's office, Curling had to run a gauntlet of reporters, who speculated to his face about the portfolio he'd be getting. Once inside, the premier revealed to Curling the debate he and his staffers had been having about the rookie's political future.

"People wanted me to give you Citizenship or Culture," the premier told him. In some respects, that would have made sense. Curling's strength was certainly in knowing more than most legislators about the multicultural experience of Toronto, and a junior ministry is usually a good place to start someone with no political history.

"But I won't do that," Peterson said. "I won't make you a token, Alvin. You're getting Housing. Now, I don't want you to talk to anyone about this. Don't say anything to the media. Just wink when you come out."

"How can I not tell them," Curling laughed. "*They've* already told me it's housing."

It almost didn't matter what portfolio Curling got. At first, wherever he went, the policies he pursued were never the story. *He* was the story. How well was Ontario's first black cabinet minister doing? Could he represent the government effectively? Curling was never a policy wonk. People skills were his thing. For two years, he rejoiced in an intense high for his role in making history. And simultaneously, he suffered through constant headaches for the same reason.

"The high was very frightening in a way," Curling says. "I became clumsy. I didn't want to speak and look stupid. When I was the minister of housing, each time I'd stand up to speak, I'd remember those faces from election night. Don't let them down. Don't let them down. The pressure was enormous."

Whenever Curling had to give a speech, he'd look at the crowd and sense that the black people in the audience were almost holding their breath.

"They're telling you in a way, 'Please don't screw up. Because if you screw up, I screw up,'" he recalls.

And those headaches. Curling says he had them almost the entire time he was minister. The pressure to be in command of his ministry, to know the facts, not to look foolish, to be able to represent himself—and by extension, other blacks—effectively in Question Period.

That was a constant challenge for Curling because the reality was, he had no experience at the parry and thrust of Question Period. Moreover, the first issue to grab headlines was his ministry's attempt to find a new rental formula on which landlords and tenants could agree. The numbers, the acronyms, the bureaucratese sounded like a foreign language to someone who hadn't spoken it before. Curling seemed to be grasping at straws, trying to answer pointed opposition questions about the formula.

Then one day, he heard the opposition leader, Larry Grossman, interviewed on the radio about the issue. A reporter wanted to know why Grossman kept hammering away at Curling on the formula.

"Because he doesn't know the answer," Grossman answered.

"Do you?" the reporter asked.

In fact, he did. Grossman, a cabinet superstar when the PCs were in power, then explained quite effectively what Curling had been unable to explain. And the media made sure everyone understood that the opposition leader knew the issue better than the minister.

The next day at Question Period, Curling was ready. When Grossman rose to ask him, yet again, to explain his new housing policy, Curling said, "Mr. Speaker, I am appalled to know the leader of the opposition already has the answer yet wastes our time here asking me." The whole place broke up.

However, while Curling was fighting for his political life, his sister Madge was fighting for her actual life in a hospital in Orlando. Curling was delayed getting to Florida to be by her bedside. By the time he got there, his sister was on life support, falling in and out of coma as she fought cancer. Then he was called back to Toronto to shepherd his rent formula bill through the legislature and ensure its passage. He was unable to be at Madge's bedside when she eventually passed away, and to make matters worse, couldn't even fly back to Florida in time for the funeral.

But the sun was setting on the Liberals. Curling was having a lot less fun at his job. For one thing, his relationship with the premier had deteriorated.

"Please, Alvin, you know my door's always open," Peterson told him. "Come on by."

"Stop bullshitting me," Curling responded. "The door's open but there's nobody home. And once you get through that door, you have to get through another door as well."

After the Liberals fell prey to an NDP upset, life changed a great deal for Curling. He retained his seat, unlike sixty of his colleagues, but found the transition to opposition difficult.

"When I wasn't the minister any more, there were some frightening parts about it, both emotionally and physically," he says. "Just the routine of what you do. I drove through a stop light without realizing it, and I really got frightened about that. I hadn't driven in four years. I'd gotten accustomed to being driven by a chauffeur. I couldn't drive for about a month." Curling was also learning lesson number one about politics—people treat you a lot differently when you're in opposition than when you're a minister. "And the phone doesn't ring that much any more."

But his relegation to the opposition benches didn't mean Alvin Curling was through making history. In fact, in 1996 he was at the centre of one of the most celebrated incidents of civil disobedience against the new Progressive Conservative government.

Mike Harris wanted to move with lightning speed, so he introduced an omnibus bill which touched on so many different aspects of life in the province, you almost needed a forklift to pick up the bill. It would have given extraordinary powers to cabinet ministers to make decisions quickly, without much scrutiny from the provincial parliament or the public. Even the future Speaker of the legislature, Conservative MPP Chris Stockwell, thought the bill was dangerously close to being anti-democratic.

The bill was so huge no one could read it, and yet all MPPs were being asked to vote on it immediately. Curling was so disgusted, he considered simply not showing up at all for the vote. The Liberal caucus met and found a clever way within the rules to stall the bill's passage. Curling missed the meeting, but in his absence, the caucus decided each member would cause a ruckus, forcing the sergeant-at-arms to eject each of them, one by one. It might not have been elegant, but they were all furious at how the Tories were riding roughshod over their rights. Twice Curling had tried to get the Speaker's attention to rise on a point of order and protest the proceedings. Twice he was rebuffed. He was angry.

Alvin Curling's regular seat in the legislative chamber was in the front row of the Liberals' section, two seats in from the end closest to the Speaker. Once the plan went into action, the Speaker started ordering the ejection of MPPs, starting with those closest to him. Bernard Grandmaître, a soft-spoken gentleman from eastern Ontario, was the first to go. Then the sergeant-at-arms came to Curling, who, having missed the caucus strategy session, wasn't in on the plan. The Speaker ordered the sergeant to eject Curling.

But Curling refused to budge. He was asked again to leave. And again, he shook his head. The sergeant-at-arms at the Ontario legislature is a tall, wiry man who carries a sword. But it was pretty clear he wasn't about to use his superior strength or weaponry to carry out the Speaker's orders.

Suddenly, opposition members from both the Liberals and New Democrats realized Curling had accidentally stumbled on a brilliant means of filibustering. Many of them began to converge around Curling. They surrounded him, as if to say to the Speaker, if you want to physically remove him, you're going to have to go through all of us first. It was an incredible scene.

"There's a word—*uhuru*. It's a Swahili word meaning 'freedom at any price,'" Curling says. "I felt that way. I thought, I really don't care. So I won't move. I was angry that democracy was being hijacked."

The situation was unprecedented and no one knew what to do. The business of the legislature couldn't continue—the opposition had seen to that. So the clerk's office called Westminster to ask for advice. What do we do? the mother country was asked. Well, nothing like this had ever happened there either. England's response: you're on your own.

The Tories wanted their omnibus bill passed but realized they were at the precipice of a public relations nightmare if they tried to get security guards to bully their way towards Curling and have him physically removed. Such an approach might actually have worked if it were a different Liberal MPP, say someone younger, stronger, with a bigger mouth, and with more of a reputation as a troublemaker.

And frankly, someone less black. Behind the scenes, everyone was buzzing that the government, which had been accused of bullying many minority and special interest groups in society, couldn't allow the legislature's only black member to be roughed up and tossed out.

So Curling, and the many MPPs who surrounded him, waited. And waited. And waited. If he were to leave to go to the bathroom, the filibuster would be over. So some members held up a blanket while Curling hid behind it and relieved himself, one assumes, into a bottle.

Curling's filibuster started at three o'clock in the afternoon, lasted all night long, until eleven-thirty the next morning. He never slept. He never stood. He sat for twenty and a half straight hours. But during that time, negotiators from all three parties struck a deal and arranged for public hearings on the omnibus bill. When Curling did stand up to leave the chamber, he collapsed. "The place started to spin," he says. Both opposition leaders, Lyn McLeod and Bob Rae, had to escort him out, his legs were so stiff.

"What I love about public life is that people don't need a lot," he says. "The potential of what you can do is enormous." So Curling actually gets his kicks returning constituents' phone calls and solving their problems. Maybe he'll write a letter supporting someone's bid to get into a certain school. The little things. Without fail, people seem shocked that he returns his own calls. It makes their day.

"Sometimes they just need a little smile," he says. "You can sit in the house every day in opposition and ask the question that you hope is going to bring the government down. Well wake up, you're not going to bring the government down. I prefer the joy of helping people."

SHE'S NOT SURE WHY, BUT THE EVIDENCE just kept piling in. Brian Mulroney had his eye on Kim Campbell. He accorded her the singular honour of giving the reply to the 1988 Speech from the Throne. It would be the first speech of the new session, and Campbell's first ever address in Parliament. Then, just two months after winning her seat, Mulroney appointed her to the Indian Affairs and Northern Development portfolio. Almost immediately, people started whispering about her as a possible future leader of the party.

Campbell's stay in the Indian Affairs Ministry only lasted thirteen months, but she felt she was able to leave some footprints by moving the land claims agenda forward. She was the first British Columbian since Arthur Laing twenty-three years earlier to have the position.

Then on February 23, 1990, Campbell's career got another huge boost. Mulroney appointed her minister of justice and attorney general of Canada, made her the political minister for British Columbia, and gave her one of the coveted positions on the "inner cabinet," the priorities and planning committee. Plain and simple, it was an enormous promotion.

"The day I was sworn in as minister of justice was just the most amazing thing," Campbell says. Her fondest memories of public life happened in that portfolio. "Hammering out an issue and just enjoying it so much, enjoying the collegiality, the challenge of it, the stimulation of it, knowing that you were inspiring and motivating the people around the table." Campbell loved it all.

It also marked the beginning of an unusual and confusing relationship with the man who clearly tabbed her for greatness.

"I have a lot of respect for Brian Mulroney," Campbell says. "He's a very smart guy and did a lot of very, very good things. When he could see that I could handle things and I wasn't going to tear the caucus apart, he just left me to get on with it. And so it was a huge pleasure to work for him."

Having said that, Campbell always felt shy around Mulroney and never talked to him much, despite the fact it was obvious he was championing her career. That was typical. Mulroney didn't socialize with his ministers much. But the prime minister often did things that left his justice minister perplexed.

Perhaps the most controversial file on Kim Campbell's desk in the Justice portfolio was the one with David Milgaard's name on it. Milgaard had been convicted in 1970 of murdering a nurse named Gail Miller. He spent twenty-three years in prison for a crime which, it later emerged, he did not commit. His mother, Joyce, was a tireless campaigner to have the evidence in her son's case re-examined, and her public confrontation lobbying Campbell in Winnipeg was caught by a phalanx of cameras. Campbell's response to Joyce Milgaard's entreaties may have been legally appropriate, but politically it looked cruel. "Madam, if you wish to have your son's case dealt with fairly, please do not approach me," Campbell said, before scurrying through the closest door. Technically, Campbell may have been right, since, as minister, her handling of the case had to be seen to be completely free from politics and decided strictly on the merits. But it looked bad. It looked even worse when, months later, Prime Minister Mulroney met Joyce Milgaard on a street in Winnipeg and went out of his way to praise her courage and determination.

"We were all floored," Campbell said in her autobiography *Time and Chance*. "We just couldn't understand it. The prime minister had blindsided me on one of my most difficult issues."

Why did Mulroney do it? Campbell tells me she still doesn't know.

"He's his own worst enemy in that sense," she says. "Sometimes he just can't help himself."

Did Campbell ever seek a private moment with Mulroney to discuss the matter? She says not. It just wasn't the kind of thing ministers did with him.

"It depends on whether the leader creates an atmosphere that makes that possible," she says. "And I don't think Brian Mulroney did." Campbell says, eventually, she did get an apology from the Prime Minister's Office and an assurance that no promises had been made. However, Campbell's ire was raised several years later when DNA evidence exonerated Milgaard, and "Brian Mulroney was then quoted as saying that he was the one that was responsible—which annoyed me because he had nothing to do with it at all."

Having said all that, Campbell enjoyed some of her most intellectually and politically stimulating moments in public life while tending to the Justice portfolio. Her championing a Canadian Human Rights Act amendment towards the end of 1992 was a major undertaking. Campbell wanted sexual orientation to be included on the list of prohibited grounds for discrimination in the human rights code. Trying to get a fundamentally conservative caucus to agree was an enormous challenge.

"I actually put my job on the line," Campbell tells me of that effort. "Had caucus not approved it, it would have gone down. That was a very exciting moment because that was really the culmination of a couple of years of manoeuvring and lobbying. It meant a lot emotionally."

Campbell continued to win high-profile, challenging portfolios. After three years as Canada's first female justice minister, she became the first woman ever to be awarded two of the cabinet's most macho jobs: minister of defence and minister of veterans affairs. She became the only woman ever to sit at a table of NATO defence ministers. But her stay in Defence lasted only a few months. On February 24, 1993, Brian Mulroney walked into a meeting of the Progressive Conservative caucus to a thunderous ovation and with the news he was quitting politics.

That started a chain of events that would lead Kim Campbell to blaze a trail no one ever had before or has since.

Timing one's departure from office is one of the trickiest political exercises any first minister undertakes, and for the Tories it was doubly problematic. Twice in the twentieth century, the Liberals demonstrated they were more expert at renewing the leadership and maintaining power, having successfully done so from William Lyon Mackenzie King to Louis St. Laurent, and from Lester Pearson to Pierre Trudeau. As Brian Mulroney contemplated whether to leave politics, he had to consider the reality that no two Tory leaders had successfully passed the baton and maintained power since Robert Borden and Arthur Meighen did the trick in 1920, and even then, Meighen was only able to remain prime minister for eighteen months.

So Mulroney was essentially trying to achieve something that the Tories hadn't done in almost three-quarters of a century. As Kim Campbell watched the nation's political agenda unfold, she knew events were conspiring to make a smooth transition even more difficult.

"I understand how hard it would have been with the defeat at Charlottetown," she says of Mulroney's second effort to secure a national unity package. "He couldn't go out on a defeat." Campbell speculates if Charlottetown had passed, Mulroney might have run with the victory and retired, but even then, there would have been less than a year for a smooth transition.

During the national debates over the Charlottetown Accord, Campbell ran into Manitoba's Liberal leader Sharon Carstairs. The two women were on opposite sides of that debate, but shared a concern over who would be the next to lead the federal Tories.

Carstairs's advice was to the point: "Don't become Mulroney's sacrificial lamb."

What did she mean by that?

"I think she felt that Mulroney would have so poisoned the well that nobody was going to be able to win."

Was Carstairs right?

"You can't say, I don't want to run 'cause I don't think we can win," Campbell says. "We all knew that it was a real long shot and yet, how can you resist the opportunity to become prime minister even for a brief period of time?"

At this stage, Campbell appeared to be the flavour of the month as Mulroney's successor. But what was really required? Why did Campbell want to be leader? Was she doing it for the popularity or validation? Did she truly grasp how difficult the process would be?

"I wanted to be very clear in my own mind what I was going to be encountering and that was going to include a considerable amount of loneliness," Campbell says, recognizing her closest friends who could keep her grounded were in British Columbia, hardly a hop, skip, and a jump from the capital. Campbell also had to do something no male contender ever had done or ever will do, and that's to consider whether contesting the leadership would help or hurt others of the same gender, who might want to follow the same path in future.

"I had to weigh the question of, would it put women back to win, become prime minister, and then not win the election?" Campbell asks. "And I decided that it would not."

Once Mulroney told his caucus he was retiring from politics, the question was no longer academic. There would be a leadership convention. There would be a new prime minister by June. And that new prime minister would only have a maximum of five months to restore the PC party's lustre and bring it back from the disastrous 18 per cent popularity ratings it was suffering through at the time.

Somehow, even though she was still just a rookie MP with relatively little time in the party to make those valuable connections, Kim Campbell shot to the top of the list of potential replacements for Mulroney. She made two hundred calls over a three-day period to size up her chances, and obviously she liked what she heard. She appeared to so dominate the field that almost none of the expected challengers from cabinet came forward.

On March 25, 1993, one month after Mulroney announced his resignation, Kim Campbell took the next giant step in her political career. She gave one of the most original campaign-kickoff speeches in Canadian history. She spoke with no notes. She was relaxed. She told jokes. She talked about "changing the way we do politics in this country."

Even though Campbell was heading towards an easy victory, not everybody was pleased about that, in particular, the man she was hoping to replace.

"Well, see, Brian Mulroney is a control freak," Campbell says. "And he had this vision that the leadership campaign was going to be a hotly contested campaign that would show off all the Conservative strength." In fact, what the party appeared to want was quite the opposite—not a brutal, divisive, five-ballot drama, but something closer to a coronation so the party could regroup quickly and re-craft itself in time for the next election.

"And so what happened for me was that I then became everybody's target," she says. "So it really turned out to be very bruising for me."

In public, Mulroney was saying how important it was to have a seamless transition from him to his successor. Privately, he was urging other candidates, in particular Jean Charest from Quebec, to get in and give Campbell a tough fight. As Campbell thinks back on it almost a decade later, she's dumbfounded at Mulroney's strategy.

"It was just amazing," she says. "Although he kept saying, 'I want to pass it on to a new leader who can win,' blah, blah, blah. It was bullshit. It really was."

In the final week of the campaign, Joe Clark talked about the importance of having a leader that's "stable." Another cabinet minister, Bill McKnight, said he couldn't believe Tory delegates would drink "Campbell Kool-Aid," a bizarre reference to the mass suicide at Jonestown, Guyana. The insults were getting thick and personal. Ultimately, the only purpose they served was to chip away at Campbell's image, although not necessarily her convention votes. On June 12, 1993, in Ottawa, she convincingly defeated Jean Charest on the second ballot by 187 votes. In the end, it wasn't a bad showing by Charest. However, it was a decisive victory for Campbell, who would now join a most exclusive club of female world leaders.

"After I'd won, and at the celebration that night, the euphoria, the excitement, it was this sense that people had of having made history," she says. "You know that tough stuff is going to come. But that was a night when I really allowed myself to savour the accomplishment, the significance of it and what it, meant to other people. I mean the party, the celebration, people were just in seventh heaven."

And not just the women. Paul Curley, a veteran of many Conservative campaigns, was in tears. "This is for my daughter," he told Campbell that night.

Campbell wasted little time trying to restore Tory fortunes. She was sworn in as Canada's first female prime minister at Rideau Hall on June 25, 1993, then hit the hustings. She wanted to show Canadians she was not only different in gender, but also in style. Where Mulroney constantly came under criticism for running an imperial prime ministership, Campbell earned kudos for her informal, accessible approach. She spent much of the summer hitting the barbecue circuit, and the public responded. Her approval ratings soared. Canadians seemed genuinely excited to have a woman as prime minister, even if she did represent the hated Tories, and they gave Campbell the highest job approval ratings in thirty years.

Campbell didn't have much time before the government's five-year mandate was over, but she did manage to enjoy some of the trappings of being prime minister. For example, she had a couple of private meetings with U.S. President Bill Clinton.

I know it's tacky, but I have to ask. "Did he ever hit on you?"

"He's very nice, very charming, very easy to get along with," she says. "But no. Somebody once said I don't have big enough hair."

Campbell was also just one of two women ever to attend the G-7 Summit.

However, because Mulroney had left his departure to the fifth year of the mandate, Campbell had little time to make an impression. She could shuffle her cabinet and try to dramatically restructure departments, but there was no time for a parliamentary session. So she called an election for October 25, 1993—less than one month before the five-year term was up—and crossed her fingers.

To this day, understanding all the complexities of that '93 election campaign is difficult. The media were merciless in their coverage of Campbell, but gave Liberal leader Jean Chrétien virtually a free ride. That may have simply reflected what the public wanted. Vast segments of the population wanted to get back at the Tories, but Mulroney was gone. Campbell was the handy target.

Campbell also discovered how the media can choose to make a

huge deal out of something trivial, but ignore something much more significant. On the first day of the campaign, when asked about the prospects for lowering unemployment, Campbell pulled a chapter out of Howard Cosell's book and told it like it was. She forecast—accurately and honestly as it turned out—high unemployment rates for several more years. She was crucified for not offering Canadians hope. Chrétien, on the other hand, offered a good old-fashioned Liberal make-work program—and a fairly insignificant one at that—and somehow he was said to have a vision for leading Canadians out of their unemployment doldrums. As the *Globe and Mail's* Ed Greenspon so accurately put it, Campbell's biggest problem was "new politics, old media."

With just over two weeks to go before election day, a reporter asked Chrétien about some aspect of his program. His answer: "Let me win the election and after that you come and ask me questions about how I run the government." Chrétien actually said that, and no one in the media batted an eyelash.

Not surprisingly, given the way the campaign was being covered, Campbell's numbers started to fall. In hindsight, she also has come to realize that she couldn't handle the sleep deprivation that was a feature of the campaign. She recently read *Sleep Thieves*, a book by University of British Columbia professor Stanley Coren, about what happens to the body when it's denied the sleep it needs. Campbell felt she was reading her biography.

"I was exhausted," she says. "Everybody else, after the leadership campaign, took time off. I couldn't. I did have to hit the ground running the next day. And every time, I kept saying, 'God I need to get some rest,' and the campaign team would say, 'Oh yes, yes, yes, we're going to set this time aside.' And it never came."

Campbell's campaign staff evidently didn't realize how important it was to give their candidate a chance to regain her stamina, which had been put to the test with almost non-stop campaigning since the Charlottetown referendum in 1992.

"I could feel the disaster coming," says Campbell, who made more mistakes, and whose French deteriorated as she became more fatigued.

What irritated her more was the ghost of Brian Mulroney, which always seemed to be hovering above the fray.

"It annoys me when the people who'd been close to Brian Mulroney said, 'Brian Mulroney would have done this.' Well, Brian Mulroney never operated under those circumstances. You know he never dealt with that kind of a time frame."

Campbell says Mulroney's allies in the party seemed to be more concerned about the reputation of the outgoing leader than the party's prospects for re-election.

"Mulroney would phone the campaign team every day to make sure that his legacy wasn't being besmirched," Campbell says.

Campbell recalls discussing this situation with a friend of hers who happens to be the former president of Bolivia. That man told his would-be successor, "Say whatever you like about me. Don't spare my feelings if you want to be critical of me. Do whatever you need to do."

Campbell never got the same speech from Mulroney.

(For his part, Mulroney disputes much of this. He says he was in China and Europe during the campaign, spoke to Campbell twice to buoy her spirits and checked in with other party insiders a few more times to see how things were going. Further, "I'm not offended at all by the idea that she had to distance herself from Brian Mulroney any more than John Turner distanced himself from Pierre Trudeau or Al Gore distanced himself from Bill Clinton," he says. "This is absolutely normal. It was fine by me.")

On election night, Kim Campbell had no idea what dramatic events would unfold. She knew the Tories were only polling at sixteen per cent, but had no idea how that would translate into seats. She got her answer soon enough. The PCs would capture more than two million votes nationwide, but those votes were scattered too broadly. A rout of historic proportions was on. The Tories went from 169 seats in 1988 to two. Campbell couldn't keep together the coalition which Mulroney had assembled in 1984. As a result, those voters created two new parties, Reform in the West and the Bloc Québécois in Quebec. As a percentage of the national tally, Reform only captured 2.5 per cent more votes than the Tories, but it was a much more efficient vote, and translated into fifty-two seats. And the Bloc, under

Lucien Bouchard, astonished everyone by becoming the official opposition with fifty-four seats, winning almost half the votes in Quebec.

"Election night 1993 was devastating but it wasn't something that I didn't see coming," Campbell says. "I think what was devastating about it was that I knew it was the end of my political career. It had been high-stakes poker and I knew what the implications were."

Campbell did entertain thoughts of sticking around and trying to rebuild the Conservative Party. But she had two problems. First, she had no seat in Parliament. Second, she says even after the debacle, her predecessor's influence was still being brought to bear.

"It became very clear that particularly the Mulroney people in the party were not going to let me do that," she says. "They're so committed to making sure that Brian Mulroney is never criticized."

So Kim Campbell made the painful decision to leave The Life. She resigned the PC leadership six months to the day after winning it.

It's not uncommon after crushing defeats for leaders to go into a funk, even a depression, for several months. Campbell didn't. She instinctively reinvented herself to deal with her post-political blues. She went to Harvard University the following year, in part to teach and in part to get away from having to read the Canadian media every day.

"I knew that it would be cruel," she says of the post-election coverage. "And so I just went into survival mode."

Campbell dove into her new life with the same energy she'd shown throughout her political life. In a classy gesture, Prime Minister Chrétien appointed her Canada's consul-general in Los Angeles. She became chair of the Council of Women World Leaders, an organization based at Harvard, whose members either are, or have been, female presidents or prime ministers. At her first meeting, Poland's former prime minister Hanna Suchocka approached her, saying, "You're the one I wanted to meet." Everybody knew about Canada's first-ever female prime minister.

Last year, Campbell co-chaired a conference in Yemen on emerging democracies. She's a senior fellow at the Gorbachev Foundation in Boston, a think tank which tries to spread the gospel of democracy and economic liberalization. And she's on a dozen other organizations dealing with foreign affairs, post-secondary education, and global security.

Time is, of course, a great healer, and Campbell's election showing is no exception. She wrote in her autobiography, "I will always be haunted by what we could have done differently in '93." She seems less haunted today.

"People say to me, 'Don't take the loss personally. We liked you, but you were in the wrong place at the wrong time.' So I don't think that it put the cause of women back. It's past. I've turned the page a long time ago."

Interestingly, when Campbell is asked whether she'll ever run again, she doesn't answer with a direct "No." She'll say she can't imagine it, or can't see how it could happen. But there is something about most politicians that requires keeping the door open, even one per cent. The notion that The Life is gone forever is hard to stomach.

"I was sad because I had enjoyed it so much," she says of her departure from politics. "I loved it. It was the thing that I was best cut out to do."

POLITICIANS, MORE THAN MOST OF US, have a sense of their place in history. Making that contribution which journalists might chronicle or historians might analyze for years to come is part of their makeup. Even more so, if you've been fortunate enough to blaze some trails along the way.

However, there appears to be a price for that uniqueness. There are myriad examples that suggest the more history-making the accomplishment, the more devastating the experience will ultimately be.

Both Kim Campbell and Audrey McLaughlin suffered huge reversals of fortune after achievements of historic proportions. Rita Johnson, the first female premier in Canadian history, found her government utterly rejected by British Columbians. She not only dropped out of politics, but also out of sight. The first woman *elected* premier, Catherine Callbeck of Prince Edward Island, found herself winning every seat on the island but one, then was hounded from office still in her first term, admitting her performance was a terrible liability for her party. The first NDP governments in Ontario and British Columbia—led by Dave Barrett and Bob Rae, respectively—lasted only one term and were crushed at the polls in the ensuing elections.

Blazing trails can assure you a place in the history books. But another adage seems just as valid. The bigger they are, the harder they fall.

THE CHILDHOOD DREAM

In 1938, Herb Gray was a grade two student at Victoria School in Windsor, Ontario. Gray would go on to an enormously successful career in politics, pre-dating Jean Chrétien's arrival on Parliament Hill by one year. He won his first election for the Liberals in 1962, and seven years later, became the first Jewish-Canadian to sit at the federal cabinet table. Eventually he became Chrétien's deputy prime minister in 1997.

But the politics of his life in 1938 were a bit different. That was the year David Croll was running for re-election as the mayor of Windsor. Croll was the first Jewish cabinet minister in Canadian history, having served on Ontario Premier Mitch Hepburn's executive council in the 1930s. But now he was in a tough battle against Colonel E.S. Wigle for the mayoralty.

Each day when Gray arrived at school, he and his male classmates waited in one basement room, while the girls waited in another, until they were led upstairs to their classes. Then, during the mayoralty campaign, one group of boys would yell, "Yeah, Wigle!" followed by the other group (including Gray) which would chant, "Yeah, Croll!" This would continue until the teacher opened the door and led everyone into class.

Not everyone gets "involved" in politics as early as Herb Gray did. But for many, dreams of The Life begin long before their name actually appears on any ballot.

TOM LONG IS LATE. TWELVE MINUTES LATE. He's also unfailingly polite as he apologizes and gives his excuse.

"I resigned from my firm this morning. That's why I am a little late coming," he says.

Long has had a very successful career at the Swiss executive search firm Egon Zehnder for the past ten years. The timing of his departure is curious to say the least. "What are you moving to?" I ask.

"I have no idea," he says.

"Come on, you quit without having something else?"

"Yeah. I have nothing else," he insists.

"Are you insane?" I admonish him.

"No, I'm not," he says. "Looking for a job's a job. You can't do a proper job of figuring what's out there if you're somewhere else."

The timing of Long's resignation is so interesting because the old Reform Party is in the midst of recasting itself as the Canadian Alliance, and a leadership contest is afoot. Reform leader Preston Manning is in. So is Alberta treasurer Stockwell Day. But there's no serious candidate from Ontario, and at the moment that's a glaring omission for a party that's desperately trying to be taken seriously east of Manitoba. Long gave a spectacularly well-received address at the United Alternative convention in January, 2000, at which time delegates opted to create the new Alliance. Eight standing ovations, a blistering and well-publicized attack on Tory leader Joe Clark, and a take-no-prisoners style prompted many delegates and pundits to start wondering whether Tom Long might be that credible candidate from Ontario the Alliance has been waiting for.

Two months after the convention drama, Long and I are having lunch together. So I ask again. "Tom, what the hell are you going to do now?"

"I don't know," he says. "I'm very excited and scared out of my pants all at the same time." Long goes on to describe what he'd like in a new job, and the only thing that's clear is it's definitely going to be in the private sector. Some "consumer-driven business" is how he describes it.

It seems perfectly obvious to me that Long's quit his job to clear his calendar for a leadership run. The only thing wrong with my theory is that Long's already told everyone who'll listen that he's not interested in running for the leadership. He wants to help build this new, national, neo-conservative movement, but not lead it.

"Tom," I begin, "you go to this [United Alternative] convention. You rock 'em sock 'em. You got great press."

"Yeah," he says.

"They're looking for an Ontario candidate." Do I have to spell it out?

"I didn't want the job," he says.

"How could you not want the job?" Everything I've ever read about Long suggests he's wanted to be prime minister since he was in diapers. He was born in 1958 in Sarnia, the petrochemical capital of Ontario. His parents, Lorraine and Stan Long, weren't at all interested in politics. Neither were any of the four Long children, of whom Tom is the oldest.

The first political involvement he remembers was as a grade six student. As part of a school project, Long had to help some candidate running for some office. He chose a New Democrat seeking a seat on the school board. Obviously, nothing took.

"Even at that young age, I was more sensible," he deadpans.

Long credits his parents (who always voted Liberal) with instilling in him his core conservative values of hard work and less reliance on government. But it was a neighbour working for PC candidate Andy Brandt in the 1972 federal election who gets credit for turning Long on to partisan Conservative politics. He was pounding lawn signs into the front yards of Sarnia at age fourteen. Active involvement in Tory youth clubs followed. Not surprisingly, Long was seen as a bit of a loner at school. He was serious, committed to a cause, and old beyond his years.

At this lunch, he was trying to convince me he had no interest in being prime minister.

"There's a great new phrase that management consultants are using," he says. "It's called a 'clear line of vision.' The clear line of vision in this race is through to the Prime Minister's Office. Because unless you can sit down and say to yourself, this is a job I want and that I can do, and that is a good match with who I am, you can't take the first step down the road. You can't run for something just because it's going to be fun."

Long also points out another obvious impediment—he and his wife, Leslie Pace, are about to have a baby. Due date is right in the middle of the final weeks of the campaign.

"I am not going to do something I don't believe in," Long says firmly. "It wouldn't be a good match for me. What they do in Ottawa isn't anything I want to do."

About one month later, Tom Long was in the race.

THE ALBANY CLUB IS THE QUINTESSENTIAL Conservative hangout in Toronto. Ever since Sir John A. Macdonald founded the place more than 120 years ago, it's been the slightly stuffy, establishment place to be seen by mostly older, established Tory party members. The fact that Tony Clement joined the Albany Club as a University of Toronto student tells you a lot about Tony Clement. He knew this was a place where an up-and-coming Conservative could make myriad contacts, but was street smart enough "not to discuss it with normal folks."

Clement (pronounced Cle-MENT) seems to have enjoyed a reasonably good childhood, despite encountering several obstacles that were unusual for a kid growing up in Hamilton and Toronto in the 1960s. He was born Tony Panayi in Manchester, England, the only child of a Greek Cypriot father and Jewish mother. The family came to Canada when Tony was four years old. His parents separated six years later.

Tony's first brush with politics almost happened before the 1972 federal election. His friend Vern Freedlander invited him to a barbecue hosted by his local MP, who happened to be David Lewis, the NDP leader. Tony declined. To this day, he wonders.

"What if I'd gone?" he asks rhetorically. "Would I be a raving socialist right now? As fortune would have it, I didn't go."

He may have missed the 1972 campaign, but before long, Tony did become riveted by current events. His mother bought him a subscription to *Time* magazine and he became fascinated with Watergate, the Vietnam War, the energy crisis, and the dwindling popularity of Pierre Trudeau's government.

In 1975, Tony got introduced to PC politics in a very direct way. His mother, Carol, got a job at Queen's Park as an administrative assistant to a Tory MPP. But her timing wasn't the greatest. She was hired just in time to watch Premier William Davis's popularity plummet. So she enlisted the support of everyone she could get her hands on, including her fourteen-year-old son, Tony, to knock on doors and hand out leaflets. The MPP kept his seat, Mom kept her job, and young Tony got bit by the bug. Throughout his high-school years, Tony dove deeper into politics and began to entertain his first serious thoughts about standing for office some day.

"I became known as the political guy," he says. "I got my friends involved in campaigns. They were always saying to me, 'You're going to be premier, you're going to be prime minister.' So of course, you start thinking about that."

He showed unusual perspective for a young kid. His ambition, while no doubt simmering below the surface, seemed held in check, perhaps because of the experience of one Davis cabinet minister in particular, John Clement.

John Clement was elected the Tory MPP for Niagara Falls in 1971. In 1972, Davis put him in cabinet as consumer minister, and a few years later, Clement had worked his way up to attorney general of Ontario. And then it all ended. Clement was the highest-ranking cabinet minister to lose his seat in that nearly disastrous 1975 campaign.

In 1978, he married Carol Panayi and adopted seventeen-year-old Tony, who opted to take his stepfather's surname.

"John Clement was Exhibit A for the other side of politics," Tony Clement says. "He was the cautionary tale." The unmistakable lesson: "If I was interested in running for politics, I'd better be prepared to lose, because politics is never forever."

His name was now Tony Clement, and before long, people across the country would be reading it in their newspapers.

JOLIETTE IS A SMALL TOWN OF TWENTY THOUSAND inhabitants, about forty minutes northeast of Montreal. It's almost entirely francophone. The majority of people voted in favour of sovereignty in both the 1980 and 1995 referendums and turned thumbs down on the Charlottetown

Accord in 1992. Its local member of the Quebec National Assembly has represented the Parti Québécois since the party formed its first government in 1976. And the Bloc Québécois has taken the Joliette seat since its inception on the federal scene in 1993.

They've never been much on voting for Liberals in Joliette. Even when Pierre Trudeau was running up big majorities in Quebec—for example in 1980 when he won seventy-four of seventy-five seats—the lone holdout was Joliette, which voted for Conservative Roch LaSalle.

So it was a very blue neighbourhood in which Anie Perrault was born and raised. There was some political activity in her family. Her grandfather, Guy Perrault, was a close friend of Antonio Barrette, the premier of Quebec in 1960, who was also from Joliette. And granddad was also an organizer for Daniel Johnson, Sr., when he was Quebec premier later in the 1960s.

As a child of eleven, Perrault can remember watching the news with her father and offering a running commentary on current affairs. But her indoctrination into politics really took place in the late 1980s. Perrault was in her late teenage years when her father, who was also politically active, took her to a Progressive Conservative convention in Montreal. The Tories rolled out some of their Quebec cabinet ministers, who fielded questions from the delegates. On occasion, things got tense. One minister, Pierre Blais, got a tongue-lashing from some of the youth delegates.

"I was really impressed by that," Perrault recalls. "I thought, this is cool. I like that." She enjoyed the atmosphere so much, she became president of the Tory youth club in her riding.

And so it started. Perrault became an organizer at the next youth convention, got on the executive, and worked to keep Joliette in Tory hands after Roch LaSalle retired and Gaby Larrivée took over in 1988. By 1990, Perrault was president of the entire province's Tory youth wing and listening to colleague after colleague tell her she had to run for office some day.

Her position as head of PC Youth in Quebec also meant she was in occasional contact with Prime Minister Brian Mulroney, who'd call her from time to time to talk shop. On one occasion, the Tory caucus met in Rivière-du-Loup and Perrault wanted Mulroney to meet the members of her executive. After all, they were, if you like, the chief lieutenants in Mulroney's youth army. She went through the proper channels to get the meeting on the PM's schedule, but was consistently rebuffed by Mulroney's staff. Perrault was invited to attend a meeting in which the prime minister would be present. As Mulroney was making the rounds, shaking hands, Perrault seized the moment.

"I'm Anie Perrault, president of PC Youth in Quebec," she said.

"Yes, yes, yes, of course," Mulroney responded.

"Your PC Youth executive is meeting here at the same time and we would really like to meet with you," Perrault continued. "Unfortunately some member of your staff doesn't consider it priority."

Mulroney exploded. "Who told you no? Who said no?"

The poor chap who had said no happened to be standing beside Mulroney at the time—and Perrault couldn't help but point that out.

Mulroney turned around and in front of everybody said, "The PC Youth are people that are working hard for this party. I should meet with them at least once a year and she is right." Perrault got her meeting. The assistant got a prime ministerial earful.

Anie Perrault was on her way.

MOST SIX-YEAR-OLDS ARE CONTENT TO GO to school, play outside with their friends, attend birthday parties on the weekends, and leave the big issues in life to their parents.

Jason Kenney wasn't like most six-year-olds. The dinner-table conversations in the Kenney household consisted of young Jason interrogating his parents about what the president of the United States knew, and when he knew it. Just because he was only six didn't mean he was averse to offering an opinion or two of his own about the Nixon presidency. By the age of seven, he was reading the front section of the *Winnipeg Free Press* daily.

"My parents must have been thinking, we've got a kind of idiot savant in the house," Kenney quips. "He can't do math, doesn't have any musical talent. But he talks about American politics. From an early age I was interested in current affairs. Instead of watching cartoons, I was watching the Watergate hearings."

To this day, Kenney finds his childhood interest in politics inexplicable. Ask him when he first got interested in public life and he says, "It must have been in utero." He had two older brothers, neither of whom was interested in politics. His parents were interested but not at all involved. In fact, the only significant political connection Kenney can find in his background is his grandfather, Herbert Martin Kenney. "Mart" Kenney, nicknamed "Canada's Big Band King," once ran against future Liberal cabinet minister Barney Danson for a nomination in north Toronto. (Mart failed in his political career, but spent nearly seventy years in show business, playing saxophone and clarinet).

Jason Kenney was born in Oakville, Ontario, in 1968. His father was a teacher at the prestigious Appleby College. He went on to become president of Notre Dame College in Saskatchewan, best known for its hockey team, the Hounds. Alumni include Toronto Maple Leaf favourites Curtis Joseph, Wendel Clark, and Gary Leeman. Consistent with Jason Kenney's personality, he spent most of his time trying to organize mock elections, while his friends were considering the bigger issues in life, such as whether to play hockey or soccer.

Kenney sounds as though he was number one on the list of campus nerds. But the underpinnings of his interest in politics weren't that unusual. Other students loved the competition of the hockey arena. Kenney loved the competition of ideas in the political arena. At fifteen, he got involved. He formally joined the Liberal Party, then attended his first national convention in Halifax the following year. Kenney was looking for a way to get more actively involved in Liberal politics and noticed there was one position on the Young Liberals of Canada executive which for some reason wasn't being contested. There was only one candidate for the YLC spot on the party's national policy committee, and at that moment, a twenty-four-year-old medical student, who became a Rhodes Scholar, had the field entirely to himself. That is, until Kenney came along and thought it would be an interesting experience to put his name forward too. He worked the rooms, stayed up all night printing and distributing brochures, and despite the confident predictions of others that this young punk would lose, he won. He was sixteen years old.

Kenney now found himself in the company of a number of soon-to-be-prominent Liberal comers, including future Paul Martin supporters David Herle and Richard Mahoney. Though he was just a teenager, he started to think about the day he might stand for office.

"I've read about teenagers who decided they were going to be prime minister of Canada, who laid out this grand plan and they adjusted everything in their life to that plan," Kenney says. "I decided that I never wanted to be that kind of obsessive lifetime politician, for whom the end became so important it justified any means. I was open to the prospect of running for the federal parliament some day, but I was never the kid who had this grand life plan to get elected."

Nevertheless, everything pointed to Jason Kenney's becoming a major star on the Liberal firmament—until he met his first roommate at the University of San Francisco. And then everything changed.

HOW COULD TOM LONG LOOK ACROSS the table and say with utter conviction that he had no interest—*none*—in running for the leadership of the Canadian Alliance, then do a complete 180 a matter of weeks later?

His enemies—and there are plenty of them—would seize upon this as an example of Long's burning ambition at the expense of all else to get to the top of the mountain. Who is this man who inspires such hatred in some and passionate loyalty in others?

Long spent his teenage years immersing himself in the politics of the time. There was Trudeau and the FLQ. Living so close to the American border made stories about Vietnam and Watergate that much more important to him. He had a natural interest in history. Long was also building his own network of political contacts. High up on the list were men such as Sean O'Sullivan (at twenty, the youngest MP ever elected) and Peter White (business associate of Conrad Black's and political associate of Brian Mulroney's). Running for office seemed inevitable, so a year before the 1979 election that brought Joe Clark to power, Long ran for the PC nomination in Sarnia. He was nineteen years old. O'Sullivan had urged him to do it. Even John Diefenbaker sent a letter of recommendation. His Aunt Catherine, who had always voted Liberal, bought a PC party membership solely to support her nephew.

"She came to the meeting," Long recalls, "looked distinctly

unhappy for three hours, then came up to me afterwards, ripped up the card and said, 'That's what you can expect from the Conservatives,' and walked out." Long placed third, which also happened to be last.

It was a setback but only a temporary one. Graduating from law school and practising law would follow (he was Liberal cabinet minister Allan Rock's junior at Fasken and Calvin for awhile), as would a brief stint in Prime Minister Mulroney's appointments office, working for Peter White. Long actually soured on the experience because he found Mulroney's government too pragmatic and rootless, and not committed to conservatism.

Instead, Long set his sights on the Ontario Conservative party with a view to bringing his neo-conservative agenda to Queen's Park. Of course, the pragmatists under William Davis were firmly in control of the party and wanted nothing to do with an ideologue such as Long, whose political heroes were not John Robarts and Leslie Frost but Ronald Reagan and Margaret Thatcher.

However, after Davis's retirement, the Tories fell on some very tough times. Their forty-two-year dynasty ended in 1985, then the party spent the next two elections mired in last place, still trying for half that time in the wilderness to sell a more pragmatic message to the electorate, but with no apparent prospects in sight.

With the party in disarray, these were the ideal circumstances for Long, who's always preferred to be the insurgent rather than the establishment man. He sought and won the party presidency, then used the post essentially to launch a coup, taking the party away from the pragmatists and delivering it to a group of neo-conservatives who'd come to be known as the Common Sense Revolutionaries. By his own count, Long made five hundred visits to virtually every riding in Ontario, making a lot of friends and enemies in the process.

"I wouldn't have been president of the party if I hadn't been such a pain in the ass a few years before," Long admits. "The fact that I actually am the way I am has helped me out quite a lot."

But not as much as he'd hoped. It was at this time that Long made a premature bid for the PC party leadership.

"The most devastating line I heard was, 'Tom doesn't understand that there's a difference between ambition and leadership,'" he recalls. Long hated the accusation but today admits it was true. "I didn't know the difference. I was thirty-one years old."

Long could read the writing on the wall as well as anyone, so he quit the race for leader before he really got in and did one of the smartest things he could have done. He backed a guy named Mike Harris. Why did he do it?

"I wasn't fit to be the leader of the party," he says flat out. Given what the PCs had been through, Long came to realize the party needed a likeable leader. He was also smart enough to realize he had a polarizing effect on people. "At that age, I didn't need five more years of people finding new reasons to intensely dislike me."

In 1990, when he entered the race for the PC leadership, Mike Harris had been an MPP for nine years, but was always one of those politicians with his face pressed to the outside of the window looking in. He was definitely not part of the Bill Davis crowd and was one of just two MPPs in 1990 seeking the leadership. The lack of interest in the job spoke volumes about how most Tories viewed the state of the party. But Harris's victory started the long climb back for the Ontario PCs. Even though they came a bad third in the ensuing 1990 election, Harris's team ran on a platform of cutting taxes and spending, and getting tough on crime, all of which would be the foundation of the party's platform for the next ten years.

Long wasn't hugely involved in that 1990 campaign, serving from time to time on an advisory committee. The breakup of his first marriage prevented greater involvement. Long's married life was constantly in competition with his political life. When the couple temporarily separated in 1985, they'd already had one child. Then they got back together and had another child. But in the end, the marriage didn't survive.

"I can't blame it on politics," Long insists, implying there were other problems as well. It was a dark time in his life.

"My personal life was not ideal, I had burned myself out and I had burned countless bridges as president of the party," he says. "I was a very polarized figure in the Conservative Party. There were people who frankly thought I was the worst guy they'd ever met."

However, 1990 did turn out to be the dark before the dawn in Tom Long's life. Three years later he married Leslie Pace, with whom he worked at a Toronto law firm. He describes his second wife as someone who "knows more about politics than anybody I know."

With his personal life now intact and the party in the hands of like-minded neo-conservatives, Long felt freer to reimmerse himself in politics. Just as he considered challenging Mike Harris for the leadership but thought better of it, Harris too put aside their prior rivalry and appointed Long co-chair of the 1995 PC campaign. When Premier Bob Rae called the election for June 8, it seemed as if the Tories' ten years in the wilderness would continue. The party was twenty-five points behind the front-running Liberals. Conventional wisdom held that the Tories' campaign platform, the Common Sense Revolution, was simply too right-wing for moderate Ontarians.

Conventional wisdom would soon be reading its obituary. The 1995 Ontario election represented the beginning of Tom Long's comeback in politics. He had success on the political battlefield and forged some remarkable friendships.

"There's a bond that gets formed that I don't think people outside of politics can ever truly appreciate," he says. "You get your back to the wall and you're counting on people to come through. You have a shared sense of purpose."

For Long, June 8, 1995, was the culmination of years and years of slugging it out in the political trenches. His brand of conservatism, rather than something at the fringes, was now considered mainstream in the party. And the campaign he co-chaired with Leslie Noble unfolded exactly as he'd predicted. (Long told me at the beginning of the campaign the Tories would need two or three weeks to define their issues, define the Liberals' weaknesses, and then the numbers would move after the leaders' debate. He was exactly right. The Liberals went into free fall, the Tories' numbers were on the ascent, and before you knew it, Mike Harris became the first party leader in seventy years in Ontario to go from third place to the premier's office.)

It was one of those nights when everything came together, as Long puts it, "Where you really see the wonder that is politics—the thing that would explain to people why we do what we do." In one night, the

Common Sense Revolutionaries were rewarded for all those four-hour drives to deliver a twenty-minute speech to a room filled with fifty people. "It has moments of magic that you could never find anywhere else, unless you're having a child," Long explains.

More important, the victory afforded Long something rarely offered in politics—an opportunity for a fresh start, an opportunity to change people's views of him.

"I think I left that campaign in '95 without any significant enemy left in the party," Long recalls, and he thinks he knows why. "I guess I got something done for the party that wasn't related to my getting somewhere." In fact, after the election, Long went back to his head-hunting job at Egon Zehnder and was happy to provide occasional advice to the new government as needed.

But, as you may have discovered by now, Tom Long is no ordinary politico. He's a backroom ideologue who also yearns to be the guy counting *X*'s beside his own name on election day. He's also a serious policy wonk. While it would be easy to say Long's best moment in politics was the night the Ontario Conservatives came back to power, the truth is it wasn't.

Before Mike Harris won that election or was even leader of the party, Long and several other young Tories had an idea as to how their new leader should be selected. This group disliked the old delegated conventions, where a few thousand élite party members gathered to wheel and deal and choose their new chief. It was often very dramatic, but not as democratic as Long and company preferred. Once party members voted for the delegates to attend the convention, their influence in selecting the leader was finished. Long, and others such as Tony Clement, a future party president, wanted a more direct election for leader. Each member should get to vote directly for the leader, something more akin to a regular election.

There were other more political motives for changing the system. The pragmatists, who'd owned the PC Party for decades, had solid connections among riding association presidents and party stalwarts. But the younger insurgents such as Long felt they could take the party away from that group by appealing to the broader party membership. Now that the PCs were out of power in Ontario, the majority of party members were small-c conservative, grassroots types, who'd be more inclined to take the party to the right than the red Tories. Furthermore, a radically new method of choosing the leader might garner the party some much-needed attention. The question was, what alternatives were out there?

The young turks started doing their research and discovered the only leader in the country who'd ever been elected by a one-member-one-vote system was Pierre Marc Johnson, the former leader of the Parti Québécois. Coincidentally, Long's mentor, Peter White, had once worked for Premier Daniel Johnson, Sr., Pierre Marc's father. Long asked White to arrange a meeting.

Politically speaking, Johnson and Long couldn't have been more different. But Johnson was intrigued with this zealous group of youngsters, so he asked Long to bring some of his people to the Club Ste. Denis in Montreal, where Johnson and some of the people who worked on his leadership effort would explain some of the fine points of their new system for electing a leader.

Could there have been an odder mix of political participants? In one corner, a group of French, social democratic, bilingual sovereignists. In the other, English, right-wing, unilingual federalists. "Actually, it made it kind of cool on both sides," Long admits.

Despite their differences, the two groups met from 7:30 p.m. until two in the morning. "We just talked politics and life and philosophy," Long says. Johnson and Long established a friendship that endures today. Long says it was the most extraordinary night of his political life.

(As a postscript to that meeting, the Tories did use the new one-member-one-vote system in their 1990 leadership race. And for Long, the new system had the desired effect. The neo-conservatives took the party away from the red Tories, as Mike Harris defeated Dianne Cunningham, an MPP from London. The new system seemed to perform without any serious glitches. It was also the most boring leadership convention in recent memory. A few hundred people gathered at the Coliseum on the grounds of the Canadian National Exhibition in Toronto to watch the returns come in. It couldn't have been a less dramatic event. But, of course, that wasn't the point.)

The other significant event of Long's life at this time was meeting an American political consultant who'd go on to help the Ontario Tories revolutionize the way they would fight election campaigns. Peter White and Long flew to Washington to attend a campaign seminar. There, they met Mike Murphy, campaign consultant to some of the most popular right-wing insurgents in American politics (Oliver North and John McCain to name just two). Murphy is nicknamed the "Merchant of Mud." There was a story going around that once upon a time, his car licence plate read "Go Neg," a reference to the advice Murphy always gives his candidates—when in doubt, go negative with your advertising campaigns. The story sounds more apocryphal than anything.

Long and Murphy met, then bonded in a twenty-five-minute drive to a Washington restaurant, where they became fast friends. Long didn't quite go as negative as Murphy would have in the two consecutive Ontario election campaigns he co-chaired. However, his ads did contain a certain *punch* to differentiate Mike Harris from his Liberal challengers that wasn't typical of Canadian election campaigns. The result: two Conservative majority governments, something that hadn't happened in Ontario in three decades.

"Mike [Murphy] helped me regain my hobby," is the way Long puts it. "He helped make politics fun for me again." Murphy was best man at Long's wedding to Leslie Pace.

Tom Long was no longer a pariah. His professional, personal, and political lives were all on the upswing. And then he decided to jeopardize it all.

The Canadian Alliance hoped it had solved its Ontario problem when a little-known cabinet minister in Mike Harris's government put his name forward. Frank Klees wasn't on anybody's A-list of potential candidates, but he did have some things going for him. He represented a riding in suburban Toronto, the heart of the Harris government's base of support, and presumably a potential launching pad for Alliance votes. He seemed to have access to buckets of money, so running a competitive campaign wouldn't be a problem. And he had access to the best political strategists in the country—the strategists who'd just helped Mike Harris win back-to-back majorities.

For a couple of weeks, Frank Klees was in the eye of the media hurricane. He did every talk show in town, got his profile up, and looked as if his would-be campaign had some decent momentum behind it.

Tom Long had been nothing if not encouraging to Klees's ambitions during this time. He was so confident that Klees was going to throw his hat into the ring and run a well-organized campaign that he didn't cancel his annual golf vacation. He and Leslie and a group of others (which included Ontario's then attorney general Jim Flaherty and the premier's former chief of staff Ron McLaughlin) went off to golf school in Las Vegas and had a blast.

However, when the group returned a few days later, Long found a panicky Peter White on the phone.

"It's Frank Klees," White said. "He's gone off the rails."

Long called Klees right away and listened to a story that was right out of an Allen Drury novel. Klees said one of his chief contributors would pull the plug on his extremely generous donation unless Klees promised to support that contributor's preferred candidate on the second ballot. The assumption was, Klees would come third on the first ballot, behind Preston Manning and Stockwell Day. Klees said his judgement and principles weren't for sale, so he was going to turn down the money, drop out of the race, and call a news conference to expose the entire sordid mess.

"Whoa, Frank," Long responded. "If you're not comfortable, you shouldn't run. By all means, don't go into debt. But don't call a press conference."

The next day, that's exactly what Frank Klees did.

Long called him afterwards. "We had a candid exchange of views," he says. That's what politicians say when they want to rip somebody's lungs out through their nostrils.

For the Alliance, the withdrawal was doubly bad. First, the party was back to square one. There was no Ontario candidate. Second, the Alliance purported to be a party different from the others. But Klees had confirmed for all the country to see that backroom shenanigans were just as much a part of this party as the others. Long was devastated.

"I watched, over the next three days, everything we'd worked to accomplish slip into the garbage," he says.

For the Common Sense Revolutionaries, the problem was more

acute. They were ready, willing, and able to fight another leadership contest, but now didn't have a candidate.

On Friday, April 7, 2000, conservative author David Frum returned home to launch his latest book. Family members threw an intimate party for him at their north Toronto home. Several high-flyers from the worlds of conservative politics and journalism were there to eat, drink, buy a few books, and swap gossip about the state of the Alliance now that Klees had dropped his bomb.

At one point in the evening, Frum was chatting with Tony Clement and Tom Long, when Hal Jackman, Ontario's former lieutenant-governor, joined the gathering. Jackman reached into his pocket for a coin, and looked at Clement and Long.

"Let's flip this right now to see which one of you is going to replace Frank Klees," Jackman joked.

Clement had been in on the ground floor of the United Alternative movement, but had no interest in the leadership. His sights were firmly set on staying in Ontario politics and he said so to Long. If Long wanted to be the Alliance candidate from Ontario, Clement was all too happy to be an ally, not a competitor.

"Well, one of us ought to do it," Long told Clement.

Two days later, Frank Klees started musing about getting back into the race. He thought he might be able to raise enough money from other sources after all. So he called Tom Long at noon, both to ask his advice and tell him he just might reconsider.

Long's response shocked Klees. He told him he'd discussed it with his wife, and he'd decided to get into the race himself. Leslie Noble, his co-chair from two successful provincial campaigns, would be in charge of his own leadership effort.

It was an incredible change of heart. What about Long's lack of a "clear line of vision" to the prime minister's job? What about the fact that his wife was only days away from giving birth to the couple's second child? What about the fact that both Manning and Day had huge head-starts over Long, making his prospects a Long-shot at best? What about the fact that he didn't speak French, had only ever been to half the provinces in Canada, and had spent most of his adult life in downtown Toronto?

"Apart from all that, I was a dream candidate," Long jokes.

One of Long's friends, speaking not for attribution, speculates on the debate raging within the candidate's soul.

"He's a very complicated, complex person," the source says. "Dr. Jekyll and Mr. Tom. The evil Tom is back."

The comment suggests Long's ambitious, more ruthless side was prevailing over the good judgement he'd shown during two previous Ontario election campaigns. In fairness, there's another more charitable interpretation. Long always believed in his guts that Canada needed a truly conservative alternative to the Liberals. He thought the Progressive Conservative Party was dead, and worse, in Joe Clark, not led by a true conservative. He also knew the Alliance would never be taken seriously as a national force unless and until the leadership race got a seal of approval from a legitimate Ontario candidate.

"So I dove in," he says.

There were other factors too. First, the Reform Party already had seventy-five thousand members. Most of them would no doubt be loyal to Manning. But Long was convinced he could get a good chunk of that vote, because of his barn-burner of a speech to the UA conference.

Second, Long and his team were convinced they could use their aggressive campaign tactics, which worked so well for Mike Harris, to Long's benefit. Some campaign officials speculated Long's team could sign up two hundred thousand new Alliance members in Ontario alone.

And finally, if the campaign fell short, it would still serve as an excellent dress rehearsal for Long's other ambition, which he'd always had in the back of his mind since the late 1980s—to be the leader of the Ontario Conservatives and premier of Ontario.

"The speech he gave didn't touch what he's capable of and he still got eight standing ovations," one of Long's advisers and friends told me. "He hasn't been truly engaged in a personal campaign in ten years (when he thought about challenging Harris for the Ontario leadership) so he's ready for bear."

What about the imminent birth of his child?

"His wife hates politics but knows what drives him and she loves him," the associate said. "So she'll support him through this in a way his first wife wouldn't."

Long says that characterization of his wife is not quite accurate. "Leslie doesn't hate politics," he says. "In fact she loves it. She is just more realistic about how it works and what it can do to you than I am."

Meanwhile, Long's fourth child, Veronica, was born in the midst of his leadership run.

But there was one problem. A huge problem. Long and his team must have been reading too many articles in the media about their superior organizational abilities. They may have started believing in their own invulnerability. Because when the team hit the ground running trying to sign up supporters to vote for Long's leadership, the effort fell surprisingly flat. The *National Post* did its best to keep the flame burning for Long, devoting significant resources and fawning coverage to his every move.

And yet in the end, the campaign fell embarrassingly short. Observers discovered Long was much less effective on the stump and during the all-candidates' debates than his reputation suggested. He told everyone he'd be Jean Chrétien's worst nightmare because only he, the Ontario candidate, could deliver Canada's largest province to the Alliance. And he suffered the embarrassment of having his organization caught red-handed in a bit of vote fraud in the Gaspé, Quebec. Long claimed to know nothing about it and disavowed the votes anyway. He called all the other candidates personally and apologized. They all accepted his apology graciously.

On June 24, 2000, the man who was promising to deliver Ontario to the Alliance in the next election lost on his home turf. Stockwell Day shocked the country by leading all challengers on the first ballot. (Jason Kenney, the co-chair of Day's campaign, was hoping Day might manage a strong second. He would call this his greatest day in politics. "It just blew me away. I was such a happy camper.")

Day also won Ontario by more than eleven hundred votes over Long. And that wasn't the most depressing number for Long that evening. With hopes of signing up two hundred thousand new members in Ontario alone, Long had to content himself with the fact that only 12,015 Ontarians voted for him to lead the Alliance. He got fewer than ten thousand votes in the rest of the country.

Long's quixotic run was over. For him, his next move was clear. He called Manning after the first ballot votes were announced.

"How are you?" Long asked him.

"I'm doing marginally better than you," Manning joked.

"You going to stay on?" Long asked.

"Yes," Manning answered. "The party needs it."

"Well then," Long said, "I'll support you."

There was ample speculation that Long was supporting Manning as a quid pro quo for Manning's keeping the Reform Party out of Ontario politics, thus enabling Mike Harris to create a united conservative movement provincially. Long says no. That favour was repaid when Long joined the United Alternative movement several months earlier.

No, Long endorsed Manning simply because he grew to admire and respect him during the leadership contest. He thought Manning had a better-defined vision for the country. Frequently during the course of the campaign, the two candidates shared a helicopter ride across Ontario and Alberta. Manning would act as tour guide, showing Long the landmarks of Western Canada.

"I thought he deserved better than what he got," Long says. "At least he got a couple of days of good news" from the endorsement.

But why endorse Manning when it was obvious to everyone that Day was going to win on the ensuing ballot?

"Politics isn't about winning every time," Long says. "Les and I have made great friends out of Sandra and Preston Manning. They're great people."

After Day's victory, things got a bit awkward. Relations between the Day and Long camps were never the greatest. Some Day operatives made some disparaging comments about homosexuals, fully aware that Long had some gay staffers in the fold. And there weren't any significant efforts made by the Day campaign to reach out to Long's team for some post-convention healing.

Often, leadership runs enhance a politician's image, even if the campaign fails. Think about Jean Charest losing to Kim Campbell. Jean Chrétien losing to John Turner. Joe Clark losing to Brian Mulroney. All of the losers emerged with their dignity intact, their reputations enhanced. Such was not the case for Tom Long. His team of advisers had clearly confused his currency in the world of political élites with his stock among the general public. Was he concerned that the leadership run had tarnished his image?

"I don't really care," he says bluntly. "Opportunities present themselves and sometimes you have to strap on the flak jacket and take a chance."

If Long did feel used by the leadership process, he wasn't saying so. Without his entry into the race, the Alliance leadership fight would have essentially been between two Albertans. It would have been next to impossible for the Reform Party to claim it had made the transition from a Western-based regional party to a national force.

"He legitimized the race, then they tossed him over," was the way one of Long's friends put it.

Long did have a role in the November, 2000, federal election campaign, but nothing close to the influence he enjoyed when he was helping Mike Harris to victory. He spoke to Day only twice during the entire campaign. Friends say he offered advice when asked, but it was rarely taken. The main piece of advice he offered was that if the Alliance were defined as a party espousing socially conservative values, they'd lose. Two seats in Ontario suggests Long was spot on.

Perhaps it was fortuitous that Long's run for the Alliance leadership ended as it did. Having given a year of his life to this new venture, he looks forward to pulling back from politics for now. After all, he's still got to get a new job.

Over the years there has been ample scuttlebutt that he lost his first family to politics even though he denies it. Don't suggest to him that history might repeat itself.

"Tom Long is not going to lose his second family. Period. Regardless of what I do," he says emphatically. "I'm older. I'm a better father and husband than I was ten years ago. I'm a better listener."

Long may be a bit down for the count at the moment, but it's hard to imagine that lasting.

"Anything you and I do will be demanding, stressful, absorbing, interesting or we wouldn't do it," he says. "I think that the biggest single sin that you can make is to be bored and indifferent. I never want to be bored or indifferent."

IN THE MID-1980S, THE UNIVERSITY OF TORONTO became the locus of an intense and occasionally uncomfortable debate about apartheid. An international law organization invited South Africa's ambassador to Canada to speak at the U of T. Many students found the invitation unacceptable, that South Africa's system of government was so offensive, the invitation was akin to asking a representative of Nazi Germany to expound on the virtues of the master race. The university administration felt sympathy for the protestors and urged the ambassador's invitation be rescinded, which it was.

Enter Tony Clement. To him, this was a case of freedom of speech infringed upon—of all places—on a university campus, where law students such as Clement were learning about the freedom of speech provisions of Canada's new charter of rights. So Clement kick-started an organization called Lawyers for Fundamental Freedoms and reinvited the ambassador, this time to debate law professor (and future Liberal MP) Bill Graham. Rob Prichard, the dean of the law school and future president of the U of T, tried to stop the invitation until the media got hold of the story. Then Clement became a minor celebrity, doing numerous interviews with the media, defending free speech. The ambassador came and debated apartheid, despite a major protest outside the hall, which required police on horseback to keep things from getting out of hand.

Tony Clement eventually got his law degree. But he discovered the lure of participating in the great issues of the day was much more appealing. In 1990, he'd seek and win the presidency of the Ontario PC Party and contribute to a coming revolution in his province—a common sense revolution.

There are two important things you have to know about Tony Clement. First, he's one of the very few people in politics who's seriously thought through some of the truly big issues of our time. Second, he's the closest thing to a Boy Scout you'll find in public life. That's not to suggest he's not ambitious. He is. That's not to suggest he's not capable of playing political hardball. He is. But it is to suggest that some of the things that come out of his mouth would sound totally cynical and ridiculous from anyone else. Clement believes them. Ask him why he's attracted to The Life, and you get an answer such as this:

"Why are we on this earth?" he asks. He has an answer. "Is there something you can do with the postage-stamp portion of the earth that we inhabit that is better for civilization and the community than when you got there? That's about the only thing worth doing."

And there's more. "When school kids ask me why I'm in politics, I say, 'It's to change the world.' That's the short answer. What else could I do with my life that's as meaningful?"

Clement started by trying to democratize his party. He was instrumental, as chairman of the party's constitution committee, then party president, in researching, then helping to create the new one-member-one-vote system for choosing the new leader. The system is almost commonplace in Canada now, but in 1990, the PCs became the first party in English Canada to implement the new system.

"Everyone said it would crash, but it didn't," Clement says. In fact, it worked rather well, particularly since Clement's preferred candidate, Mike Harris, won. (Technically, Clement was neutral, given that he was the party's chief election officer. But his heart *was* with Harris. After his term as president expired in 1992, Clement was appointed assistant principal secretary to Harris.)

Tony Clement seemed to be on a roll, so two years later, he decided to fulfill his childhood dream of running for office. He ran for a seat on Metropolitan Toronto Council, hoping his efforts among the Tory grassroots and his increasing profile would propel him to elective office. Then, the best thing that could have happened to him did. He lost. Badly. To a New Democrat named David Miller. In fact, Clement came third.

"I thought, as long as I don't repeat this too many times, it's a learning experience," Clement says. "At the time you're miserable, but you have to learn how to lose. It's all part of being a better politician."

As fate would have it, Clement wouldn't have to wait too long to try his luck again. Bob Rae's government was limping to the end of its mandate, so Clement offered himself up as a candidate in the 1995 election for the Tories in Brampton. (No less a figure than Bill Davis, the former premier from Brampton himself, urged Clement to run in his old stompin' grounds.)

Clement looked as if he were taking on another impossible task. A second consecutive defeat just half a year after his municipal failure seemed inevitable. And then the wheel turned. Clement started hearing unusually supportive things while going door to door. People would tell him to save his spiel, he'd gotten their vote, and leave a sign while you're at it. Mike Harris's support shot up twenty points in a week, and suddenly, Tony Clement's move to Brampton didn't look so stupid. In fact, Brampton represented the most solid part of the Harris government's foundation—the "905 region," named after the telephone area code of all the municipalities in suburban Toronto.

Mike Harris won every seat in the 905 region. And Tony Clement had finally fulfilled his childhood dream. He was an elected politician—the honourable member for Brampton South.

The first thing Tony Clement discovered about being an MPP was that it was infinitely more rewarding than being a backroom boy.

"People in the premier's office or on a campaign team," he says, "they'll never know the satisfaction of having a constituent with a problem, battling the big bad bureaucracy, and getting something done. That's a great feeling."

One of Clement's first tests came from a constituent who had, in fact, been battling the bureaucracy for two years but to no avail.

"You're the MPP," Lyn Callahan told him. "See what you can do. If you can get this solved, we'll vote for you in the next election."

The problem centred on Callahan's son Tim, a teacher, who was told by the Ministry of Education that if he took certain courses and did another kind of field work, he'd get his teaching certificate.

"He does all that and they say, we can't possibly give you your teaching certificate," Clement tells the story. "They're saying jump through five more hoops."

Clement gets involved and finds out first-hand how even the simplest thing in government isn't simple. He talks to the minister of education's staff who "regurgitate" the bureaucratic answer.

"You're talking like a bureaucrat," Clement upbraids the minister's staff. "We're elected representatives. Stop talking like a bureaucrat."

Next, Clement talked to the minister's chief of staff, his deputy minister, and eventually the minister himself. It took far more time and effort to get that teacher's certificate than it should have, but in the end, Clement did get it. Then he returned to Lyn Callahan's doorstep, rang the bell, and handed her the certificate.

"It was a feeling... let me tell you, it beats one million cabinet submissions," Clement beams. "That's what it's all about. That's part of the job no backroomer will ever appreciate."

What makes the story deliciously ironic is that the teacher Clement helped was the son of Bob Callahan, the former Liberal MPP for Brampton South, whom Clement had defeated.

Constituency work notwithstanding, Clement's great hope, of course, was to be asked to join Mike Harris's cabinet. He had several things going for him. First, he was president of the party after Harris was chosen leader, so unlike many of the members of the PC caucus, the new premier actually knew him and liked him. And Clement had repeatedly proved his loyalty to the new premier. Second, Clement represented the 905 region that Harris simply had to reward because the region had been so good to him. And third, Clement deserved to be in cabinet. He was smart and experienced about politics, intelligent about policy, intellectually curious, and in Bill Davis, had the longest-serving Ontario premier of the twentieth century as his chief mentor.

But it was that mentor who stopped Clement at a community event shortly after the new government was formed to give the rookie MPP some bad news. Phone calls to new ministers were going out the next day.

"You're not going to get a phone call," Davis told him. "Don't take it too badly. You've got a bright future."

Mixed with the disappointment Clement was naturally feeling was the curiosity of how Davis knew that information to begin with.

"I don't know how he knew, but he knows everything," Clement says. "He did give me advice on how to make a name for myself. He said to take a couple of issues and champion them."

So Clement did, ironically, probably much to Davis's chagrin. Clement became the new government's point man on what he called the "direct democracy" file. Mike Harris made Clement parliamentary assistant to the premier, in charge of crafting a new bill that would offer people more referendums on key issues (something Davis would have found far too populist). And Clement also became deeply involved in something that truly offended Davis's partisan sensibilities. If nothing else, the former premier was a Progressive Conservative Party loyalist. Tony Clement decided to try to help bury the PC Party by creating a new United Alternative with the Reform Party.

How does he possibly justify that to Davis? Again, from anyone else, this answer would sound as phony as a three-dollar bill. From Clement, it rings true.

"I tell him what I tell you," he says. "I have to be prepared to look my kids and grandkids in the eye and tell them I've done everything I can do because I love Canada. I love my country and I want to help my country. That's something Mr. Davis, of all people, can understand."

Clement was there as co-chair when the United Alternative convention voted in favour of creating a new party, which would become the Canadian Alliance. He'd put innumerable hours into trying to bring Tories and Reformers together and took great pride in the birth of the CA.

"Moments like that are better than sex," he says, using a well-worn phrase in politics. (Author's note: I doubt Bill Davis would describe anything in politics quite that way, and for the sake of Clement's ego, I hope his wife wouldn't either.)

In October, 1997, Tony Clement's sense of purpose and history were both rewarded. Premier Harris was shuffling his cabinet and invited Clement to join as his minister of transportation. The swearing-in ceremony took place twenty-five years to the week after Clement's stepfather, John, was sworn into Bill Davis's cabinet. Clement used the same Bible his stepfather used. On one page of the book are the signatures of the premier, the clerk of the legislature, and the lieutenant-governor of Ontario from 1972. On another page are the signatures of the premier, the clerk of the legislature, and the lieutenant-governor of Ontario from 1997.

Clement couldn't afford to soak up the historic significance of his appointment for too long because one of the very first things he encountered in cabinet was a fight over his very first bill as transportation minister. Big cities across Ontario were finding it increasingly difficult to clamp down on drivers who'd run red lights, occasionally causing accidents or even fatalities. The public was demanding action and the favoured solution seemed to be placing cameras at selected intersections to catch the offenders. The premier thought that was a good idea. So did the mayor of Toronto. So did much of the PC caucus. Guess who didn't like the idea.

The new minister of transportation.

"I've never been sold that they're going to do the wonderful things everyone says they're going to do," Clement admits. Only trouble was, Mike Harris wanted the cameras. In fact, he pulled Clement aside one day and said, "We're going to do this."

So Clement faced the most ironic of prospects. He'd waited his whole life to become a Conservative cabinet minister. Now he *was* one, but the first bill he would ever introduce into the legislature in his name, he really didn't support.

But Clement is also smart enough to know two things. When the premier wants something, he gets it. "And he might be right and I might be wrong," he admits. "So where we clash on a public policy issue, I don't have so much ego that I can't say, you know what, he's probably right and I'm wrong."

The discomfort Clement may have felt over his first bill paled in comparison to a much graver moment. One night, Clement was out for dinner with his wife, Lynne Golding, whom he'd met in PC youth politics. As the couple dropped their three children off at Clement's parents' home, his stepfather broke the news.

"You've just been called a crook on television by Dalton McGuinty," he said.

Actually, it was a little worse. In an interview with veteran television host Robert Fisher, the Liberal leader had called Clement "corrupt." The word so offended the normally unflappable Clement that he launched a $1.7 million libel action against the Liberal leader, who refused to apologize. Several efforts to negotiate a settlement failed. Clement got some good news last fall, when a judge struck down most of McGuinty's defence. Eventually, Clement got his apology.

Whether it's the slings and arrows of opposition politicians or the battles within the Tory party, Clement seems to have it all in perspective.

"Half of politics is stamina," Clement says. "They keep kicking you and they keep beating you and you come back for more. This is a test. If I can get through this test, I'll be a better person."

Is he passing the test? Depends which test you're talking about. Clement is one day younger than the greatest hockey player of all time. "I always measure myself against Wayne Gretzky," he says. "So far Gretzky's winning."

Whenever future leaders of the Ontario PC Party are discussed, Clement's name is always on the list, even though he's only forty years old and has only been an elected politician for six years. But his stepfather's experiences a quarter of a century ago, mixed with his own perspectives on The Life, are an impressive combination, giving Clement wisdom beyond his years.

"We deal with the big issues of life, justice, and destiny," he says. "It's a big theatre we're playing in."

AFTER GRADUATING FROM THE UNIVERSITY OF OTTAWA with her law degree, Anie Perrault started doing corporate and civil law with the Montreal law firm Phillips & Vineberg. She liked practising law well enough, but it really wasn't a passion for her.

In 1993, after Brian Mulroney retired, she got a call from Jean Charest, who told her she should take a breather from her legal duties and come work for him on his leadership campaign.

"Take a leave of absence," Charest told her. "It's a great opportunity for you to get a lot of experience."

Perrault didn't need much prodding. The fact that the senior partners at the law firm liked Charest meant getting that leave of absence wasn't too tough a sell. So at the ripe old age of twenty-two, she joined Charest's inner circle. She did communications, media relations, organizing—whatever needed doing. And when Charest lost, her heart broke just a bit. Maybe more than a bit. Perrault declined to do much work for the Tories on that 1993 election campaign, which would soon enter the annals of Canadian history as one of the most disastrous for any party at any time.

"I think a lot of things would be different if Charest had won in 1993," she says. "I don't think we would have won the election, but we would not have lost it to two seats. Never."

In the fall of 1995, Quebec and the rest of Canada would experience perhaps the most gut-wrenching evening of the second half of the twentieth century. The second Quebec referendum on sovereignty was consuming the country, and the federalist forces in her home province wanted Perrault to quit the law firm again to help save the country.

She was asked to organize "Generation 18–35," a group of young federalists who'd hit the campaign trail to take on the young separatist movement.

"The law partners saw me thriving and happy when I was doing politics and not that happy when I was practising law," she says. "If you want to be successful in what you do, you do have to put your heart into it, and obviously I was not putting my heart there."

Her heart was in keeping Quebec in Canada. So Perrault quit law and spent the next nine months driving to every college and university in the province to argue the federalist case and recruit her generation to the cause. The 1980 referendum was ancient history as far as twenty- and thirty-somethings were concerned. This was their turn to make their mark on history and Perrault wanted to be equal to the task. She successfully convinced programmers at RDI (the French equivalent of CBC Newsworld) to host a "live," one-hour program every Saturday for eight weeks, featuring two young federalists against two young separatists in a series of debates.

On October 30, 1995, Perrault took immense satisfaction from the results and the role her generation played. The baby boomers, who'd lost the 1980 referendum, plus the eighteen- to twenty-four-year-old demographic, made up a significant percentage of the "Yes" forces. But to the surprise of many Péquistes, the majority of twenty-four- to thirty-five-year-olds, whom Perrault's organization targeted, voted "No."

"I think that without the work we did, the 'Yes' could have won," she says.

However, she also remembers the evening for another, more sinister reason. In 1980, the leader and most eloquent spokesman for the "No" side was the prime minister of the day, Pierre Trudeau. In 1995, that was not the case. Jean Chrétien came under considerable fire for almost blowing what seemed an insurmountable lead at the outset. Clearly, he was feeling an enormous burden to succeed, as evidenced by his breaking down into tears in caucus one day. The most widely recognized and effective leader of the "No" forces in 1995 was the guy with only two seats in the House of Commons, PC leader Jean Charest.

At midnight, when all the votes had been counted and the federalist side had won the narrowest of victories, Anie Perrault went to a microphone to introduce her friend and leader Jean Charest. Quebec Liberal leader Daniel Johnson had just finished his remarks and the television producers were giving Perrault the cue to bring on Charest, which she did. As the massive cheers for Charest subsided and he began to speak, something felt wrong. The buzz in the room was no longer directed at Charest, but at the television sets around the hall. It was Prime Minister Chrétien. He was delivering his speech from Ottawa. Anie Perrault could feel her blood begin to boil. For weeks, Chrétien and Charest had put partisanship aside and worked together. Now, when the Marquis of Queensbury rules dictated that Charest should enjoy a few moments in the spotlight, Chrétien was taking it away. It was particularly galling to Perrault because there was no doubt in her mind or in the minds of other federalists in Quebec that Jean Charest saved the "No" side from defeat.

Chrétien staffers insisted the timing of the PM's speech was accidental, that they meant no disrespect to Charest.

"You're never going to convince anybody that he didn't do that on purpose," is Perrault's still-irate response to that. "He did that on purpose. I am convinced of that. Convinced."

She may have only been twenty-six years old, but Anie Perrault had already experienced more in politics than some people twice her age. So in August, 1996, she found herself co-chairing a PC policy conference in Winnipeg, designed to roll out some of the Tory platform for the federal election, still ten months away.

One of her tasks was to give a speech to a crowd of more than twelve hundred delegates. The party leader, Jean Charest, was in the front row. Her father was there too. Perrault had been thinking for some time about whether to embark on her first run for elective office. She knew Charest wanted a group of talented, young candidates to run alongside him. With the Tories in fifth place in the House of Commons, the prospects for putting that team in place seemed bleak.

But Perrault quit law because her heart wasn't in it, and now was the time when her leader and her party needed someone with heart to set an example. Charest had asked her several times to run for the PCs in the ensuing campaign, but to this point, Perrault had remained uncommitted. So, in the middle of her speech, with tears in her eyes, Anie Perrault told a packed hall she intended to be the PC candidate in Joliette in the 1997 election.

"I told Jean that I really believed in him, and I was going to run for him, and be part of his team, and encourage other young people to run, and make a difference," she says.

Perrault had practised the speech in her hotel room before giving it. She knew she wanted to deliver the line about running with conviction and heart. She delivered it in English, which made her more nervous than she might otherwise have been (her English is excellent but she's certainly more comfortable in French). That, plus seeing Charest and his wife just a few feet away, was an emotional combination.

"Jean was really happy," she says. "I knew I was making him really happy by doing this. I guess that was a big day when I did that."

After the speech, Charest approached her. "We're going to make a hell of a team," he said.

And they did. When Chrétien called the election in April, 1997, Perrault was a major player on the Quebec political scene, frequently subbing for Charest when his national responsibilities took him elsewhere. Once, she did a debate in English on CBC Newsworld against the Liberals' star cabinet minister Stéphane Dion and the Bloc Québécois' Daniel Turp.

"I was so nervous in English, I was sick," she recalls. "Really, physically sick."

Campaigning was a wonderful experience, but Canadians weren't quite ready to welcome the PC party back from oblivion. The Tories did manage to win 22 per cent of the votes and five seats in Quebec, but Perrault's wasn't one of them. She came second, losing to Bloc Québécois MP René Laurin by more than five thousand votes. However, in the 1993 election, Laurin had defeated the incumbent Tory MP by thirty-two thousand votes.

Of course, that "hell of a team" didn't stay together much longer. Nine months after leading the Tories to twenty seats in the '97 campaign, Jean Charest left federal politics to assume the leadership of the Liberal Party of Quebec. Joe Clark ran for the Conservative Party leadership for the third time and won back his old job. And Anie Perrault was his director of communications.

But Charest wanted Perrault back on his team. So it wasn't a complete surprise when the new Liberal leader called and asked her to run for him again, this time in the provincial riding of Joliette. Actually, he called four times. But as much as she wanted to help Charest, Perrault found she couldn't. She enjoyed her job with Joe Clark. Furthermore, her rival this time wouldn't be an opposition Bloc Québécois MP, but rather Guy Chevrette, a Parti Québécois cabinet minister and veteran of a quarter century in Quebec provincial politics.

"As much as people might want to see him retired, they're not going to kick him out, and they're not going to put an *X* beside another name," Perrault thought. She also didn't want to run the risk of losing her second consecutive election in less than two years.

"I thought it could burn me and I didn't want to do that," she says.

Ironically, the PQ was a lot more concerned about the prospect of Perrault's candidacy than she evidently was. She later heard scuttlebutt in the riding that had she run for the Liberals, Chevrette might have used the occasion to retire from politics. Adding credence to the story is a conversation Perrault had with Lucien Bouchard during a meeting between the Quebec premier and Joe Clark. "You're the one from Joliette," Bouchard said after meeting Perrault. "We did some polling and you could have done some damage."

Perrault was convinced that leaving the law for politics was the right decision. Her "significant other" wasn't so sure. During the six years they lived together, he watched Perrault often work seven days a week, traipsing all over the country, trying to rebuild the PC Party. He was proud of her high profile, but at the same time, a little uncomfortable with it, given that politics didn't run as deeply through his veins as it did hers. The relationship ended in the midst of her attempt to help Joe Clark regain the leadership.

"Politics had a big impact on it," she says of her relationship. "It's a really tough job on families. I see this every day, marriages being broken up."

Anie Perrault hasn't given up her childhood dream of someday becoming an elected official. But at the age of thirty-one, she's simply decided she needs to bring more to the dance—more credibility in the "real" world. So she left Joe Clark's office towards the end of 1999 and got a job in Ottawa as director of communications and public affairs with Rx&D, the organization that represents Canada's research-based pharmaceutical companies. (Even if she'd wanted to, Perrault couldn't get too far away from politics. The president of Rx&D is Murray Elston, a former Ontario cabinet minister.)

She was asked by Joe Clark to run in the 2000 election but opted not to. Then in the spring of 2001, she joined Genome Canada as its vice president for communications.

"Right now, I am not prepared to go back to the riding every weekend and do events and meet people," she says bluntly. "I spent too much of my life travelling with Mr. Clark and others, and spending my weekends in hotels and convention centres."

Perrault is doing something else on weekends now. Playing tennis. Going to movies. Reading books. All things "normal" people take for granted, but never generally featured in her previous life.

"I do think that one day I'll want to run again," she adds. "But I do think I will be a much better candidate and a better MP if I'm elected, if I have experience in the private sector."

She's making more money now (another fringe benefit of the private sector). Her life has more balance. She has more control over her world. And yet, The Life still beckons.

"It's on the edge," Perrault says. "That's what political life is. The edge. It's a crazy life. But I love it."

THE UNIVERSITY OF SAN FRANCISCO was as good a place as any in the mid-1980s for young, idealistic, committed students to get a classic liberal arts education. Jason Kenney wanted all of that and more. His program consisted of nothing less than an intensive study of western civilization—its history, philosophy, and theology.

"I went down there with all the prejudices of a typical young Canadian," he says. "A liberal, nationalist, anti-American, knee-jerk supporter of the welfare state."

Kenney's first roommate at USF was Mark Pecha, and quite by accident, he may have been the single most important person influencing the *virage* Kenney's political thinking was about to take. His secret weapon? He subscribed to *National Review*.

"I used to ridicule him and tear him apart for being this jingoistic, right-wing American," Kenney says. "When he wasn't in the room. I'd start peeking at his *National Review* like I was looking at *Playboy*—furtively glancing at articles by William F. Buckley."

It was the first time in his life that Kenney was exposed to conservative ideas. He'd never been much on Canadian conservatism, but plugging into the American conservative political scene prompted a thorough re-examination of everything Kenney had believed.

At the same time as he was in the process of undergoing a political conversion, Kenney was having second thoughts about religion too. He was baptized an Anglican, but at age twenty decided to convert to Roman Catholicism. The spiritual conversion was, perhaps, a longer work in progress. When he was thirteen, Kenney visited a Benedictine monastery in British Columbia and was deeply moved. He wanted at that moment to attend the junior seminary but was rejected because he wasn't Catholic.

"They didn't think I was old enough to make the decision," he says. Seven years later, he was and he did.

Kenney's political transition continued after his graduation and through the 1990s. He found himself increasingly at odds with his Liberal friends, to the point where by 1994 he became president and chief executive officer of the Canadian Taxpayers Federation. The organization was allegedly non-partisan, but its championing of tax cuts, smaller government, and more direct democracy jibed nicely with the platform of the emerging Reform Party.

So it wasn't a complete surprise when Kenney announced he would seek Reform's nomination in Calgary Southeast before the 1997 election. The riding had previously been held by Jan Brown, who'd left the party, creating a vacancy in one of the safest Reform seats in Alberta.

So anxious was Reform to have Kenney's name on its candidates' list, its leader, Preston Manning, called him one of the party's "star" candidates.

In Kenney's former party, the prime minister had the power to appoint star candidates to their nominations, much to the chagrin of local party members. That policy was anathema to Reformers, whose raison d'être was more local control. So star candidate or not, Kenney would have to run hard to win the nomination and represent Reform in the election. And he did. He defeated three other candidates and took 80 per cent of the votes on the first ballot.

But Kenney's association with Reform almost ended right then and there. So adamant was the party to show its bona fides on local control and differentiate itself from the other parties that it had a plank in its charter forcing members to vote against their own conscience if their constituents clearly favoured the other side of the issue. In fact, every Reform candidate had to sign a form pledging to do just that.

"I took strong exception to this. I refused to sign this form," Kenney says. "I could never abnegate my conscience in matters of fundamental human rights. Democracy is predicated on the inviolable dignity of the human person. No democratic majority, no parliamentary majority, no majority of constituents can alienate inalienable rights."

Reform and Kenney were at a standoff. Some senior party members were threatening not to sign his nomination papers. Reform's critics were licking their chops at the prospect of the party turning its back on one of its most highly touted future stars. And then the issue just went away.

"I called their bluff," Kenney says. "I was a 'star candidate.'" Eventually, the party accepted his position.

The 1997 federal election would firmly establish Reform as the dominant national party in Western Canada. The party would take twenty-four of twenty-six Alberta seats, most of them by huge margins. Still, Jason Kenney was nervous. As a veteran of political back rooms, he knew all too well that individual candidates had much less influence on the outcome of election night than the performance of his or her leader during the campaign.

"It can be extraordinarily frustrating," Kenney says. "You sit there watching the leaders' debate, and any single flaw by your leader can kill your chance of getting elected. It's all so far beyond your control. I just had a sense of resignation because, even though we'd run a pretty good campaign, I knew it could only make a modest difference in the outcome."

Kenney had a lot at stake. He'd quit his job with the Canadian Taxpayers Federation and had no source of income for six months after winning the nomination. He'd spent almost all his life savings in pursuit of serving in Parliament. He woke up on election day, went to church for mass and essentially left the evening's outcome in God's hands. Having said that, he did spend the whole day going from poll to poll, church to church, school to school, visiting all 180 polling stations in the riding and thanking volunteers for their support. His brother ("an extremely high-priced lawyer from New York") flew into Calgary to help the "get out the vote" effort. It all worked and Kenney won his riding by more than fourteen thousand votes, taking 55 per cent of the vote in the process.

"It was the culmination of months and months of dreary effort," he says. "It's a huge relief to have this burden lifted off your shoulders."

While the victory was thrilling, the night wasn't without its stranger moments. Some people showed up at Kenney's victory party, tooting their horns at how much they'd done for the candidate, when, in fact, they hadn't done a thing ("fair-weather friends" Kenney now calls them). It's traditional on election night for the losers to visit the winning campaign headquarters or at least telephone to offer congratulations. None of Kenney's opponents did so. (In fact, none of them showed up at the all-candidates' debates either. "I never met them. It was kind of like a phantom election.")

Next, Kenney joined what should have been festivities at Reform's national headquarters. After all, the party did win sixty seats and was unquestionably now the official opposition in Parliament. However, the mood was morose and many eyes were moist because the party failed to make the all-important breakthrough in Ontario. When Kenney's head did hit the pillow in the wee small hours of the morning, he received a couple of threatening phone calls from people not altogether happy with the results.

"In retrospect, you look at the numbers and say this isn't so dramatic. This is Calgary, you won by a big majority," Kenney says. "But it's such an all-consuming project that it's hard to describe the emotional investment in a campaign."

For Jason Kenney, it was an investment that had paid off. He was going to Ottawa to become a member of Parliament. It was two days past his twenty-ninth birthday.

For a first-time member of Parliament, Question Period can be a surreal experience. When the chamber is full, there are 301 MPs vying for attention. It's a raucous atmosphere, much like a hockey arena. The national media are lying in wait to pounce on every mistake. If that weren't enough to get the adrenaline running, opposition MPs have just thirty seconds to keep their focus, ask their questions, as other members heckle them. The first time Jason Kenney stood up to ask a question, he thought his heart was going to break through his rib cage, he was that nervous.

"You can't even hear yourself think sometimes," Kenney adds. "But when you know you've hit a bull's eye, it's very gratifying. You feel like you've just scored an overtime goal in the Stanley Cup finals."

Being on the opposition benches means Kenney never gets to exercise real power in politics. But what he can do is hit those bull's eyes and hope people take notice. "The power we have is the power to create facts," he says, "creating an agenda that the government has to respond to."

At the top of Kenney's agenda was his crusade to end discrimination in the tax code against single-income families, who decide to have one parent stay home full-time with the kids. Kenney had been championing that cause for years, without success. Then, with a series of deft questions and one cabinet minister's unfortunate answer, he brought the issue unprecedented attention. In March, 1999, in response to a question from Kenney, the Liberals' Jim Peterson suggested government policy discriminated against single-income families because two-income families work harder and have more expenses. Politically, it was a unwise thing for any minister to say, but particularly so for Peterson, who has no children. (Peterson is one of the truly decent guys in politics, but given his personal circumstances, he opened himself up to being out of touch on the issue.) When Reformers put a motion on the floor of the House of Commons that the child-care deduction should apply to dual-income, single-income, and single-parent families, the Liberals used their majority and voted it down.

Peterson's comments and the ensuing vote created a three-week frenzy and a national debate. "Had we not been there pushing consistently, it never would have happened," he says. That's what Kenney calls "creating the facts others have to respond to." (The government struck a committee, which agreed to examine the issue further. The committee made recommendations, but to date, the Liberal government has yet to enact any of the recommendations.)

On the opposition benches when the government has a majority, there are certainly more defeats than victories. That's expected. What's troubled Kenney more are the defeats that are self-inflicted, such as Reform's internal brouhaha over MPs' pensions—an issue that so agitated him, he briefly considered quitting the caucus over it.

The Reform Party garnered a tremendous amount of attention by campaigning against MPs' so-called gold-plated pensions. Many Reformers, when offered an opportunity by the Liberals, opted out of the plan. The government then closed the option to opt out. However, some time later, the Liberals reopened the issue, in essence to set a trap for some Reform MPs who were privately muttering about the unfairness of not having pensions, given that they were working every bit as hard as those who had them. But how could the Reformers, who'd campaigned so hard against the MPs' pensions, do such an about-face? In fact, some did, and it made Jason Kenney crazy. He'd been so proud of his caucus, which had given up potentially millions of dollars in pension benefits to show their commitment to public service, not self service.

"That was a consistent message in my campaign in 1997," Kenney says. "So to see some of our people consider going back in and breaking their word and essentially making a liar out of me was very painful. I had staked a lot of my own personal credibility on the leadership of these people. So we had some very raucous debates in our caucus."

One night, Kenney was filled with such anxiety at his colleagues' actions he left the caucus meeting early "and was just considering saying to hell with it all. I'm just not going to put up with this. My integrity is more important than caucus solidarity." Kenney briefly flirted with the notion of quitting the caucus entirely, if any of the Reform MPs rejoined the pension plan. Instead, he made some rather blunt comments to the media, which cost him some friendships but preserved his consistency on the issue.

Meanwhile, Reform leader Preston Manning sensed the burgeoning split in his caucus, so he summoned Kenney to his office to let him vent, which he did.

"We're there to fight for more important convictions," Kenney says. "I never wanted to let myself be put in the position where the end justifies the means. I thought that was the case here."

However, on another occasion, Kenney showed some old-fashioned team spirit by supporting his party when he disagreed with it. The issue was the scandal surrounding the 1997 Asia-Pacific Economic Cooperation (APEC) summit in British Columbia, where demonstrators were pepper-sprayed by overzealous police, perhaps acting on the wishes of their political masters in the Prime Minister's Office. The government called a public inquiry into the melee, and to tweak the government's nose a bit, the Reform Party urged that the Liberals pick up the legal costs of the protestors.

"I really wasn't comfortable with this," Kenney admits. He figured, if Reform was in government, they'd be doing the same thing as the Liberals. "We were just trying to take a position for political advantage," he says. "Nobody should get funding. Why should these guys, just 'cause they've got political savvy?"

Kenney very much wanted to vote against Reform's resolution providing legal assistance. But the party twisted his arm and urged him to "take one for the team."

When it came time to vote against Reform's resolution, "I glued myself to the seat not to vote against it," Kenney says.

Does he still regret that vote?

"Yeah, I really do. I really came to Ottawa with the determination never to vote against my conscience."

Kenney's unusually steadfast commitment to the job even extends to his personal life, which he's essentially put on hold while he's an MP.

"One of the reasons I decided to run at this stage of my life was I thought it would be extremely difficult to be both a good father and a good MP," he says. "It must take heroic virtue to be a good parent, good husband or wife, and a good representative, especially at the national level."

Kenney marvels at some of his caucus colleagues who do attempt to do it all. For example, Reed Elley represents Nanaimo–Cowichan in British Columbia. To get home, he takes a five-hour flight from Ottawa to Vancouver, then hops another flight to the southern part of Vancouver Island and Nanaimo. The entire trip takes eight hours. There's a three-hour time change. And Elley has eight children, several foster children among them. "How he does that just blows my mind," Kenney says.

Or take Grant McNally, MP for Dewdney–Alouette east of Vancouver. He has that same five-hour flight, then a two-hour drive home. "To put his kids to bed Sunday night, he takes the red-eye into Ottawa, arrives at 7 a.m., then works a twelve-hour day," Kenney says. "I don't know how these guys do it."

Ask most MPs who their political heroes are and you'll understandably get Pierre Trudeau, Wilfrid Laurier, John Kennedy, Abraham Lincoln, Winston Churchill, and so on. Who's Kenney's political hero? William Wilberforce. William Wilberforce?

"He's the man who over a forty-year period in the British Parliament in the early nineteenth century brought an end to the slave trade in the British Empire," Kenney explains.

An obvious history buff, Kenney's job has given him a front-row seat on many historic events. He once met twenty World War I veterans on Remembrance Day in 1998, men who'd fought at Vimy Ridge and Ypres. They're now in their second century of life. "I was just in tears," Kenney recalls. "That was a pretty moving experience."

Kenney would become a major player in the new Canadian Alliance's efforts to abandon its old Reform image and create a broader party Canadians east of Manitoba could embrace. Jean Chrétien called a federal election on Sunday, October 22, 2000. That meant that Stockwell Day would be unavailable to launch his party's campaign because of his refusal to work on his Sabbath. Who would step into the breach for the Alliance? Deborah Grey, the Reform Party's first-ever MP? Preston Manning, the man who created the Alliance movement in the first place? Nope.

Jason Kenney found himself before a phalanx of microphones on the day of the call. He was thirty-two years old, appointed co-chair of the Alliance's campaign because of his early and dedicated support of Day, and was now, with co-chair Peter White, front and centre at the launch. After watching its predecessor, Reform, pick up just one seat east of Manitoba over two prior elections, Kenney boldly predicted the Alliance would take twelve to twenty seats in Ontario alone, or even more if the wheel turned as much as party officials dared dream.

"I think if the change dynamic takes hold during this campaign, as we anticipate, we will be winning forty or more seats in this province," Kenney said.

Of course, it didn't quite work out that way. Stockwell Day did manage to increase the Reform Party's tally in Ontario by 162,000 votes. In fact, the Alliance was the only party in Ontario to gain support—the Liberals, PCs, and NDP all lost votes compared to the '97 campaign. But all those extra votes only translated into two seats. Out West, Kenney was still as popular as ever in his own Calgary Southeast constituency, taking that prize by more than 21,000 votes.

Jason Kenney still has days where he wakes up and wonders why he's still in the game, why he hasn't given up long ago. The lack of power individual MPs have is still a constant frustration to him, but he tries to maintain his sense of humour, if only to preserve his own sanity.

"You see people who are psychological zombies, MPs who take themselves too seriously," he says.

So what keeps him coming back for more? Two things really. The competitive fires still burn inside Kenney. He likes to win in his chosen arena. And one can't mock his dedication to be of service. His personal hero is Pope John Paul II, who once wrote that only in self-abnegation do we really find ourselves.

"At its most fundamental level, this is what I'm most motivated by," Kenney says. "It's difficult to live that in politics because you're surrounded by the trappings of power. But that's what motivates me."

WHAT'S SO INTERESTING ABOUT ALL THE PEOPLE in politics who've followed it since they were kids is their inability to explain what drew them to it in the first place. Tim Murphy, a former MPP from Toronto, started subscribing to *Time* magazine while in elementary school. He had a thirst for politics and current affairs even then. Others such as Tom Long and Jason Kenney started craving politics even though no one else in the family seemed particularly interested. Richard Mahoney, a former president of the Ontario Liberal Party, recalls organizing a group of nine-year-olds to get on their bicycles and engage in the time-honoured tradition of ripping down the lawn signs of Liberal opponents. His bedroom featured two posters at the time: Mick Jagger and Pierre Trudeau.

"It was incredibly cute or incredibly pathetic, I'm not sure," he says.

Perhaps Kenney comes closest to explaining how a love for this very tough and often unforgiving business can suddenly appear in the minds of young children.

"All I can ascribe this to is a deep genetic flaw," he says with only a slightly bemused look on his face.

THE ACCIDENTAL CANDIDATES

There is a widely held belief among the public that the vast majority of candidates who stand for office do so out of a burning desire to fulfill their personal destiny or ambition. To be sure, that description fits some politicians. But there is another group, which has not seen the flame burning since age eight. Their parents weren't politicians. In fact, their entrée into politics may have been entirely accidental. Their lives were heading in a completely different direction when politics called, or more likely, when some friend in politics called.

They are the accidental candidates.

Jean Pigott had no intention of running in an Ottawa by-election in 1976 until she received a phone call from John Laschinger. The Tory backroom boy was conducting a poll in the Ottawa–Carleton riding, testing a bunch of different names to determine whose candidacy might be the strongest. Laschinger asked Pigott if he could include her name.

"In a moment of weakness, she said yes," Laschinger says. "Three weeks later I went back to her and said, 'You led the poll. Now you've got another decision to make.'"

Pigott agreed to run in the by-election and won. Strangely enough, three years later when Joe Clark became prime minister, she lost her re-election bid by seven thousand votes. Pigott went on to become chairman of the National Capital Commission and had a building, Jean Pigott Place, on Lisgar Street in Ottawa, named for her. Not bad for an accidental candidate.

Oftentimes, professional athletes become accidental candidates. They are people who have approached their craft with a singular devotion, yet somehow find their way into the "other" arena. Perhaps it's because the comparisons between sports and politics are so obvious. Former U.S. President Theodore Roosevelt referred to politics as life "in the arena." So does National Hockey League Hall of Famer and former MP Leonard "Red" Kelly.

"The House of Commons is the arena," he says. "The Speaker is the referee. The sergeant-at-arms is the linesman." Kelly played hockey against some tough customers but says, "Some of the slipperiest people I've ever seen are politicians."

Kelly was a member of the Toronto Maple Leafs when he got a call from the Liberals' legendary Rainmaker. Keith Davey wanted Kelly to come to a meeting with Prime Minister Lester Pearson at Toronto's Park Plaza Hotel. Davey was most keen on having Kelly run for the Grits, and thought brushing shoulders with the PM might seal the deal. Kelly didn't even want to attend the meeting, let alone run for office. But eventually he agreed to see Pearson.

The meeting didn't go particularly well. In fact, by the time it was over, Pearson was trying to convince Kelly *not* to run. That offended Kelly's athletic pride. "So I took another look at it and thought, why not?" Kelly says.

The sixties would prove to be a pretty memorable decade for Red Kelly. He won four Stanley Cups with the Toronto Maple Leafs and two elections as the Liberal MP for York West. In his second election, he thumped a PC candidate named Alan Eagleson, who thirty years later would go to jail for defrauding hockey players such as Red Kelly. Kelly also voted for the new flag, despite Maple Leaf owner Conn Smythe's constantly leaving him notes in the dressing room urging him not to abandon the Red Ensign ("We fought for that flag," Smythe would admonish him).

One day, Kelly found himself in Prime Minister Pearson's office with influential cabinet minister Jack Pickersgill and Keith Davey. Suddenly, the "red phone" rang. The White House was calling the prime minister. The phone may have been ringing, but no one would answer it because no one could find it. Apparently, Pearson used to hide the phone because his grandchildren would play with it when they visited. And now Pearson had forgotten where he'd hidden it.

"So we all got down on our knees and looked for it," Kelly recalls, laughing hysterically at the memory of the prime minister, one of his top cabinet ministers, one of his top advisers, and a future Hall of Famer looking for a telephonic needle in a prime ministerial haystack.

Howie Meeker was another Maple Leaf and another reluctant player in that "other" arena. "The first political meeting I ever attended in my life was my own nomination meeting," Meeker laughs. He was ordered by Conn Smythe to suit up for the Tories to help the major's fellow military man and leader of the Conservative party, George Drew.

Meeker won a by-election as the Conservative MP for Waterloo South in 1951. And just like Red Kelly, he won four Stanley Cups in a Maple Leaf jersey and played in both arenas simultaneously.

"The arena in the House of Commons is no different than the arena of any rink around the country," says Meeker. "You sit there and you fight and argue and bitch and complain. It's the same kind of game with the same kind of emotions as hockey."

Meeker loved politics, but didn't love the precariousness of the business. He had little formal education and no business to return to if he lost (his playing days were coming to an end). When a minor league coaching job came up in Pittsburgh, he jumped at it. Ironically, had he hung around, he certainly would have been re-elected. John Diefenbaker was on the verge of taking over the Conservative Party, and the greatest landslide in Canadian history was just around the corner. It may have been brief, but golly gosh, Howie Meeker was a parliamentarian.

"It was great fun, honest to God," says Meeker.

Sometimes, the most fun you have in politics is totally accidental.

HOW MANY POLITICIANS IN CANADA can say they were the first member ever elected in the history of their party?

Deborah Grey can.

And the amazing thing about this woman's date with the history books is, it all happened by accident.

In a way, it's surprising that Grey had no interest in politics until she became the Reform Party's first-ever member of Parliament. Her great-grandfather was Ted Applewhaite, an MP from Prince Rupert, British Columbia. Grey remembers, as a three-year-old, meeting Applewhaite at the train station in Vancouver and seeing him off to Ottawa, having no idea what his job was all about. If that connection to politics weren't enough, her great-uncle Byron Johnson was the last premier of British Columbia before W.A.C. Bennett owned the job for twenty years, starting in 1952. By the time Grey knew her great-uncle, he was already out of politics and victimized by a stroke. Grey remembers sitting on Johnson's knee, but unable to converse with him because of his condition.

Grey's next encounter with politics didn't take place for another thirty years. "I was never really interested in it because I thought they were a bunch of crooks," Grey says with characteristic bluntness. "Especially out west, because they'd disappear into Ottawa until election time. So I paid precious little attention to it."

Some young people are born to be politicians. Others are bred to it. Deborah Grey was neither. And nothing that took place between sitting on the knee of a former premier of British Columbia to her first hearing about something called the Reform Party suggested politics would ever be in her future.

Grey was born and raised in Vancouver, one of five children to a saintly mother and an alcoholic father, who disappeared from her life when she was just nine. For the next several years, she fought with internal demons who'd convinced her she drove her father away. As a result, she became the local troublemaker at school. Her principal, Ken McPherson, put her on probation after grade eight, which was a bit of a wake-up call, since Grey knew disappointing her mother was an absolute no-no.

And then that summer, something happened that changed Deb Grey's life. She went away to summer camp and began to hear that Jesus Christ died for everyone else's sins. Grey found that rather unconvincing. Why would he die for her? she wondered. She was bad news. She drove her father away.

But something made her re-evaluate her skepticism. On August 5, 1966, she decided to become a Christian, which made the next encounter with her principal rather eventful. Grey explained that she wouldn't be causing him any more problems because of her new-found faith. It was a new one on the principal, but he promised to give Grey the benefit of the doubt. Just as well. She kept her word and left her troublemaking days behind.

The seventies saw Grey attend Bible college, work with a missionary organization in Spain, and make friends with some school teachers at Fort Chipewyan in northern Alberta. She fell in love with the area and decided to stay, eventually getting a job as a teacher on the Frog Lake Indian Reserve. "I taught them how to read and they taught me how to fish in a creek with my bare hands," she says. "It was a great tradeoff."

The following year, 1980, a permanent teaching job opened up in the county of Vermilion River in northern Alberta, and Grey jumped at it. She'd always wanted a husband and kids, but it didn't appear to be in the cards. So, she became a foster mother instead.

After eight years of that, Grey was a little burned out and needed a break. Her foster-parenting term was due to end, so she told the administrator she wanted to pull back for a year.

"We can't do it without you, Deborah," they told her.

"If I got hit by a bus, I bet you a dollar you'd manage anyway," she replied.

One thing you discover when you talk to Deb Grey—being a born-again Christian doesn't mean you can't have a pretty blunt sense of humour.

In the fall of 1988, Grey and a bunch of friends got together to celebrate one of their birthdays. They started grumbling about Brian Mulroney. "We thought he'd smarten up when we put him in, in 1984," Grey said at the party. "Now it's worse."

Then someone mentioned a new, Western-based political party, led by a former Alberta premier's son. And Deb Grey's life was about to change in an unimaginable fashion.

JUST LIKE DEBORAH GREY, IONA CAMPAGNOLO'S first exposure to politics took place in Vancouver at age three. And the incident was equally as memorable.

"My father informed me that he carried me through a food march in the early thirties," she says. "My mother always said it was a disgraceful thing to do, and he always said that was my first political act."

There were two encores to that first political act, but they'd be decades away. Forty years later, Campagnolo would become a cabinet minister in the government of Canada. And fifty years later, she'd make her mark as the first-ever woman to be president of the federal Liberal Party.

Like so many politicians, Campagnolo's path to the job was unexpected. She got her start in broadcasting, where she had to keep her political opinions to herself. But there was municipal politics, where you didn't have to show your partisan stripes, and so Campagnolo worked her way up through that system, first as a school board trustee, then "alderman," a term she didn't much care for. (Now they're called councillors.)

"I just thought about doing my duty, improving society, and doing my piece of public service," she says of that time. Even though it wasn't the rule, Campagnolo would voluntarily take herself off the air for two months during election campaigns.

But then the broadcaster Campagnolo did an interview that would ultimately change her life. The year was 1967, Prime Minister Lester Pearson had announced his retirement, and Liberals were engaged in mounting what would become an historic leadership convention. One of the young hotshots vying for the leadership was a man named John Turner, whom Campagnolo interviewed for her morning radio program on CHTK in Prince Rupert. The interview itself wasn't terribly eventful. But the hour-long conversation Turner had with his interviewer after the microphones were off was significant. The future Liberal leader (but not this time) made a pretty strong pitch for why Campagnolo should give public life a shot. Campagnolo listened. Six years later, she acted on Turner's advice. Completely by accident, of course.

SAINT JOHN, NEW BRUNSWICK, SEEMED as nice a place as any for Richard and Elsie Wayne to make a life together. She was born in Shediac, two hundred kilometres away, but moved to Saint John at an early age. She and Richard had purchased a house in the east end of the city, which seemed fine and good, except that one day it started to rain and the water wasn't going away. Elsie called Richard at work.

"The water is rising on our street," she told him.

"Well, it *is* raining," he answered.

"But it's rising," Elsie pointed out. "It's not running off." Richard came home from his Wayne TV repair shop later that day, and sure enough, the street was submerged.

That's how the Waynes found out their new home was on a flood plain. That was also Elsie Wayne's entrée to politics. Many of the families affected by the flooding met at the local church. Who knows what made them decide to choose Elsie as their champion, but that's what they did. It would be her job to make the pitch at city council that this problem needed rectifying. If she needed any incentive, all she had to do was look inside her home. There were tens of thousands of dollars' worth of damage to her furniture, appliances, beds, basement—just about everything.

Elsie made her case rather forcefully, then realized solving the problem was going to take a lot more than just one solid performance before city council. So she turned her kitchen into a sort of war room on the issue. She typed letters every day to the federal and provincial environment ministers, urging them to spend some money to fix her problem.

Then one day, the federal environment minister knocked on Elsie's front door. It was Romeo LeBlanc, who also happened to be the MP for Beausejour, two hours' drive from Saint John. LeBlanc expected to get a warm welcome because he was bringing news that the federal government was prepared to contribute $2.2 million to getting the Waynes' neighbourhood on to a more secure footing. No doubt, he was surprised by Wayne's reaction.

"What's $2.2 million going to do when I said I needed $4.4 million?" she said. In fact, an engineering study had been done that suggested the federal contribution would only get half the job done.

"It's a beginning," LeBlanc told her. "And knowing you, you'll get the other two-point-two."

Today, when reminded of the story, LeBlanc laughs and says, "Elsie wasn't shy."

LeBlanc wasn't wrong. Wayne did manage to get the other governments on side and, voila, the battle was over.

In another respect, it was just beginning. Wayne's success at her first foray into politics prompted some of her neighbours to urge her to stand for city council to ensure the money was properly spent. So she did, and out of the thirteen victorious councillors, tallied the third-highest vote count. She spent a whopping $685 on the campaign.

Although her extended family had some experience in politics, Wayne knew absolutely nothing about the game. Her maiden name is Fairweather. Her cousin is Gordon Fairweather, a former Diefenbaker cabinet minister, the first-ever chairman of the Immigration and Refugee Board, and former chief commissioner of the Canadian Human Rights Commission. But fortunately for Wayne, Saint John's mayor, Samuel Davis, took her under his wing and taught her much about how government works. He sent her to the United States with the Canada Mortgage and Housing Corporation to learn about public housing projects. He put her on the planning commission, where she got a greater understanding of how cities work.

But Davis lost the next election and Wayne did not get on at all with his replacement. So she challenged him next time out and beat him. She became the first female mayor of Saint John, a job she held for ten years.

Wayne discovered she quite liked the life of a politician, although there were those days where she wondered why she ever got in—such as the day someone put her home in the cross-hairs of his pellet gun.

Wayne's husband and youngest son, Stephen, were watching television when they thought they heard someone knock at the front door. Stephen got up and answered the door. At that moment, someone drove by and shot out the front windows of the home. Wayne later learned the action was related to her efforts to take away the Saint John police force's right to strike. A disgruntled city worker was hired to do the job, in hopes of frightening Wayne into changing her mind. Police eventually caught the perpetrator. Wayne wanted to talk to him.

"How much did they give you?" she wanted to know.

"A hundred bucks," came the reply. "I'm an alcoholic," who apparently needed the money to feed his habit.

"If they'd have given you a thousand dollars, would you have killed me?" Wayne asked.

"Probably," the man said.

Wayne found the response chilling, but her next move was anything but conventional. The police wanted the man charged. The city manager urged at the very least that he be fired. Wayne disregarded both options. Instead, she invited the assailant to her office and told him she wanted to send him to a rehabilitation facility in Ontario. If he cleaned up his act and stayed sober, he could keep his job. If not, he'd be terminated.

He chose door number one, dried out, and eventually moved to Prince Edward Island, where he called Wayne again to apologize for what he'd put her family through.

Elsie Wayne proved she was no ordinary politician as mayor of Saint John. But her story was about to get really strange.

MARILYN JEAN HURST GREW UP IN A COMPLETELY non-political family in Manitoba. She has some recollection of John Diefenbaker's election in 1957, but truth be told, it didn't make much of an impression. Politics just wasn't that much of a big deal.

Even after marrying Dr. Neil McLeod and moving to Thunder Bay, Ontario, there was no immediate evidence that the family was going to get any more involved in politics. Marilyn, or Lyn as she was always known, did what most women in rural Canada did in 1966. She started having children. In fact, when a group of parents was trying to enlist some support for a run at a school board position, it was Neil they approached, not Lyn. The only women on the school board in those days were much older—women whose children had already gone through the school system, women who were looking for something else to do now that the kids were out of the house. It also wouldn't have occurred to anyone to approach a young mother of two children when her better-known husband, a respected physician yet, might be available.

But Neil McLeod gave the group a most unorthodox reply when asked if he'd stand for a school board trustee's position. He told them he didn't think he could do it, but have you talked to my wife? She'd be great.

Frankly, they hadn't thought of his wife, because there had never been a female school board trustee in Thunder Bay with children still in the system. But the more they thought about it, and the more Lyn thought about it, the idea made sense. Besides, "I was not meant to be at home looking after the kids," Lyn thought. She had a degree in English and French literature from the University of Manitoba. She wanted to put that knowledge to work. Not that she didn't love being a wife and mother. She just needed more. And so she ran, and won a seat on the school board in 1967, and seemed content to make her contribution to local education. She'd be on the school board for seventeen years.

A year later, Pierre Trudeau burst on the national scene. A local school principal was running for the Liberals in Thunder Bay, so Lyn took the next step, although not a terribly big one. She bought a party membership, made some phone calls, and put a sign on her lawn. She did it as much out of respect for the local candidate as for any enthrallment with Trudeau. ("I was intrigued with Trudeau, but I wasn't a Trudeaumaniac. I was too old to be a groupie.") But throughout the course of the campaign, one thing did crystallize for McLeod. She now thought of herself as a Liberal. Not a future Liberal politician, but a Liberal nonetheless.

That didn't stop others from trying to enlist her services. One night leading up to the 1984 federal election, three Conservative Party officials visited the McLeod home, cracked open a bottle of wine, and tried to convince McLeod to run on Brian Mulroney's ticket.

"But I'm not a Conservative," she told them.

"That doesn't matter," said Peter Michalyshen, one of the officials, "as long as you're not on the executive."

"I'm a Liberal," McLeod reiterated, concerned that the Tory trio wasn't quite getting it.

"Well, if you don't run in this next federal election, you'll be past your prime," Michalyshen warned her. "This is your last chance." Apparently, this almost forty-five-year-old mother, now with four children, had a "best before" label on her she wasn't aware of.

McLeod thanked them for coming but said running for the Conservatives was out of the question. Besides, she'd just gone back to school for five years as a mature student and was working on a master's degree in psychology from Lakehead University. She'd just started a new job, doing psychological assessments of children and adolescents in a general hospital setting, and she was loving it. She wasn't going to leave that for anybody, particularly some Tories who'd just insulted her. Thunder Bay politics were a little unpredictable that year anyway. On September 4, 1984, when 211 Conservatives swept into office, Thunder Bay voted for the NDP's Iain Angus. The Liberals, who'd held the seat since 1935, came third.

McLeod continued to aid the Liberal cause from time to time, attending party meetings and creating lots of buzz in the community that she might be a potential candidate some day. However, the 1985 Ontario election approached—an election that would see the Liberals returned to power for the first time in forty-two years. McLeod could have been a candidate, but passed.

Less than two years later, election rumours were in the air again. Premier David Peterson had been governing with the support of Bob Rae's New Democratic Party. He hoped to turn his unprecedented popularity into his own majority government.

A friend of McLeod's returned from a conference in Winnipeg. "I hear you're running," Susan Braun, former chair of the Lakehead Board of Education, told McLeod.

"I'm not even thinking about running," came the response.

"Well, I'll give you two weeks to make up your mind, because one of us should run, and if you don't, I'm going to. But it should be you."

Finally, it was time to fish or cut bait. That weekend, Lyn and Neil McLeod went to their cottage at Lake Shebandowa. The couple intended to hash out all the reasons why Lyn should *not* run. She was tempted—how could she not be? The Liberals were virtually guaranteed to win the election, and as a competent woman from the North, the chances of a cabinet job were tantalizingly close.

But there seemed to be a long list of reasons why taking another pass made more sense: the five years of upgrading her education to win a job she loved; Queen's Park was so far away; only two kids were out of the house (the youngest was fourteen).

After a vigorous discussion, McLeod went to bed, then woke up at two in the morning and resolved she couldn't pass up the opportunity. Still, she wanted to hear from her kids. The next day, the McLeod parents gathered their two younger daughters in the living room and asked their opinion.

"Mom, I don't think I could manage if you were going to be away that much," said Kristen, the youngest of the four McLeod girls.

Dara, now in grade nine and ever the pragmatist, offered another view. "Kristen, by the time Mom gets elected, you'll be in high school and it won't matter to you if she's there or not."

The issue was now resolved. McLeod called the Liberal riding association and asked if they were still looking for a candidate. They were, and McLeod took the nomination by acclamation.

But the tough sledding was still to come. Peterson may have been popular province-wide, but in Thunder Bay, the Liberals hadn't won the seat McLeod was contesting in twenty years. And the local polls didn't look that good.

But fortune smiled on the reluctant candidate on that September night in 1987. McLeod defeated ten-year Tory veteran Mickey Hennessey by fifteen hundred votes—a narrow victory, considering some Liberals won their seats that night by more than twenty thousand votes.

Lyn McLeod was on her way to Queen's Park. *Really* on her way.

DEBORAH GREY HAD ALMOST NO INTEREST in politics. But she had heard of Western Canada's latest foray into national politics, and what she'd heard wasn't good. "The Reform Party?" she asked her friend Liz White at that birthday party in 1988. "Aren't they a bunch of Western separatist wackos?"

White's answer surprised her. On the contrary, she said. In fact, White herself was a member of the new party. Grey knew her friend to be a farmer and a nurse, and not much more politically active than she was. And yet, something Reform was saying struck a chord with Liz White. Then something White said struck a chord with Deb Grey. She heard Reform's message of less government, lower taxes, attacking the deficit, getting more power for the West in Ottawa, and it interested her. Because of redistribution, Grey lived in what would become the new riding of Beaver River. To show her commitment to the new party, she told her friends she'd go to an all-candidates' meeting. But that was it.

Did she think of running herself at this time? In answering the question, Grey's voice went from a moderate tone to eight octaves higher in two seconds.

"No! Never!" she replied.

Liz White had other ideas. At that same birthday party, while Grey was watching television, she got a phone call from a Reform Party official named Pat Chern.

"I've been talking with Liz," Chern told Grey, "and she tells me you're thinking of becoming a candidate. Are you?"

"No I'm not!" Grey replied, thinking at the same time she was going to give her friend Liz a piece of her mind the next time she spoke to her. "I'm a school teacher and it's September. But thanks anyway." Grey asked for some literature and ended the phone call.

Grey soon found herself at the Edmonton airport, on the way to Vancouver for her brother Shaun's wedding. She was killing time, reading the Reform Party literature. She noticed a man looking over her shoulder, eyeing the material. It turned out to be Gordon Shaw, vice-chairman of the party. The two struck up a conversation.

"You could call it coincidence, fate, providence, whatever," Grey says. "I always say the common denominator is the same. The hair on the back of your neck goes *boing* when something big happens."

Something big was happening. Grey enjoyed being a teacher, although after ten years, she confesses to being a tad restless for something new.

"I could remember saying, 'Okay God, maybe you're getting me ready for a bigger classroom.'"

And so she took the plunge. She took six weeks of unpaid leave from her teaching job and sought the Reform Party nomination in the northern Alberta riding of Beaver River. She was acclaimed.

What Deb Grey knew about politics and how to contest an election probably could have been written on one or two pieces of confetti. Not only that, she was running in Alberta, where every single seat in every single general election since 1972 had gone to the Conservatives.

The 1988 election would be different. Unfortunately for Deb Grey, she wasn't the candidate that would make that difference. The Tories won every single Alberta seat again, except one. The NDP's Ross Harvey took Edmonton East with a 1.5 per cent margin of victory over his Tory opponent.

On November 21, 1988, Deb Grey would come fourth in the fight for Beaver River. In fact, if you were looking for signs that Grey was about to launch a national Reform revolution, you'd have been hard-pressed to find any in her constituency that night. Not only did she come fourth, but she also managed to capture just 13 per cent of the votes. Twelve other Reform candidates in Alberta (out of a total of twenty-six) managed to capture a higher percentage of the vote than Deb Grey.

Grey took two days after the election to write some thank-you notes, then returned to the classroom and expected to resume teaching.

And then she got the phone call that would change everything. Throughout the 1988 election campaign, Conservative candidate John Dahmer, a college instructor, was sick. But no one had any idea just how serious his illness was until he passed away just days after winning.

Deb Grey's phone was ringing because party officials wanted to know if she was ready, willing, and able to contest the upcoming by-election. After lifting her jaw off the ground, Grey said she'd have to call Preston Manning, whom she'd actually never even met.

"You probably don't know my name," Grey said to the Reform leader.

"Oh, you're Deborah Grey. You're our candidate out there in Beaver River," Manning responded. (As Grey tells this story, she does a marvellous impression of Manning's high squeaky voice.)

Grey told Manning her life was now back to normal, and that he should consider her the "warm-up act" for the riding. Given that Manning only lived four miles from the Beaver River border, she fully expected and encouraged him to run in the by-election. Manning said he understood, and that was that.

However, unbeknownst to Grey, Manning drove all over the riding, seeking feedback on who should contest the by-election. On December 1, 1988, Manning and Grey met in Smokey Lake, about an hour and a quarter northeast of Edmonton.

"I think it would look a lot like political opportunism if I jumped in here," Manning told her. "Would you be willing to run again?"

Grey's reaction? She just about burst into tears. "I thought, 'Holy smokes, this isn't the way I thought this was going to go.'"

There were some obvious practical problems Grey would have to overcome if she wanted to run again. She was in the middle of a school year with still no clue about when the by-election would be called. The board of education was dominated by Tories, who weren't crazy about giving her time off to run the first time, let alone to reprise her candidacy.

"They weren't real happy about this cheeky, young pup," Grey says of herself.

Yet, somehow, the party convinced her to give it another go, despite the unimpressive results in the '88 campaign. Grey would soon discover a new definition of the word hectic. She'd teach all day, then campaign all evening through December, January, and February. It was dark and freezing every night across her 28,000-square-kilometre constituency.

"Then try to mark Shakespeare essays on the back of it," Grey laughs. "I think a lot of it was, I'm up for the dare. I believe in what I'm doing. I'm no policy wonk. I'm a communicator. If you can give me this stuff, I can communicate it. I thought, it's high time these guys got a good kicking."

Grey's motivation for knocking the Tories down a peg got a huge shot in the arm the night of the Progressive Conservative nomination meeting. It took place in Glendon, Alberta (population a few hundred), at the local hockey arena. Forty-five hundred people showed up. It was the biggest political event Deb Grey had ever seen. Mind you, by this time, she was beginning to figure out a few tricks of the trade. Her campaign ran off brochures with her picture on the cover saying, "If your candidate didn't win tonight, maybe you'd like to have a look at me." Grey got a bunch of kids together and asked them if they wanted to spend an hour in forty-degree-below-zero weather, putting her brochures under the windshield wipers of the cars at that PC nominating meeting. Believe it or not, she found some takers.

"A few of us just cooked it up," Grey says of the idea. "I have to have some fun every day. I thought, what a pack of laughs."

The laughs didn't last long. After a nine-hour marathon, the convention nominated Dave Broda to carry the Tory colours into the by-election to be held March 13, 1989.

Jack Shields, MP for Athabasca, saw Grey at the meeting. While he was at the microphone, he took aim at her.

"We'd like to welcome another candidate from another party here tonight to show her how a real nomination meeting runs," Shields taunted her. Then Dave Broda chimed in. "Tonight is election night," he said from centre stage. "March 13 will be the coronation."

What did Grey think of that show of bravado?

"Not if I can help it, honey. If you get coronated March 13, it's because you did a lot of work and that's the only way you're going to get this sucker."

Even though it had been less than four months since the last general election, the political landscape in Alberta was changing. Disillusionment with the Mulroney government was already on the rise, and an apparently meaningless by-election, which wouldn't affect the Conservatives' ability to rule, seemed the perfect opportunity to send the government a message.

Still, the Reform campaign in Beaver River didn't appear to be striking much fear into local Tories. Deb Grey was operating out of a flower shop on Main Street in St. Paul. Her chief source of campaign funding seemed to come from the proceeds of garage sales. But she did have one thing in her favour. She was the only candidate who had run in the previous general election four months earlier. Her signs had been up from the previous October, and her name was becoming better known.

By-election night was surreal. As Grey's team gathered to receive the returns, a reporter from *Maclean's* magazine showed up. "We thought, wow, in St. Paul, Alberta?" Grey says. Then a reporter from the Canadian Press wire service arrived. Then CTV. Then the CBC.

"You guys are welcome here and I love to see you, but what are you doing here?" Grey asked.

"We think you're going to win," came the response from one of them.

Had Grey done any polling to corroborate what the reporters' presence was telling her? She shoots me a stare, suggesting I'm the biggest idiot she's met in a year. Polling? Was I kidding?

In any event, the returns started to come in. Grey had no scrutineers, and no "get out the vote" machine to rely on. She was completely in the dark as to what her fate might be by the end of the evening. Polling station after polling station would report, showing her ahead, but the overall significance of it never dawned on her. "I had no idea that people do trends and Peter Mansbridge makes predictions," she says.

Finally, with her campaign team watching *Hockey Night in Canada*, the CBC ran a bulletin at the bottom of the screen. It said, "Reformer Elected." And then she knew.

"We just said, 'Yikes,'" Grey recalls. "It was just unreal."

"You really had no idea you were winning?" I ask.

"Not a clue. Not a clue," she insists.

Grey took the by-election by more than four thousand votes over Broda, capturing almost 50 per cent of the votes in the process. And just like Robert Redford at the end of *The Candidate*, her reaction was complete confusion about what comes next.

"I can remember thinking, now what do I do?" says Grey, who didn't even understand that she now had to go to Ottawa. Given that it was March, she was actually expecting to finish up her teaching duties, then assume her political duties. Whatever that meant.

"I am a campaigner, but we were so green on the other stuff, we just did not have a clue," Grey says.

One thing she did know for sure. March 13, 1989, was the greatest night of her political life. She may not have had a family of her own, but Deb Grey had just given birth to the Reform Party's presence in the nation's Parliament.

When she finally got to Ottawa, Grey was scared and utterly ignorant about how things worked on Parliament Hill. She didn't know how a bill became law. She didn't know what a petition was. "Greener than grass, I'm telling you," is how she describes herself.

She soon discovered she could count on one hand the number of other MPs who would welcome her to their club of 295. The Tories, quite naturally, regarded her with suspicion and antipathy, since she'd stolen one of their seats. The Liberals were coming off their second consecutive election defeat and were wondering how and when to get rid of John Turner (he'd oblige them the following year). And the New Democrats were filled with dread at the thought of Reform policy ever being implemented. She ate a lot of meals alone, while watching other MPs point at her and whisper things to one another.

On her first day in the house, Grey was escorted to the chamber by fellow Alberta MP Ross Harvey and Liberal MP Doug Young, whom she sat beside when the house was in session. Some years later, Young would provide Grey with her first significant encounter with the meanness of politics.

In the meantime, Grey was learning how to be a politician. One of the first things she did was get a plaque for her desk, which had inscribed on it some words to live by, courtesy of Nellie McClung, the women's rights activist, who served one term in the Alberta legislature. The plaque read: "Never retreat, never explain, never apologize. Just get the thing done and let them howl."

One of Grey's favourite political heroes was Agnes MacPhail, the first women ever elected to the House of Commons, in 1921. One time, another MP, a male of course, approached MacPhail with the intention of cutting her down a notch.

He asked, "Agnes, have you ever been mistaken for a man?"

"No," she responded, "have you?"

To know Deb Grey is to know she has a lot in common with MacPhail, not necessarily on policy matters, but certainly as it relates to a sharp tongue. When critics would accuse Reform of trying to send women back into the Stone Age, Grey would point out that Reform was the first party to have 100 per cent female representation in its caucus. Liberal MP Hedy Fry from Vancouver Centre once accused Grey of wanting women to be barefoot in the kitchen.

Grey's response: "Honey, I'll go toe-to-toe with you any day. Even when I'm home, I'm not in the kitchen, honey, I'm at Swiss Chalet."

After two hard-fought campaigns, Grey was used to rolling up her sleeves and working hard. But the schedule of an MP was something else. She'd leave home Sunday afternoons, not arriving at Ottawa until midnight. She'd arrive at work at seven in the morning, filling her days with committee meetings, interviews, Question Period, receptions, answering correspondence, and staff meetings. Thursday nights, she'd fly back to Alberta and take appointments with constituents on Fridays, then attend functions in her riding all day Saturday. Sunday, she'd start the cycle all over again.

Besides getting elected, the highlight of Grey's first term in Ottawa had to be meeting the man who'd become her husband. She was beginning to think that marriage was something she simply would never experience in life. Until she met Lewis Larson in October, 1991.

"We had a long-distance love affair, with long-distance phone calls," Grey says. "Now we've got a long-distance marriage."

It's also quite a coincidence that the two most influential men in Grey's life were both carpenters: Jesus Christ and Lewis Larson.

"He's a builder," Grey says of her husband. "So am I."

At this point in her political life, Deb Grey was still a bit of a novelty. Then came the 1993 election. And everything changed again.

The two federal elections in the 1990s represented one of those sea changes in Canadian history, and Deborah Grey had a front-row seat. Instead of being the lone wolf in a strange town, Grey was joined by a sizeable contingent of Reform MPs. In 1993, her home province turned its back on the Conservative Party with ruthless disregard for the party's past electoral success. Reform took twenty-two of twenty-six Alberta seats—fifty-two nationwide, good enough for third place in the House of Commons. The party just missed out on official opposition status by two seats, as the Bloc Québécois took fifty-four seats.

The 1997 election was a virtual repeat of the previous campaign. The Liberals formed a majority government again, albeit reduced in size. Reform supplanted the Bloc as official opposition by capturing eight more seats, bringing its total to sixty.

Deb Grey's party was clearly a threat to Liberal hegemony in Ottawa, and the increasing viciousness of the rhetoric on both sides of the house reflected that. One of Grey's worst days in politics happened, ironically, because of a slur made by one of the first friends she made in Ottawa.

Liberal MP Doug Young, who represented the New Brunswick riding of Acadie–Bathurst, had been Grey's seat-mate after she won her by-election in 1989. They weren't best buddies by any stretch of the imagination, but they got on well enough for two people with sharp tongues. A few months before the Liberals would go back to the polls seeking re-election in 1997, Young and Grey were involved in a nasty exchange in the House. The incident was memorable because it demonstrated, as well as anything, how hurtful politics can be, and how vicious relations between the Liberals and the Reformers had become.

Grey rose from her seat to ask a question about MPs so-called "gold-plated pensions." She pointed out the unfairness of Canadians contributing increasingly more of their salaries for relatively little payback from the Canada Pension Plan. She cranked the rhetoric up to another level when she blasted "parliamentary porkers" such as Jean Charest and Sheila Copps, whose pensions from politics would be six times higher than the average Canadian's. "That is scandalous," Grey thundered.

The question was to Marcel Masse, president of the treasury board of cabinet. But before he could consider his response, Doug Young, now defence minister, shouted back: "There is more than a slab of bacon talking there." Grey, who's had endless battles with her weight for years, was cut to the quick and reduced to tears.

"I sat with Doug Young," Grey says. "He was my seat-mate. So that's why when he did his shot at me, that was particularly hurtful."

Young didn't apologize at the time or since. "He could have sent me a note and said, Deb, that was stupid. I'm a really forgiving person."

Sometimes in politics, what goes around comes around, and for Doug Young, it came around a few months later, in the 1997 general election. He lost his seat. His gruff, speak-before-you-think manner may have caught up with him. Even today, four years after the incident, Grey still has people coming up to her when she visits New Brunswick, offering the apology Young declined to give.

"I feel sorrier for Doug Young than I do for myself," Grey says.

(Ironically, Grey was hoisted with her own petard earlier this year. Tossing aside her long-standing opposition to the pension issue, Grey bought back into the MPs plan, citing the need to look after her future. It cost her just over $80,000 to get back into the plan. When she leaves the house, that plan will pay off one million dollars.)

In some respects, Young's loss of temper was understandable, if not acceptable. Grey had become perhaps the foremost expert on the opposition benches on how to get under the skin of Liberal cabinet ministers. Her staccato-style of attack, combined with a knack for the twenty-second clip, got her plenty of ice time on the evening newscasts.

However, how can someone who feels Jesus Christ so deeply at the core of her being at the same time be so caustic with her parry and thrust across the floor of the Commons?

Her explanation is classic Grey: "Well, Jesus wasn't exactly a wet noodle."

During her eleven years in the house, Grey admits to having gone too far just once. It was in 1998 during the debate on how to compensate victims of Hepatitis C. The Liberals were being stingy on who should be eligible for compensation, so much so, that even Mike Harris, Ontario's premier, was getting rave reviews for his much more compassionate approach to the issue. Grey was looking up in the public gallery of the house. She watched the Hep C victims eyeing the Liberal majority, which was voting against a more generous compensation package. Her temperature started to boil. Liberal MP Carolyn Bennett, a doctor and a founding member of the board of the Hepatitis C Society of Canada, voted with her party and against her profession (fighting back tears all the while). Grey shouted at Bennett, "How could you just let these people die?"

Later that year, Grey read a newspaper account of that day. The piece quoted Bennett, who was in enough agony over the vote, but felt completely devastated by Grey's heckle. She suggested to the reporter that Grey seemed to be a hateful individual.

Grey immediately wanted to phone Bennett to straighten things out, but thought better of it.

"I thought I'd sooner do this face to face," she says. "And I went over to her the first day of Parliament and said, 'Look, whether I am or not that's not the point. But you perceived that, and I'm really sorry about that, and I want to ask you to forgive me.'" Bennett did. The incident served as an important lesson for Grey.

"It's often that your greatest strength is your very greatest weakness too," she says. "So my gift of being able to be quick-witted and queen-of-the-one-liners often is your very, very greatest weakness too."

Grey and I conclude our conversation because she's got to catch a flight home. At one time, her candidacy may have been accidental. But for the past twelve years, everything has been very intentional. Everything is designed to transform Deb Grey from a one-seat-wonder to a minister of the Crown. She tried again in November, 2000, taking more than 50 per cent of the votes in Edmonton North. She may be an Alliance MP now instead of a Reformer, but the result was the same—another term on the opposition benches.

"I want to see that those Liberals are not in power any more," she says, with fierce determination in her eyes. "And all the things I've fought about and harangued about for so many years, I want to see them implemented. The only way you're going to do it is form the government." That seems more remote given her very public break with Stockwell Day. "I don't expect to do this for the rest of my life," she says, "but boy, I tell you, I want to get across the aisle."

THE YEAR 1974 WAS A DIFFERENT TIME in the worlds of politics and journalism. Iona Campagnolo was still working in radio as a broadcaster, but also wrote commercials for the political parties as part of her job description. Since she wrote for all three parties, she considered herself non-partisan.

That nicety was probably lost on the station manager, Roy Last, who clearly was a partisan and wanted Campagnolo to be one too. He was a huge fan of Pierre Trudeau's and had been waiting for just the right moment to run for the Liberals in Skeena, a riding so far north in British Columbia, it touches the boundary with Yukon Territory and Alaska. He decided the 1974 election was the time and that Campagnolo would be his campaign manager.

About one month before the nomination meeting, Last took Campagnolo out to lunch. And he sprung some pretty heavy news on her.

"I can't do this," he told her. "My wife is ill. But you could do it."

Campagnolo's reaction was interesting, inasmuch as she didn't choke on her lunch or reject the suggestion out of hand. She remembered what John Turner had told her. She'd already had some experience in politics, albeit at the local level. But that was a far cry from taking a seven-hour trip to get to work every week. But the more she thought about it, the better the idea sounded. Equality between the sexes was a huge issue for her. Coming from northern B.C., so was aboriginal self-determination, which she thought the country had failed at miserably. What better place to promote those issues than in the House of Commons?

But could she win? Her modest political experience, mixed with her exposure from being on the radio and running the local theatre group, and many other civic ventures, were all positives, particularly in a small town.

"Well, there are women all over Canada trying to break into political life," she told him. "So, yes." At that lunch, an accidental candidate was born. Campagnolo became the candidate. The station manager became the campaign manager.

So much of the success of one's political career depends on things over which one has absolutely no control, and that was particularly true for Campagnolo. Her first general election run culminated in a Liberal majority government on July 8, 1974. It was sweet news for the Grits, who'd watched Trudeaumania fizzle, yet survive two years of minority government between 1972 and 1974. Campagnolo was also one of just nine women MPs in a house of 264 members. Right timing, right geography, right gender—the perfect political trinity. As a result, she was immediately appointed parliamentary secretary to the minister for Indian and Northern Affairs. Her first day in the house, she had to introduce a bill on the Northern Canada Power Commission. Her critic was her neighbour to the north, Yukon's Erik Nielsen ("the dreaded Erik Nielsen" as she calls him).

"I thought, 'Dear God, do I really have to do this?'" Campagnolo recalls. And then someone offered a helping hand. The NDP's Stanley Knowles, a legend in parliamentary procedure, wandered over and gave her the Coles Notes version on what to do.

"He just came to help," Campagnolo recalls. "A lovely man."

The learning curve was huge for Campagnolo, but she was up for the challenge. She enjoyed taking on constituency issues and forcing them through a "reluctant" system. She also earned a bit of a "reputation." She was, after all, rather different.

"I was thought of as being vaguely uncivilized," Campagnolo remembers. "First of all, because I was British Columbian. Second, because I was a woman. And third, because I was from the North, and, you know, we all go home on weekends and shoot bears."

Jokes aside, there were plenty of tough times too. Because of her portfolio, Campagnolo was frequently on the receiving end of tongue-lashings from aboriginal groups.

"I had a conscious sense of simply squaring my shoulders and taking the heat that was being meted out as part of your duties on behalf of the country," says Campagnolo, who also felt she represented, in British Columbia, the worst of all of the provinces when it came to government relations with native communities.

"So there are times when it's simply your duty to take it. It's unpleasant, but it's part of making the society function," she says.

That was a tough part of the job Campagnolo understood. There was another side to The Life that she quite disliked.

"I don't think many people know the truth, the bitterness of being in public life," she says. "And I also think that we early women had rather a double dose of it. We were such aliens in the system in those days."

Campagnolo had gone to Ottawa a divorced woman. In fact, eight of those nine female MPs from the class of '74 flew solo, either because they were single or divorced.

"I just gave my staff orders," she says. "No men, period. Keep them out of the way."

Easier said than done. The nine MPs wanted to be treated as equals, but virtually everything they did (or didn't do) was cause for comment. What they wore, how they conducted themselves, what they said, who they sat beside in caucus, were all scrutinized to the *nth* degree. Campagnolo didn't think of herself as blazing any trails in Ottawa. She thought that honour belonged to former MPs such as Ellen Fairclough (the first-ever female cabinet minister) or Judy LaMarsh. But upon further reflection, she now thinks she and her colleagues (Flora MacDonald and Monique Bégin, for example) were pioneers.

How ridiculous did it get? One time, Campagnolo and Bégin showed up at an event wearing the same style of dress. Some Prime Minister's Office staffer felt it important to note that on Campagnolo's file as an indication of her poor judgement.

"Somewhere you would think with the resources that they're commanding, they could manage to get dresses that were different," the note in her file read.

Perhaps the biggest surprise about coming to Ottawa and working in a chamber with 255 men and nine women is that Campagnolo never got "hit on." She was single. She was attractive. But apparently, in an overwhelmingly male chamber where power is the ultimate aphrodisiac, no one made any passes at her. At least, that's what she says.

"Oh, no. Our caucus guys were so careful," she insists. "I can't say sex was ever an issue. We were just out of the sixties. We all had this heady sense that equality was here."

Moreover, Campagnolo didn't want a social life. "I didn't have time for one," she says. "Besides which, if you're going to be doing a job in your constituency, in your province, in your country, or for your party, you're not going to be there. But I am a cat of a different colour on that subject. And as far as I'm concerned, there are lots of people who were not cut out for more than one marriage, and I am one of them." Campagnolo believed she had already had a good marriage, and besides, her two daughters came ahead of any future relationship she might get into.

After two years on the job, Campagnolo apparently impressed Prime Minister Trudeau enough that he promoted her to a full cabinet position. Rumours had been flying, but Campagnolo didn't pay too much attention to them.

"What do you hear?" she once asked Stuart Legatt, a New Democrat MP. Before he could answer, she said, "I'll take anything except all you jocks."

In fact, Campagnolo got the ultimate jock ministry. She became Canada's first minister of state for amateur fitness and sport. But Campagnolo never planned to have a very long career in elective politics. "No Liberal in British Columbia ever had long," she muses. So it wasn't a complete shock when she and every other Liberal MP from B.C. except one lost their seats in the 1979 election.

Campagnolo went back to broadcasting, hosting a CBC-TV show called *One of a Kind* and interviewing the movers and shakers of the day. When Joe Clark's government was unexpectedly defeated just nine months after taking power, everyone expected Campagnolo to repeat a familiar pattern in her life—leave broadcasting and get back into politics. But she didn't.

"I didn't feel I could break the contract with the CBC and then go to the people and say, 'I'll never break my word to you,'" she says. (Ironically, two years later, the CBC broke its contract with her. A parliamentary committee decided that a former cabinet minister shouldn't be allowed to work for a federal Crown corporation. So Campagnolo was fired.)

But the blow wasn't as harsh as it might have been because, before her firing and out of the blue, one of Prime Minister Trudeau's closest friends and cabinet ministers called her with an idea.

"Mr. Trudeau will be going in the foreseeable future," Marc Lalonde said, "and we need someone to cover off the black hole between his leaving and the new leader being elected. We think it's you. Will you run for president of the party?"

Lalonde was correct in his speculation, if not exactly accurate in his timing. Trudeau's departure would turn out to be two years away still, but Campagnolo liked the notion of taking another shot at The Life. So she took Lalonde up on his offer and entered what would turn out to be a bitterly fought contest for the presidency. No one had challenged an incumbent president before, and the winner would be in a significant position either to help or hurt Trudeau's fortunes. The incumbent president, Norm MacLeod, was thought to be too close to John Turner, and the fear was, he'd use the position to launch a formal review of Trudeau's leadership. But Campagnolo defeated MacLeod, beat back the review forces, and in the process, became the first woman ever to become president of the Liberal Party of Canada. She immediately began the process of wresting control of the party out of the Prime Minister's Office and back into the hands of the party members themselves.

In her four years as party president, Campagnolo completely transformed the way the job worked. In the past, with rare exceptions, the job was designed to be unpaid and very low profile. Campagnolo insisted the job come with a salary (equivalent to an MP's). And low profile? Forget it.

Before long, she was into seventy- and eighty-hour work weeks, trying to spread the Liberal gospel, democratize the party's operation, raise money, and keep her antennae up on the state of the party's condition from coast to coast to coast. And even though these were the eighties instead of the seventies, Campagnolo still had her share of gender politics through which to navigate. For example, on occasion the chief financial officer of the party would call a meeting at the Vancouver Club. That might not seem important until you realize the Vancouver Club was a men's-only establishment. Either Campagnolo wouldn't go to the meetings, or she'd have to sneak in some back door.

"I said nothing," Campagnolo says, preferring to ignore the stupidity of it all. "I just did the job. The trick of all of this was to simply show you were an equal at every departure."

She became an even bigger star as president than she was as a cabinet minister. She travelled from St. John's to Vancouver, giving speeches and raising money for the party. And then she became a central figure in one of the most historic meetings any party president has ever had with any Canadian prime minister.

On February 28, 1984, Pierre Trudeau invited Campagnolo to 24

Sussex Drive for lunch. It had been exactly four years and ten days since the country rejected Joe Clark's government and re-embraced Trudeau for his fourth election victory. But much had changed since then. So the PM wanted an assessment from his party president on the state of Liberal fortunes in every province and territory. He also wanted to know what the grassroots were saying about his leadership.

Trudeau's closest advisers in his office were begging him not to have the meeting. They had a pretty solid sense of what Campagnolo would say and didn't want their leader to hear it. Behind her back, they were telling Trudeau their party president was overly dramatic and given to emotionalism. Everything was fine, they insisted. But Trudeau demanded the meeting and Campagnolo gave him the straight goods.

"The fundamental issue," she recalls, "was that there were a great many good Liberals, who loved him dearly, who respected and admired him, but who wanted him to leave before the party was defeated, who wanted him to go out as the great champion and the great prime minister he was, and didn't want him to remain following a defeat. And so, that's what I imparted."

"And how did he take your advice?" I ask.

"How did he take anything? Superbly, of course," she says. "The man was an enormously philosophical person."

"He wasn't disappointed to hear that?"

"No," she says. "This is a man who's a consummate actor. If he was disappointed, he didn't show it. He was controlled. That's what I always admired about him, his immense discipline."

"When you left him that day, did you have a sense of which way he was going to go?"

"I told him I thought that, if he was going to go, he had to do it in some dramatic way, because Canadians expected him to perform in a dramatic manner," she says.

"And what did he say to that?" I ask.

"He just smiled," Campagnolo says.

Later that day, Pierre Trudeau took the most famous "walk in the snow" any Canadian ever has. At ten-thirty the next morning, he telephoned Campagnolo. "I am sending you a 'Dear Iona' letter," he said. And with that, Pierre Elliott Trudeau decided to retire after more than fifteen years as prime minister.

What did Campagnolo think when she received that letter?

"That I had a little, tiny role in history," she says. "Third Act of *Julius Caesar*."

"Just curious," I ask Campagnolo, almost as a throwaway question. "Where's that letter?"

"It's in a very safe place," she says. That's not the answer I'm expecting. I'm expecting to hear it's in the National Archives or some such place.

"Do you still have it?"

"No. It's in an archives, but not the Liberal Party archives," she says, toying with me. "They have a copy in the Liberal archives."

"The National Archives?" I guess again.

"No. I won't tell you. The original is in a very safe place." I'm thinking, this is a document of historic significance that belongs on display somewhere. Campagnolo agrees it's historically significant. On the other hand, the letter is addressed to her by name, not by title. It's an interesting grey area as to whom the note actually belongs.

"Well, it was personal," she says. Coincidentally, Campagnolo and Trudeau shared the same birthday, and she's kept all those 'good wishes' cards too.

Will she ever reveal the location of the original?

"I'll put it in my will," she says. "It will emerge as public property one hundred years from now."

Controversy and Iona Campagnolo have never been very far apart. But the Liberal Party president outdid even her standards for headline-grabbing at the leadership convention to replace Trudeau in 1984. John Turner, the man who originally recommended politics to her, was the prohibitive favourite to win the prize. But Jean Chrétien had a huge contingent of emotional supporters.

Publicly, Campagnolo was neutral. Privately, she cast her first vote for her friend, the agriculture minister, Eugene Whelan, because she didn't want to see any of the candidates embarrassed. There was a good chance Whelan would be. Campagnolo wanted to be sure he got his deposit back, which he did.

On the second and only other ballot, Campagnolo voted for Chrétien. Turner won on that ballot and it wasn't close.

Now, Campagnolo had a dilemma. As she marched to the podium to announce the results, she realized a sizeable chunk of the hall would be crushed by Chrétien's defeat, and she was mulling over what to say to prevent them from exiting the hall en masse in the middle of Turner's victory speech.

"What can you say in ten seconds that will keep them here?" she thought to herself.

And so she called Chrétien to the stage with an unforgettable introduction. She called him second on the ballot, but first in our hearts.

"I thought that was simple truth," Campagnolo says of the phrase, which earned her the eternal enmity of the Turner forces, who thought she was somehow downgrading their guy's victory.

"Lots of people have said to me, it was dead wrong, why did you do it?" Campagnolo says. "I thought it was the right thing, at the time, to help keep the party together, to do what had to be done to bind up the wounds."

If Turner himself was peeved at Campagnolo, he never expressed it. Just a month after winning the convention and succeeding Trudeau, he called an election, and Campagnolo did him a big favour by agreeing to run in the same city as Turner. The leader would run in Vancouver Quadra, the president in North Vancouver. That way, when Turner was out of the province, the party had a solid backup in Campagnolo covering for him, which she did at fifteen all-candidates' forums. (Ironically, Campagnolo did so much filling in for Turner, she missed her own all-candidates' meeting. Jean Chrétien pinch-hit for her.)

The election, of course, was one of the worst disasters ever for the Liberals. Turner went down in history as having had the second shortest prime ministership ever—just seventy-eight days. Inexplicably he did win his own seat, the only Liberal in British Columbia to do so.

In 1986, Iona Campagnolo's time as Liberal Party president ended. She finally had to make the transition to private life, which had been interrupted by Marc Lalonde's call to return four years earlier. This time she made a clean break. She went to Africa with Canadian University Services Organization (CUSO), working on some water projects. In early 1987, McMaster University in Hamilton offered her a job setting up the Centre for International Health.

But her home province beckoned, and so Campagnolo returned to British Columbia and put herself back in circulation. She was elected the founding chancellor of the new University of Northern British Columbia—the first new university in the province in twenty-five years, whose main campus is in Prince George, but with outreach to all parts of the North. Some of her old colleagues in the amateur sport world raised enough money to create a scholarship in her name there, even though she hadn't been the sports minister in twenty years.

She's also on the board of the Fraser Basin Council, a non-profit organization established by three levels of government and the First Nations to enhance the sustainability of the Fraser River and its vast basin. The basin contributes to 80 per cent of B.C.'s economy and 10 per cent of Canada's gross domestic product. It contains twenty-one million hectares of forest, almost half of the province's agricultural land, eight major producing mines, as well as a salmon fishery contributing hundreds of millions of dollars to the economy.

Campagnolo hasn't been an MP in more than twenty years. But she's still one of the best-known political figures in the country. That's both a benefit and a curse.

"I was coming in the [council] building just an hour ago, and a fellow opened the door and said, 'Good afternoon, Senator.' I said, 'I am not a senator.' He said, 'Oh, yes you are.' You get this kind of stuff all the time. Public life doesn't end just because you're not in the public eye."

Others are less kind in their observations. When Campagnolo got appointed to a federal committee to help study the Nisga'a treaty, Reform MP John Cummins blasted her with this: "Why would they pick her to talk about fish? We got thousands of fishermen in B.C. who can talk about fish. She was a Liberal MP back in the 1970s and she has been at the trough ever since." Cummins's comment, besides being rude, doesn't seem borne out by the facts. Campagnolo has no federal pension. She's almost seventy years old and is still working, particularly on issues related to aboriginal land claims.

Moreover, in 1990, Campagnolo was national chair for Paul Martin's leadership campaign. Rumour had it that after her supportive comments about the runner-up at the 1984 convention, Chrétien expected her support the next time around. When he didn't get it, the prime minister froze her out for more than a decade. In fact, the jokes used to fly around Ottawa about the possibility of giving Campagnolo an ambassadorship to Somalia, or some other very undesirable place. The vast majority of her work is done gratis or for small honoraria. So Iona Campagnolo has contented herself with being a director of the Arctic Institute of North America, the International Centre for Human Rights and Democratic Development, and a member of the ethics committee of the 2010 bid for the Winter Olympics for Vancouver/Whistler.

However, in June, 2001, the man Campagnolo described seventeen years earlier as number one in the hearts of Liberals, finally welcomed her back from political purgatory. Prime Minister Chrétien put the exclamation point at the end of a long career in public service by appointing Campagnolo lieutenant-governor of British Columbia.

"I have a mass of interesting things to do with my mind," she says. "I don't intend to stop until God says so."

YOU CAN'T BE A HIGH-PROFILE LOCAL POLITICIAN, particularly in the Maritimes and particularly if you're a woman, without coming to the attention of the senior levels of government, and Elsie Wayne was no exception. She'd been a take-no-prisoners, no-nonsense mayor of Saint John for ten years. The Liberal, the Conservative, and the Reform parties all asked her to carry their banner into the 1993 general election. Wayne's family history, plus her own natural inclination, suggested a run for the PCs. So she took the plunge into national politics, confident that Kim Campbell could build on Brian Mulroney's record.

What came next offered Wayne the biggest political shock of her life. Two hundred and ninety-three Conservative candidates lost. Two won. Jean Charest. And Elsie Wayne.

The day after the election, Wayne and her husband had a heart-to-heart talk about her predicament. "Dear Lord, Richard, there's only two of us. What do I do now?"

"I don't know, darling," he answered. "You got yourself into it, and I don't know how you get yourself out of it."

As popular as Elsie Wayne was in Saint John, she still needed a minor political miracle to win. She got it in the form of a major miscalculation by the Liberals, which no doubt contributed to her victory. Before the 1993 election, in a move filled with controversy, the Liberal leader, Jean Chrétien, had been given the power to appoint candidates wherever he deemed it appropriate. The move was designed to recognize that the best candidates don't always win their nomination meetings. The leader was going to fix that by ensuring some of his favoured choices were there on election day. So Chrétien appointed Pat Landers to run for the Grits in Saint John. The move alienated thousands of local Liberals, who had the temerity to think they were actually going to nominate the candidate of *their* choice, Joe Boyce. The appointment caused a bitter family feud. Landers did run for the Liberals, but Boyce ran too, on an independent ticket. He ended up taking more than thirty-six hundred votes away from the official Liberal candidate. Had those votes been included on the Liberal tally sheet, Pat Landers would have defeated Elsie Wayne by three hundred votes and the Tories would have been reduced to just one seat.

Meanwhile, Wayne was genuinely shocked at the results. She was convinced Brian Mulroney had done great things for the Maritimes and was sure the public would see it that way too. She was furious with the Reformers, who'd cut the right-wing, populist legs out from under her party, noting that unhappy Paul Martin supporters didn't up and quit the Liberal Party and start their own.

National politics was a whole new experience for Elsie Wayne, and there was much about it she didn't like. For the first time in four decades, she was spending vast amounts of time away from her husband. She was reduced to basically the summer months for seeing her two grandchildren. While Jean Charest was criss-crossing the country, trying to rebuild a once-proud institution, Wayne was a one-person caucus, trying to keep the Tories relevant in Ottawa. Fortunately, she was welcomed into the PC Senate caucus meetings every Wednesday, reducing her sense of isolation.

"I'd go to the apartment and wonder what the blazes I was doing there," Wayne recalls. "I would always stop at Yesterday's (a restaurant at Sparks and O'Connor) and have a bowl of soup on the way home all by myself. It was a lonely life."

Ironically, her situation paralleled Deborah Grey's, when the first-ever Reform MP arrived in Ottawa. But the two never broke bread to compare notes, even though their offices were just down the hall from each other—so tense were relations between Tories and Reformers.

But to say it was all doom and gloom wouldn't be fair. Elsie Wayne is, after all, one of the funniest members of Parliament (not always intentionally so). Despite being a doctrinaire social conservative, which would have turned off many in Ottawa, Wayne dazzled people with her bubbly style and sense of humour.

One day in the House of Commons, she entertained MPs with a rendition of "Let Us Spend," sung to the tune of "Let It Snow." And so she sang:

> Unemployment rates are frightful
> Inside, the Grits feel delightful
> They say stop the cuts and then
> Let us spend, let us spend, let us spend.
>
> The Grits say we need to buy some votes back
> We must reward some old hacks
> The jobless can wait till then
> Let us spend, let us spend, let us spend.

There were two more verses but you get the drift.

Another night, she showed up at the Liberals' annual Christmas party, where twenty-six hundred friends and faithful gathered to drink some eggnog and raise some dough for the party. Wayne showed up with felt reindeer antlers attached to her head, marched to the microphone and announced to the group that she was the "horniest" woman in the room. She then challenged cabinet minister John Manley to come to the stage and dance the macarena with her. Last anyone heard, Manley was hiding under a table, declining the invitation.

When Wayne wasn't performing the comedic routines, she was the subject of them. Double Exposure's Bob Robertson and Linda Cullen set up the following premise—John Diefenbaker returns from the dead on his one hundredth birthday to host a radio phone-in show. And Elsie calls:

> CALLER: Okay, well, Johnny, listen, this is Elsie Wayne calling, and I'm a member of the Tory caucus in Ottawa.
>
> DIEF: Well, that is wonderful. And how much of the Tory caucus do you control?
>
> CALLER: Oh, half the caucus are on my side.
>
> DIEF: Well, madam, that is twice as good as I ever did.

Elsie Wayne's sense of humour shouldn't mask the fact that there are a handful of issues that are almost life and death with her. She's a member of the Main Street Baptist Church in Saint John and a forceful supporter of the pro-life side in the abortion debate. She does not fear going on about "the one hundred and ten thousand little babies who are killed through abortions."

She's also just old-fashioned enough to ignore today's political correctness, and promote "good, Christian values." Her best day in politics came when she went to bat for the Lord's Prayer, and like her original candidacy, that too was an accident.

Wayne's Ottawa office got a call from sponsors of a bill designed to take the reference to God out of the prayer, which opens each parliamentary day.

"We want you to second the motion," the caller said to an astonished Wayne.

"You want me to do what?" she asked.

"Who is this?" the caller wondered.

"It's Elsie Wayne," she said.

"Oh good Lord," the voice said. "We got the wrong number."

"You certainly do," snapped Wayne.

Now that she was on to the plot, she asked one of her staffers what she could do to stop it. Because she was one of only two MPs, she had no authority to demand time during Question Period. Instead, her staff told her to rise on a "point of order" after Question Period was over, and the speaker would have to recognize her. Gilbert Parent did that and more. He let Wayne get up on her soapbox and have her say. Next thing you know, the press gallery descended on Wayne for a "scrum," and suddenly the issue grabbed national prominence. God's place in a nearly 130-year-old ritual was, at least for now, safe.

Still, Wayne was having grave doubts that this life was for her. One day, she approached Parliament and saw a familiar figure, a Jesuit priest, who frequents the Hill. She confided to the priest that she was thinking of packing it in.

"I think I'll just go home," she said. "I don't know how much I can do for my people, being up here just two of us."

The priest set her straight. "You must never go, Elsie," he told her. "God wouldn't be in the prayer without you. No one helped you. You did it by yourself. You must stay, Elsie."

And so she did.

After the good, the bad, and the funny for three and a half years, Wayne went back to the people of Saint John on June 2, 1997, asking for another chance to represent them in Ottawa. The previous time, she was lucky to win. This time, it would be no contest. She'd capture more than 63 per cent of the votes cast and join nineteen other Conservatives in winning a seat to Parliament. The Tories were still the fifth-place party in the House. But at least there was hope.

But for Elsie Wayne, her worst day in politics was just ahead. Less than a year after Jean Charest breathed at least some new life into the national PC Party, he became the focus of a campaign, virtually unprecedented in its intensity. Quebec Liberal leader Daniel Johnson had unexpectedly resigned. The arm-twisting to have the Tory leader quit federal politics and take over the Quebec Liberal Party was so fierce, it's remarkable he didn't suffer a separated shoulder. Somehow, Charest became the sole, potential saviour of federalism in Quebec—the only man who stood a chance of competing effectively with the separatists.

Charest and Elsie Wayne had something in common as it related to those efforts to move Charest to the provincial scene. Neither one wanted him to go. As the pressure intensified, Wayne stepped up her campaign to ensure Charest would stay right where he was. She'd emerge from caucus meetings, wade into a sea of reporters and assure everyone Charest was staying put.

"No, he's not leaving," she'd say.

"How do you know?" they'd ask back.

"Well, I'm going to sit on his knee so he can't go anywhere." And sure enough, when the cameras were admitted into the Tory caucus, there was Elsie, moving towards her leader and plunking herself down on his lap. Charest and the rest of the room broke up.

But on March 28, 1998, Jean Charest could withstand the pressure no more. He called his twenty-member caucus together for one last time and confirmed he was giving up his dream to bring the Conservative Party back to greatness and become prime minister of Canada, so he could return to Quebec and fight the separatists.

Elsie Wayne started to cry. It was the saddest moment she'd ever experienced in politics. She and Charest had a unique bond, given the extraordinary set of circumstances under which they were elected. At his news conference to announce his departure, Charest referred to Wayne as "my trusted companion."

Four years earlier, she was the mayor of Saint John. Now, Elsie Wayne was the interim leader of the Progressive Conservative Party of Canada. As such, it fell to Wayne to speak for her party at the annual press gallery dinner, one of the most enjoyable nights on the Ottawa political calendar. Throughout the night, speaker after speaker ripped into Prime Minister Chrétien, with frequent references to his deteriorating relationship with Paul Martin. As leader of the smallest party on the Hill, Wayne spoke last and didn't disappoint.

"Mr. Prime Minister, you don't have a thing to worry about," she assured him. "When Jean Charest said he was going, I sat on his knee and now I'm going to sit on yours." And she did. It was a front-page picture across the country the following day. But Wayne wasn't done. She returned to the microphone and added, "I forgot to tell you. After I sat on Jean Charest's knee, he was gone in two days."

But Wayne was just as adept at capturing headlines for her social conservative crusading as she was for tickling Ottawa's funny bone.

After Joe Clark's return to the helm of the Tories, she broke rather publicly with her leader on the issue of same-sex benefits, calling it a move in the wrong direction. The bill in question, C-23, would give same-sex couples legal status equal to common-law couples. Wayne was convinced this was the thin edge of the wedge towards equal recognition for gay marriages. There were no niceties in her vocabulary. "For the government of today to give benefits to someone because of their sexual habits—no. Absolutely no way, shape or form." Wayne voted against the measure, Clark voted in favour, although he gave his MPs a free vote on the matter. Not that he had much of a choice.

Similarly, Wayne crossed her leader when the Liberal government introduced the Clarity Bill in December, 1999. Several Tories, including Wayne, were much more hawkish than Clark on the bill, which attempted to set out some rules regarding Quebec separation. Three months later, Wayne voted with the Liberals to pass the bill by a vote of 208 to fifty-five. Clark voted against. Again, the leader mollified his caucus with a free vote.

Interestingly, more than a year after the Clarity Bill debate was over, it was Elsie Wayne and not Joe Clark who was having second thoughts about the vote. Just when she thought she'd heard everything she wanted to hear about the law, PC Senator John Lynch-Staunton gave her something new to think about.

"Elsie," he said, "do you really think a bill should come forth that would allow any part of Canada to separate?"

For perhaps the first time in her political life, Elsie Wayne allowed for the possibility that she might be wrong.

"That one little quote made me start to ponder," she says. "Maybe I'm wrong. Joe is right. Just that one little quote."

As the 2000 election campaign drew nearer, there was considerable scuttlebutt that Elsie Wayne might leave politics. Prime Minister Chrétien claimed she asked for an appointment to the Senate. Wayne denies it. Whatever the case, the voters in Saint John were all too happy to return her to Ottawa. She took more than 50 per cent of the votes and obviously ran well ahead of the PC party, which barely returned to Parliament with official party status.

Incidentally, that flood plain where it all started for Elsie Wayne? She doesn't live there any more. Since she left city hall, the council has permitted a lot more development to happen. Sears, Wal-Mart, and Canadian Tire are there. The Waynes are no longer convinced flooding won't recur. So Elsie and Richard Wayne sold their home and moved to a dryer location in Saint John.

"I'm not going to go flooding in a boat, or rowing a boat again," she says. "I'm not keeping a boat in the backyard."

LIKE MOST PEOPLE WHO ARE ROOKIES in politics, Lyn McLeod had no idea what was about to happen to her life. She'd spoken with the local MP, Iain Angus, who told her the House sits seventeen weeks a year. Those weeks would be chaotic, but the rest of the year needn't be.

That was before David Peterson's office made a phone call. The staffer told McLeod to check into the Windsor Arms Hotel in downtown Toronto and stand by for a phone call from the boss. She may have been naïve about politics, but this was a pretty solid signal that she was about to be appointed to the cabinet.

"Lyn, I've heard good things about you," Peterson said to a woman he'd only ever shaken hands with, but really didn't know. "I'd like you to be my minister for colleges and universities."

"I'd be honoured," McLeod said.

"Just don't make a mistake in the first couple of weeks and you'll be fine," he told her. Peterson was no doubt trying to be helpful, but that line added to the pressure McLeod was already feeling.

Talk about a trial by fire. The new minister learned her first important lesson about media relations. When asked where she wanted to take Ontario's post-secondary education system during her tenure, she responded in the only way someone who'd had the job for five minutes should respond.

"I would have to see where it needed to go before I could say," she told a Burlington newspaper, which happily printed the following headline: "New Minister Has No Goals." Welcome to the major leagues.

It didn't take long for McLeod to realize that she'd badly underestimated the demands of the job. She learned a truism that every politician who represents a remote riding discovers—that even when you're home in the constituency, you're never really home. Local events take up a huge chunk of time. The McLeods resolved to attend as many of them as possible as a couple, otherwise they'd clearly never see each other.

The workload was brutal but thrilling. McLeod would retire to her Toronto apartment and read through cabinet papers until 11:30 every night. Her husband, because of his practice, often didn't get home until after 7 p.m. Once Dara went away to school, sixteen-year-old Kristen was often on her own. She may have been the youngest person in her community to experience the empty-nest syndrome.

Meantime, McLeod herself was lonely. "I was the one that was away from home and I was the one that was having the separation anxiety," she says.

She very much felt like a kid from the backwoods, entering the big leagues. She had no long-time friends in the party, no network of support in Toronto, and didn't know any of her cabinet colleagues. Nor did they know her.

"I was really green," says McLeod, who was dealing with all the typical doubts of a new kid on the first day of school. She felt overwhelmed. Until she tangled with the provincial treasurer, a legend in Ontario political circles, at the end of the government's first cabinet meeting.

"Sometimes there are advantages to coming into things naïve, right?" McLeod smiles.

Prior to the election campaign, the Liberals had promised to build a visitor tourism centre at Old Fort William in McLeod's riding. After the Liberals were re-elected, the tourism minister travelled to Thunder Bay to confirm the centre would be built. But at this first cabinet meeting, Treasurer Robert Nixon announced he was pulling the plug on the grant. It was just too much money.

McLeod wasn't having any of that. It didn't matter that at her inaugural meeting of the cabinet she'd be tangling with someone whose roots in politics went back almost seventy years.

"It was one thing to promise it," McLeod told Nixon. "But you had the minister of tourism in my riding telling people you were about to do it. It's too late to retreat, I'm sorry."

Nixon's response was surprising. He agreed. "You're right," was all he said.

"I might have felt a little overwhelmed by it, but there was a principle," McLeod now recalls. "I was right and Bob knew I was right."

In some respects, it was a great time to be a Liberal cabinet minister. The party was popular and the revenues were pouring in, thanks to a white-hot economy. And McLeod was loving her job.

"You really do feel as though you're at the heart of making decisions and setting policies that make a difference," she says. "That's what it's all about."

On the other hand, the size of the Liberals' majority was so big, and expectations were correspondingly so high, the inevitable screw-ups were magnified. Five years after looking as though they could create a dynasty of their own, the Liberals were out, defeated in a shocking upset by Bob Rae's New Democrats. Cabinet ministers were dropping like flies. Premier Peterson, himself, lost his own seat. Somehow, this rookie minister survived, despite having heard three times on CBC-TV through the evening that she'd lost her own seat. She held on by fewer than fourteen hundred votes.

"The night we were defeated I was devastated," McLeod recalls. "It felt to me like a personal rejection of what we'd been doing. I really believed in what we were doing."

However, amidst the depressing atmosphere at McLeod campaign headquarters that night, there were some already looking ahead. Once Liberals got over licking their wounds, there were some stark realities with which they'd have to deal; most obviously, they needed a new leader. Some people in that room thought Lyn McLeod should be that leader. But Lyn McLeod wasn't one of them. One typical feature of the accidental candidate is that others almost always see the candidate's next move before he or she does. That was certainly the case for Lyn McLeod.

After the election debacle, there was a palpable buzz in the air that the party needed something very different from David Peterson. The outgoing premier was male, tall, urbane, charming, had been in politics for fifteen years, worried too much about playing Captain Canada at Meech Lake rather than tending to his own backyard, and was politically opportunistic in calling an early election.

And who was Lyn McLeod? She was first and foremost a woman. She was short. Really short. Barely five feet tall. She was from way up north. She was genuine (too many people had come to believe Peterson's charm was phony). She'd barely got her feet wet in politics. Her cabinet jobs dealt with the post-secondary education system, natural resources, and energy, so she'd never be accused of obsessing on the national unity question. In essence, she was the antithesis of David Peterson, and so even as the Liberals were in mourning on election night, her name suddenly started shooting to the top of the list of potential successors.

That night, at about one o'clock in the morning, McLeod's youngest daughter, Kristen, burst into her parents' bedroom in tears.

"I don't want you to do it!" she told her mother.

"What?" McLeod answered.

"To become the leader and be away more," Kristen said.

"Who said this to you?" McLeod asked, caught off guard. Apparently her daughter had picked up on the leadership vibe at campaign headquarters, but the politician hadn't. She was still grieving.

"I was heartbroken that David lost and that we had lost," she recalls.

Her staff may have been too, but that didn't stop them from beginning to plan McLeod's assault on the party leadership. They were keen from the get-go. Most Liberals were still in such a state of shock, no candidates were getting out of the gate quickly.

McLeod still wasn't convinced, but at least she agreed to consider it. She wanted, in particular, to hear from some more objective voices. It was one thing for her staff or the folks from Thunder Bay to say go for it. She needed some more independent advice. She talked to some of her former cabinet colleagues, Gerry Phillips, Sean Conway, John Sweeney, and Joan Smith. She went to Deb Matthews, the long-serving party official who'd helped to convince her to run in the first place. She consulted with Hershell Ezrin, Peterson's former chief of staff.

"What would I need to do this?" she asked Ezrin.

"You've got to have a vision of what it is you want to do," he told her.

Lyn McLeod looked deep inside herself. She candidly didn't know if she had that vision, and said so to one of her staffers, Connie Craddock, who was terribly gung-ho that she seek the leadership.

"Connie, there's no way I can do this," she said. "I don't have the vision thing, I don't have a fire in my gut, to say I've got to go out and do this, and this is the stamp I want to put on it."

"Yes you do," Craddock contradicted her. "You just haven't articulated it. Everything you've done for three years in government is what you're about."

As a northerner, one thing McLeod knew that she stood for was getting Queen's Park to loosen up on its authority and let local communities use their know-how to solve their own problems. When she was natural resources minister, McLeod was constantly frustrated with needing seven signatures on a policy document to get anything done.

"And yet I would go out into the field and I'd talk to a regional director about a fish hatchery, and they would have a solution to a problem that would never have hit the tables at Queen's Park," she says. "It would never have filtered through."

McLeod was beginning to see the makings of a campaign theme—a tolerance for creative solutions at the local level. Get the Queen's Park know-it-alls out of the way. She came to realize that who she was—a consensus-building, authentic, northern woman—was part and parcel of her vision for her province.

And so she was convinced. Lyn McLeod would stand for the leadership of the Ontario Liberal Party.

But now came the hard part. Because McLeod was much more genuine than most in politics, she had little affection for the show biz of politics. She was an unusual politician inasmuch as she didn't crave the spotlight. She didn't burn to be leader. But she did have an intelligent, compassionate approach to problem-solving, which was very appealing to many Liberals.

"I had to convince myself that I was prepared to do all of that which I did *not* want, in order to do some things differently in government, which I *did* want," she says.

McLeod was also fortunate that, just as in 1987 when she entered politics, her family members put aside their concerns about what a leadership run would do to them. Even Kristen came around, immersed herself in her mother's cause and was completely caught up in the excitement of the race.

A year and a half after the Liberals' 1990 election debacle, thousands of party members and observers gathered to replace David Peterson at Hamilton's Copps Coliseum, the arena named after the city's beloved former mayor, Victor Kennedy Copps, the father of long-time Liberal politician Sheila Copps. It turned out to be one of the most thrilling leadership conventions in Canadian history. McLeod won on the fifth ballot over former cabinet colleague Murray Elston just before one o'clock in the morning. The difference: nine votes. The first thing that went through her mind? "Oh, my God, how is my life going to change?"

Perhaps surprisingly, the most excited person in the arena that night wasn't Lyn McLeod.

"Is it heady to look back on that night? Sure it is. I don't underplay that. It was phenomenal," she says of her marathon victory.

But the real revelation for the new Liberal leader was something she hadn't prepared herself for—the intense loyalty shown by her supporters to her candidacy, a kind of support only found in public life.

"There's a personal loyalty that is just really unlike anything imaginable," says McLeod, genuinely humbled by the experience. "I still don't understand why I earned that loyalty, but it's a wonderfully gratifying thing."

Once the euphoria of the victory had subsided, McLeod had some fairly stark realities staring her in the face. The truth was, she'd only been in politics for three years. She may have represented something new in politics, articulated something Liberals liked, and had strong potential, but she was still oh so green.

One more thing. With the length of the convention and the closeness of the battle, perhaps momentarily forgotten was the fact that McLeod had made history that night. She became the first woman ever to lead a major political party in Ontario history. But it would be years before McLeod appreciated the significance of that accomplishment. On convention night, her thoughts were elsewhere.

"I didn't see it as being a particularly enormous thing," McLeod says.

What did preoccupy McLeod was the road ahead. Ontario was in the midst of its worst recession since the Great Depression. The mood of the electorate was plain and simply nasty. At the moment, its ire was directed at the Bob Rae government. But the people soon wrote off the NDP as a factor in their future political choices. The next election would be a choice between a moderate, nice woman from Thunder Bay, and a revolutionary, tough-as-nails guy from North Bay. Lyn McLeod's problem—the Ontario of the early 1990s was not in a moderate, nice mood.

The 1995 Ontario election campaign was so different for so many reasons. From the outset, the NDP government was never in the game and they knew it. But if the NDP wasn't the target, who was? The Tories under Mike Harris were almost thirty points behind the Liberals when the election was called for June 8, 1995. They hardly seemed a threat. The Liberals' return to power seemed a foregone conclusion for many, so much so, the media scrutinized McLeod as if she were the incumbent running to retain office. In fact, she was the least experienced leader in the race. It was Harris's second campaign as PC leader. It was Bob Rae's fourth. No matter. Everyone thought the Liberals were returning to power, and they'd have to prove they deserved it.

Of course, the other unique aspect of the campaign was McLeod herself. Never had a woman led her party into battle in Ontario political history, and observers were keenly interested in seeing how that would play with the electorate. McLeod herself never made it a big deal. She didn't want anyone to vote for her simply because she was a woman. She also didn't want anyone to disqualify her because she was a woman.

The main event on the Liberal election calendar was the rolling out of the party platform. It was to take place at the elegant Park Plaza Hotel in downtown Toronto. Party organizers used the latest in computer graphics and high-tech presentation techniques to sell the program. The event couldn't have gone better. The Liberals presented Ontarians with a well-thought-out, moderate plan, giving specific timelines on when a multitude of measures would be introduced and achieved. While most campaigns take some liberties with their financial estimates, this one seemed to be on relatively strong foundations. And most of all, McLeod herself was dynamite. She rolled out the plan with confidence, and was never stumped by any reporters' questions.

(I had a brief chat with McLeod's chief of staff, Bob Richardson, after the event was over. I congratulated him on his leader's flawless performance and told him he could relax, the election was now over. Richardson, showing he knew much more about the electorate than I ever will, shook his head and said, "No, no. It's a long way from over." I thought he was just being polite. Turns out, he was just very prescient.)

As impressive as that event was for McLeod, the party's next decision on how to sell her in television ads was downright incomprehensible. What they had in McLeod was a genuinely sincere, warm, "people person," who could bring differing views together towards a common purpose. So it was with some surprise that the Liberals' first ads showed their leader starkly and sternly lit, sitting by herself in an austere chair, rhyming off elements of the Park Plaza Plan. There were no other people in the commercial. There was not a hint of warmth in McLeod's demeanour. Perhaps the ad wizards felt McLeod needed to project more gravitas, or be seen as a tough customer to deal with the tough times. Whatever the motive, the spots played to Mike Harris's strength and Lyn McLeod's weakness, and did nothing for Liberal fortunes.

The Tories, meanwhile, did what you're supposed to do in politics. They highlighted their guy's strengths and took aim at their opponent's weaknesses. Liberals soon encountered an electorate that was angry. Candidates would go door to door in the fanciest neighbourhoods in the province and hear voters mouthing off about welfare bums, even though the chances of their ever seeing anyone in those neighbourhoods on welfare were infinitesimal.

The Tories knew the temperament of the times and directed their ads accordingly. Two were particularly effective. One spot simply compared and contrasted the Tory and Liberal positions on what became the key "wedge" issues for Mike Harris—things such as welfare reform and employment equity—programs of social justice that the electorate was tired of paying for. The ads weren't much to look at, but they helped move the polls in the Tories' favour.

And then there was the weathervane commercial. The PCs wanted to portray McLeod as indecisive, flip-flopping between different positions on a host of issues, blown in whichever direction the wind was strongest. The most notorious example was same-sex benefits, where McLeod at first appeared to support significantly increasing homosexual rights, only to back off later. Two men dressed as giant beach shoes ("Flip" and "Flop") dogged her every move on the campaign trail. Combine that with the Tory ads showing a weathervane changing directions every few seconds, and considerable damage was done. The PCs ran the ad in the last week of the campaign.

There was actually nothing new about using a weathervane as a metaphor for indecision. American campaign gurus have used it for years. Twenty years earlier, Bill Davis's Big Blue Machine used the same technique to accuse then Liberal leader Robert Nixon of the same indecisiveness.

When Lyn McLeod saw the weathervane ad for the first time, she was disgusted. She was convinced the Tories were playing gender politics, suggesting this *woman*, rather than this leader, was employing the traditional woman's prerogative.

"Not only was it blatantly discriminatory, but it was totally unnecessary and that's what made me furious," McLeod says. "They were winning by then. Why did they need to rub it in?"

On June 8, 1995, Lyn McLeod's Liberals were a thoroughly dispirited lot. For the second consecutive election, the party had blown a huge lead. Even worse, they lost to the Tories, the third-place party in the previous legislative sitting.

"I fought that campaign with everything that I had," McLeod says. "We knew that there was a latent anger out there that could be tapped into, that it could take a huge right-wing swing."

But at some point, McLeod resolved that principle was more important than power. "We sat around the table and I said, 'If that's where Ontario wants to go, then I should not be premier, because I can't go there.' I made deliberate decisions about what I could and could not do in order to win the election."

McLeod's daughter Robin, the most politically active of her four daughters, is a little more blunt in her assessment of that election.

"I'm *still* angry about '95," she says. "I felt the people didn't deserve her. She never got the respect that Harris got."

Robin McLeod fully admits she lost her idealism about elective politics watching her mother go through that campaign. However, "As angry as I was, I still think it's an important thing to do. I am more jaded about politics but I've got a passion for it."

Almost inevitable were all the typical gender questions Lyn McLeod had hoped to avoid by winning. Did she lose because she was a woman? ("Looking like somebody's mother was a greater liability than simply being female," she says. However, one of her own MPPs, Monte Kwinter, suggested he had trouble getting more traditional Italian Canadians to vote Liberal because a woman led the party.)

"I feel real regret that my failure to win the election has reinforced the idea that a woman can't win," she admits.

And perhaps most important, would the party come to believe it had made a mistake in "experimenting" with a female leader and force her out?

"I was not prepared to put this question to the test of a leadership review," she says. "Even if I could have won it, it would have been divisive for the party and hellish for me."

So McLeod took her convention victory, her place in history, and the satisfaction that she'd done everything she could to get the chance to govern, and resigned as Liberal leader. She'd have loved another chance to face off against Harris, a man with whom she "violently disagrees." But she wasn't prepared to put up with four years of internecine warfare within the party to have that shot.

Perhaps the most telling thing about Lyn McLeod's political career is that she's still a politician. While voters across Ontario punished her party in the '95 campaign, her own constituents came out as never before, as if to say, we don't care what's happening elsewhere, we still want you here. After squeaking by in two consecutive campaigns, she won her riding in '95 by more than eighty-five hundred votes, then won re-election for the third time in 1999 with a more than fourteen-thousand-vote margin of victory, garnering 64 per cent of the vote. That's a heavy-duty landslide for an area with a relatively small population base.

McLeod has taken the message to heart. She's become one of the most effective opposition politicians in the Ontario legislature. Her desire to oppose the Harris agenda, particularly in the fields of health and education, is what still motivates her.

If being "the one" who lost to Mike Harris haunts her, McLeod doesn't show it.

"I'm not anguishing over, 'If only we'd done this,' because I think we did what we could do," she says. "But the fact that it wasn't enough was what was dismaying to me."

Meanwhile, Robin McLeod has found a venue for her interest in politics as a policy adviser to federal justice minister Anne McLellan. Would she ever run for office herself? The answer is a most emphatic no. "I couldn't take the crap," she says. "It's too irrational. To have my career dependent on all this.... If I ever run, I will eat my hat."

Sounds pretty definitive from the offspring of quite an accidental candidate.

WHEN I WROTE THIS CHAPTER, I DIDN'T INTEND it to feature only female candidates. But the more I looked at the political landscape in Canada, the more I came to realize that the vast majority of accidental candidates *are* women. A much higher percentage of men seem to plan their entrée into politics. No so for women.

The Griers are another case in point. Almost thirty years ago, Terry Grier worked for the New Democratic Party in Ottawa and after much thought had finally resolved to run for Parliament. But Ottawa was not friendly territory for the NDP. So Terry, Ruth, and their three children moved to the Toronto suburb of Etobicoke, which seemed to offer a better shot at victory. Sure enough, while Terry was running to become the next MP for Etobicoke–Lakeshore, someone in the party approached Ruth to run for municipal council.

"I'd never thought of doing it," says Ruth Grier, who had been involved in community issues but was never capital *P* political. "But I figured having the Grier name on even more lawn signs would help Terry win his seat."

So she ran. Politics loves delicious irony, and the Griers' story provides just that. Terry won that 1972 election, but lost his seat and his career in elective politics two years later. Ruth, on the other hand, served more than a decade on Etobicoke council, then spent another ten years at Queen's Park, five of them as a cabinet minister in Bob Rae's government.

Sometimes, electoral success in politics doesn't come from years of planning. Sometimes, it's just an accident.

THE BACKROOM BOYS

Some people are attracted to political life because they know it's the place where important things get done, and they want to do them. Some need the personal validation that only comes when thousands of people mark an *X* beside their name on a ballot. Others still are every bit as deeply involved in public life, yet they will never give a speech in Parliament, never vote on a bill, and never stand for office. They may not even care what policies their parties pursue, for theirs is an entirely different agenda. They will work for prolonged periods of time, for eighteen hours a day, for three months straight, rarely see their families, engage in some of the most intensive and emotional experiences The Life has to offer, and then disappear from their colleagues' lives for years at a time.

"The backroom boys are the real power brokers," says David Goyette, a former political consultant to more than seventy mostly Liberal politicians. "I wasn't sure about that when I got in, but now I'm totally convinced."

The advantages are huge. Backroom advisers don't have to live under the kind of microscope politicians do. They're not accountable to thousands of voters, just one boss, who tends to depend on them significantly. When they speak, it's assumed they speak for their political master, but it ain't necessarily so. "I carry great power," says Goyette of his former profession. "But I have total deniability, no accountability, no formal responsibility."

I asked one well-known pollster whether he ever yearned to come out of the backrooms and actually be the decision maker. His response: "What's the difference?"

Here are the stories of some backroom boys, and yes, they're still mostly boys, who crave a different slice of The Life.

WHY ISN'T JOHN LASCHINGER A LIBERAL? He was born in Montreal. He got caught up in Trudeaumania and voted Liberal in 1968. His grandfather was a big-time Liberal, having been appointed assistant postmaster-general of Canada by Prime Minister William Lyon Mackenzie King.

The first efforts to bring Laschinger into the Conservative Party ended in failure. His roommate at the University of Western Ontario, John Thompson, wanted to get Darcy McKeough elected leader of the Ontario Tories in 1971, replacing John Robarts.

"What can I do?" Laschinger asked his friend.

"Well, what I'm looking for is someone to be the security for our strategy run," Thompson told him. "Like a bouncer."

"That doesn't seem exciting enough to me," Laschinger said. After all, he was working for IBM in Toronto at the time, making a very nice living. Even though his friend rejected his overtures to work on the leadership convention, Thompson persevered. Later that year, he bumped into Laschinger on Adelaide Street in downtown Toronto and tried another pitch. Laschinger was invited to join the "advance team" the Tories were putting together for the upcoming election campaign. William Davis had won the convention and this would be his first campaign as leader.

Today, John Laschinger is one of this country's most skilled political operators. So his response to Thompson's second entreaty now sounds delightfully naïve.

"What's an advance team?" he asked.

"I'm trying to build a team of people who are successful in their own right, in their own businesses," Thompson told him. "We've got some doctors, lawyers, accountants. We've got everybody. I'm looking to put together an advance team. Would you like to meet Davis?"

Laschinger had never met a premier before, so he said, why not.

"I was struck by how shy he was," Laschinger says of Davis, whom he liked very much. And so this time he signed on. "We became, twelve of us, the Dirty Dozen. That's what we called ourselves. And we were Davis's advance team for the '71 election."

For his first-ever political campaign, John Laschinger was in charge of Toronto. He spent his nights, his weekends putting together Davis's itinerary. And he was now a Tory—although not a Tory of, perhaps, the deepest conviction.

"Had John Thompson called me and asked me to meet the Liberal premier of Ontario in 1971," Laschinger smiles, "I'd probably be a Liberal today."

FOR ALMOST AS LONG AS HE CAN REMEMBER, Michael Marzolini has been interested in people's behaviour. At Don Mills Junior High School in North York, Ontario, he'd set odds on almost anything: who'd win the Academy Awards, sporting events, and, of course, elections. That wouldn't have been a problem, except that Marzolini decided to manifest that interest by becoming a bookie. And business wasn't bad. He was making thirty-five dollars a week from his fellow students' lunch money. His home-room teacher was a man named Dennis Timbrell, who would be not so well remembered for his teaching of English and history, but better remembered in political circles as a long-time Ontario Tory cabinet minister, who would run twice and lose twice, in a bid to lead his party. But at this point in his career, Timbrell discovered Marzolini's business and unsuccessfully tried to have the kid expelled.

"I thought it was entrepreneurial," Marzolini remembers of his endeavour. "Timbrell thought it was parasitical." Marzolini may be kidding when he says he became a Liberal because of "Dennis Timbrell's lack of judgement," but then again he may not be. "I guess that's why I became a Liberal and a pollster at the same time. A love of human behaviour and being able to predict it."

Actually, Marzolini's first wish—at age twelve—was to become prime minister of Canada. "I wanted the top job," he says. "You always want the top job." His interest in public life came not from his parents, who never discussed politics in the house, but rather from a biography of Winston Churchill. "He was ambitious. Well, I was ambitious. It would have been nice to be prime minister," he says.

Marzolini got in on the ground floor of the Liberal campaign in Toronto's Don Valley riding, where the legendary Dalton Camp was running for the Conservatives. There was another element that also helped solidify Marzolini's Liberal values. The campaign of the Grit candidate, Robert Kaplan, featured the very hip Mother Tucker's Yellow Duck rock band at one of the tour's big events. Rock 'n' roll seemed infinitely more cool to Marzolini than the balloon rides Camp's campaign was offering.

Marzolini also discovered something else about politics during that election. His French was as bad as his Italian, and worse, he didn't much like what politicians did.

"I find working crowds tedious," he says. "I'm basically a lazy guy. The idea of knocking on five thousand doors doesn't really excite me all that much. Listening to all those people complain to you about everything."

Maybe so, but those were also Marzolini's first political steps. And those steps would eventually lead to 24 Sussex Drive.

WITH PERHAPS THE LIBERALS' RENOWNED Keith Davey, the "Rainmaker," the only living exception, there may not be a more quintessential backroom boy in this country than Norman Atkins when it comes to political contests. His roots in Canadian politics go back almost half a century. His influence in Tory backrooms is legendary. And yet his entry into politics was completely improbable, particularly since Norman Atkins was born and raised in New Jersey—traditionally not fertile grounds for Canadian political wizards.

True, his parents were Maritimers. His father, George Spicer Atkins, was captain of the Acadia University football team. Then one day in 1915, he played his last game, hopped on a train to Kingston, Ontario, and enlisted in the Forty-sixth Queen's Battery. The fella in line behind him was Bill Cook, who'd go on to play for the New York Rangers and eventually be enshrined in the Hockey Hall of Fame. (Cook was just fifteen years old and lied about his age to serve his country.) George Atkins fought at Vimy and was wounded three times.

When he returned to Nova Scotia in 1918, there were simply no jobs to be found. His mother and stepfather had moved to Brooklyn, New York, to start a new business, and they offered George a job there. He took it, and eventually moved to Montclair, New Jersey, where in 1934 his wife, Geraldine, gave birth to a son, Norman.

The seminal event of Norman Atkins's political life took place when he was nine years old, and it had nothing to do with anything he said, saw, or did. His sister married a man named Dalton Camp. The marriage didn't last, but Camp's influence on his young brother-in-law would endure for a lifetime.

"He was a hero of mine," says Atkins, still obviously in awe of Camp as we talk at Toronto's Albany Club. "He and I connected one way or another." And it didn't hurt that Camp was an Acadia grad, where four generations of Atkins family members, including Norman, have been educated.

Atkins's first exposure to politics came almost fifty years ago. Dalton Camp was responsible for communications for the 1952 PC campaign in New Brunswick. The Liberals had been in power for seventeen years. The Conservatives had come into the election with four seats. Norman Atkins's job was to be his brother-in-law's "gofer," to do any and all odd jobs. He ran advertising copy to radio stations and newspapers in Saint John and Moncton. He drove Camp to campaign events. The Conservatives won. Hugh John Flemming became premier of New Brunswick. And eighteen-year-old Norman Atkins had found something that excited him tremendously.

A year later, Camp was trying to get Robert Stanfield elected premier of Nova Scotia. And Atkins interrupted his studies at Acadia to volunteer. On that campaign, he would meet the manager of the local radio station in Halifax, Finlay MacDonald. Three decades later, Brian Mulroney would appoint both of them to the Senate of Canada. And they'd be roommates to boot. It's impossible to imagine any of it happening without Atkins undertaking the most brilliant political decision of his life—choosing the right brother-in-law. Given his obvious talent at organizing campaigns, would he have found his way to politics anyway?

"That's an excellent question," he laughs. "I have often wondered about that. Dalton has said if he'd been an NDPer, I'd have ended up an NDPer. If he never came along, who knows?"

TO SPEND AN HOUR IN DAVID SMITH'S OFFICE with David Smith is to enjoy one of the greatest walks down the memory lane of Canadian politics there is. Because once you see that office, the inescapable conclusion is that David Smith knows everyone, absolutely everyone, in politics. The walls of his law office at Fraser Milner Casgrain on the thirty-ninth floor of First Canadian Place in Toronto contain enough memorable moments for ten politicians' lives, let alone one.

For every picture, there's a story. There's Smith with U.S. President Lyndon Johnson. And another with Johnson's vice-president, Hubert Humphrey. Smith had arranged for the national youth director of the Democratic Party to come to Ottawa and meet Prime Minister Lester Pearson. The director returned the favour when Mr. Smith went to Washington.

There's Smith in 1967 with Liberal MP John Turner, for whom he was a loyal executive assistant. There's John Diefenbaker, who always insisted he and Smith were cousins. Smith's great-great-uncle was former British prime minister Sir Henry Campbell Bannerman, after whom Smith's father, Campbell Bannerman Smith, was named. Diefenbaker's mother's maiden name was also Bannerman. Dief had genealogists on the case, trying to prove he was related to both the former British prime minister and his great-great-nephew, but could never quite make the link.

"As long as the light shone forth, the greatest sinner could return," Dief used to say to Smith, urging him to switch to the Conservatives.

"Sir Henry was a Liberal," Smith would respond. "You're the guy that needs to return." Incidentally, David Smith has a great laugh, which is a good thing, because if you get to hear all his old war stories, you're going to hear that laugh a lot.

There's a shot of Smith with Lester Pearson, with whom he was actually quite close. Smith was national youth director of the Liberals when Pearson was prime minister. He accepted frequent invitations to 24 Sussex Drive and Harrington Lake, the PM's retreat. Why would Lester Pearson take such an interest in a pudgy kid from Toronto, even if he was youth director of the party? One day, Smith found out. Apparently, both Pearson's father and grandfather were Methodist ministers. Coincidentally, Smith's father and grandfather were also preachers.

"Pearson would put his arm around me and he would say, 'We PKs have to stick together,'" Smith recalls. "We preachers' kids." Pearson reminded Smith they were actually *double* PKs—their fathers and grandfathers were preachers—a doubly rare coincidence.

And there's perhaps the most famous shot of Smith, the one that made all the newspapers in 1982. He's standing in the House of Commons behind Pierre Trudeau, shouting "Bravo!" as the prime minister basks in the applause of securing the repatriation of the Constitution.

"I looked like Lee Harvey Oswald when he got that bullet from Jack Ruby," he laughs. "He goes ooooh, you know?" The photographer caught Smith with his mouth in the shape of a perfect *O*, as in the last syllable of "Bravo."

And there are just so many more. Chinese Premier Zhao Ziyang, Margaret Thatcher, Pope John Paul II, Bill Clinton, Queen Elizabeth, Keith Davey, many with Trudeau, Marc Lalonde, David Collenette, Jean Chrétien, a three-way shot with Lloyd Axworthy (who wrote the speeches) and Jerry Grafstein (who did all the advertising and public relations) for John Turner's 1968 leadership run, and then another one of that same gang of three when Smith and Axworthy were both in Trudeau's cabinet and Grafstein was in the Senate. And Jim Coutts, and Walter Gordon, and Paul Martin, Sr. (he dated his daughter, Paul Martin, Jr.'s sister a few times), and Joe Clark, his friend of thirty-five years (yes, Smith has friends in every party, not just the Grits).

And that's just one section of one wall. But we think by now you get the picture.

ALMOST THIRTY YEARS AFTER WORKING his first political campaign, John Laschinger and I sit down to lunch at a not terribly expensive fish place in downtown Toronto. Ironically, Laschinger's offices are at

Bay and Richmond Streets, a stone's throw from where he accidentally met his former university roommate John Thompson thirty years ago and embarked on a life-long political journey. This once-reluctant Tory has brought with him a file of letters from many of the people who have watched him run campaigns over the years—more than thirty campaigns in all.

What's striking about the motives expressed in the notes is their simplicity. A Conservative lawyer from Windsor thanks Laschinger for the privilege of taking part in a team event. "It was a pleasure to participate in your grand design, but it was even more of a pleasure as a student of the political process to watch it all work," he writes.

Another note from a man who runs a ski resort up in Collingwood, Ontario. "We lost but we won. Thank you for including me in the campaign. It was one of the most exciting and rewarding experiences that I have ever had, and a lot of fun too."

Laschinger is perhaps best known for managing the constantly entertaining, but ultimately unsuccessful, 1983 leadership run by federal cabinet minister John Crosbie of Newfoundland. Crosbie came third, but it's not an exaggeration to say with a few breaks here or there, he might have won it. One of the people who helped out on that campaign was so moved by his freshman political experience, he eventually sought the PC nomination in one of the Saskatoon ridings and contested the 1984 election. He told Laschinger afterwards: "I am truly bitten by the political bug."

"So here's a guy who got involved in Crosbie's leadership, liked what he saw and then jumped into the political process himself," explains Laschinger.

Laschinger doesn't seem to have had difficulty over the years getting high-priced talent to help him on his campaigns.

"Guys just wanted to get involved because it was exciting and fun," he says. "They were lawyers that were bored silly. They'd get to the office and by 9:10 in the morning they'd want to put their head through the wall. Just no excitement."

Jean Pigott worked in Prime Minister Joe Clark's office after having lost her seat in the 1979 election. Laschinger remembers trying to comfort her after the loss, and he received this note: "Thanks for your messages, which arrived at a time when my heart was a bit heavy. I now accept the voters' decision, but in my heart I really long to be a part of it all."

These powerful emotions, fuelled by election campaigns and leadership conventions, are John Laschinger's drug of choice. Ask him about his best day in politics and he'll tell you he's had sixteen of them—the campaigns he's won. He's also lost sixteen, and you can tell each one of those losses broke his heart a little bit, or a lot.

He adores public life, but can't imagine running for office himself. The only position he's ever stood for is president of the Shady Lane Cottagers' Association, and even that job he won by acclamation. Both the candidates and their backroom support staff crave all that public life has to offer. But Laschinger is surprisingly inarticulate on what separates those who will stand for office and those, like him, who wouldn't dream of it.

"I've never asked myself that question," he says. "I don't know what the difference is."

It's clearly not an issue that interests Laschinger. His interest is in being a player and, most of all, in winning. But if "Lasch," as everyone calls him, can't answer the question, he says he's not alone. Most candidates don't know why they're in either.

"It sounds funny to say it," he says. "They're driven, but they don't know why. There are only a few politicians I've worked for who've had a good reason that they could articulate for me as to why they wanted to be premier."

One of them was Mike Harris.

"He wrote me a three-page letter, handwritten, saying he wanted to be the next leader of the party and would I help him. And he laid out all his reasons why. When I got this letter, I decided to do it," he says.

As for the country's top job, Laschinger recalls John Crosbie giving a delightfully simple explanation as to why he wanted to run for PC leader.

"He said, 'The real reason why I ran was that I thought I was the best person for the job.' I mean, just that touch of arrogance," Laschinger chuckles. "But that's what drove him."

Brian Peckford, premier of Newfoundland from 1979 to 1989,

was another, as was the current premier of New Brunswick, Bernard Lord, who impressed Laschinger with his intelligence at the tender age of thirty-three.

"Peckford told me the first time I met him," Laschinger remembers. "He had it laid out in about six sentences." So Laschinger took the job, helped Peckford become premier, disappeared from his life for three years, then came back and did it again.

"My job is to get him elected," he says, "and if I believe enough in someone to work for them, then after I get them elected, they do their job, which is to go and run a government or make public policy. I don't pretend to want to know that part of it."

I'm surprised at Laschinger's apparent indifference to the policies he's helping implement by helping get elected the people who champion those policies. But then, one has to remember why he's in politics.

"It's the thrill of the game, and winning. Vince Lombardi was right," he says of the Green Bay Packers' legendary coach. "Winning isn't everything, it's the only thing. And a chance to make the difference. I have flown out of a province, like a Newfoundland, after winning a provincial election, and you win at nine o'clock in the evening, have a few drinks with some people, get to bed by one, two, three o'clock in the morning, and be at the airport at six and on a plane flying out. And you leave the guy. He got the job and you're on to the next one.

"It's the greatest rush in your life."

John Laschinger remembers being hip-deep in a political hothouse almost non-stop from 1983 to 1984. "The exposure to people and events. You're in the loop. You're in the centre of action. People are calling you." He looks as if he's re-living it as he tells the story. He'd just been through the emotionally exhausting Crosbie campaign and was in the thick of working on Brian Mulroney's first general election bid in 1984 when Laschinger did something quite inexplicable. He quit.

"Somebody came to me and said, 'Look, we're going to give you this bag full of money and we want you to run this insurance company,' and I couldn't turn it down." The outfit was called Bale and Company. It was located in Toronto and owned by the father and brother of former Quebec Premier Jacques Parizeau. As Laschinger tells this story, one can scarcely believe the absurdity of one of the Conservative Party's most diehard strategists sitting on the sidelines of what would become the party's greatest electoral triumph ever.

"I went into this office the first day, and there's a big desk and wood and panelling. The first thing I noticed: the phone didn't ring. Dead silence. And I'm sitting there in this big office."

Did it take a genius to realize this match wasn't made in heaven? Nope.

"Eighteen months later, I was gone," Laschinger laughs. "Got the golden parachute. It was a mutual thing." It also doesn't sound like John Laschinger worried much about the insurance business while he was there. After all, he regularly played hooky from the job to help organize two leadership campaigns for Larry Grossman, the former Ontario treasurer. And just as in the Crosbie campaign, some of Laschinger's most passionate political memories came in a losing cause.

Larry Grossman was a true long shot to replace William Davis. He was a bit too Toronto, a bit too sharp, and a bit too Jewish for a party that liked its leaders less urban, more folksy, and Waspier.

Before the convention took place, I can remember bumping into long-time Tory stalwart Eddie Goodman outside Premier Bill Davis's office at Queen's Park.

"Do you really think Larry has a chance?" I asked him. "Is this party really ready to pick a Jew as leader?"

The response was pure Eddie, an indication of his cheerful optimism about life in Canada.

"Maybe they'll figure, 'We could use a smart Jew for a change.'"

Despite his built-in liabilities, Grossman did have a few things going for him. He was arguably the most able minister in Davis's government, having moved in relatively short order from the second-last seat on the back bench to the number-two job in government, treasurer of Ontario. In Laschinger and pollster Allan Gregg, he had a couple of the most capable backroom boys in the game. Also on the team were advisers such as Leslie Noble and Alistair Campbell, who'd become an integral part of the machine that orchestrated back-to-back majority governments for Mike Harris ten years later.

Grossman didn't win the leadership convention on January 26,

1985, to replace Bill Davis. That honour went to Frank Miller, whose small-c conservatives wrested control of the party away from the more pragmatic red Tories. When Miller lost the government and resigned as leader, Conservatives gathered in January, 1986, once again to pick a successor. This time, Grossman found himself on the last ballot with Michael Marzolini's former English and history teacher, Dennis Timbrell.

Clearly, the prize wasn't as interesting the second time around. The premier's job was not on the line. David Peterson had that. So both former Davis cabinet ministers were running to be leader of Her Majesty's Loyal Opposition, something with which Ontario Tories had little experience.

"That campaign hinged on the mood of the delegates," recalls John Laschinger. "Allan Gregg went out and did some polling and all we were trying to do was figure out the mood of the delegates, the mood of the party. And Timbrell did not do that kind of polling."

Laschinger wanted to know whether Conservative delegates thought the loss of the dynasty was just a bump in the road, or was a major rehauling of the party necessary.

"These delegates were out of their minds," he smiles, "but they said, 'Ah, it's just a bump in the road. Miller's going. We'll get a new leader, we'll get it back and we don't have to change anything.' And these are all insiders. 'I don't want to lose my job as president of the XYZ riding association, etc. etc.'"

So that was the tune Grossman sang. Timbrell, on the other hand, urged the party to undergo a major restructuring, "Until the last week of the campaign," Laschinger says. "Then he realized that he was on the wrong wicket. And we won by seventeen votes."

After Grossman was proclaimed leader, he did one of the most emotional things I've ever seen at a leadership convention. He asked his father to join him on the stage. It was particularly poignant for the new leader because his father had been his one and only political hero. Allan Grossman was the Ontario Conservative Party's first ever Jewish cabinet minister. When he retired from politics, Larry successfully ran for his same downtown Toronto seat.

Sadly, this story ended in tragedy for Larry Grossman, both

politically and personally. The Laschinger strategy of telling delegates what they wanted to hear about their party may have been the right one to get Grossman elected leader. But as far as the rest of Ontario was concerned, the Tories deserved to be taken out with yesterday's trash. The Peterson Liberals cruised to a massive majority victory less than two years after Grossman won the leadership. The damage was so severe, the Tories lost every seat in Toronto, including Grossman's own. On election night, September 10, 1987, he resigned as Tory leader. His marriage had already ended during his tenure as Opposition leader, and he went unhappily into the private sector, where he was the proverbial fish out of water.

Then one day while playing baseball, he experienced double vision and headaches. He went for a CT scan and learned he'd been stricken by a rare and in this case fatal brain cancer. True to Grossman's character, he subjected himself to some of the most aggressive, state-of-the-art brain surgery, but nothing worked. He died at fifty-two.

John Laschinger had a bit of a love-hate relationship with Grossman (one supposes he does with most of his candidates). Laschinger considers the first Grossman campaign one of the highlights of his life, and his fistful of letters from participants on that campaign is ample testimony to the fact that he wasn't alone in that view.

"My experience with the Grossman campaign has truly restored my belief that political campaigns can also be fun," wrote Gina Brannan, who, Laschinger says, on the basis of that experience, sought and won a Tory nomination.

But for some reason, Grossman felt he needed Norman Atkins's expertise on his second leadership run, so he tabbed Atkins to chair that campaign. Laschinger's nose was mightily out of joint over the snub and Grossman's lack of advance warning on the appointment. "It was not done right," he says. "Nobody talked to me about it. Larry missed the odd touch from time to time. Nobody's perfect."

For his part, Atkins says, "I don't think Lasch ever forgave him for that one."

Is that true? "He's dead," says Laschinger of the former leader. 'Nuff said.

Laschinger prefers to remember the happier first run for the roses. He received this letter from Grossman himself:

> I am not an easy candidate. My chances were never good but you almost pulled it off. You were terrific and could not master more. You were calm, controlled and kind. You built the happiest and the best team.

As we prepare to finish our lunch, John Laschinger says his next campaign is a big one. His record stands at fifteen wins and fifteen losses, and he'd love to keep his record above .500. So who gets the honour of trying to keep this backroom boy in the black? He shows me a letter he's just received from an adviser to the president of the Kirghiz Republic. "I'm writing to find out if you'd consider the possibility of assisting us in the organization of the presidential election campaign in the autumn of 2000," the letter says. "[Signed] Kamil Biailinov."

How in heaven's name does the president of Kirghistan know about John Laschinger?

"Mulroney," says Lasch. "The president wanted to run a modern campaign, with polling and buttons and strategies and all that stuff. He's a member of the Academy of Science. He's a very bright man. He's a physician. And he said to Mulroney, 'I need someone to run a campaign for me here. Who'd you suggest?' And Mulroney gave him my name."

In fact, this will be Laschinger's second campaign in Kirghistan. Biailinov first came to Canada in August, 1995. He visited Laschinger at his cottage and went water-skiing for the first time in his life. "He could barely speak English. He spoke good Russian and some English. And we hit it off and so I did that campaign."

Laschinger was in charge of campaign research. He did focus groups in Russian and nightly public opinion tracking. He'd fax the raw data back to Toronto, they'd do the number crunching here, then fax the reports back overseas by 7 a.m. Biailinov did win his re-election bid with 70 per cent of the votes, tipping Laschinger over the .500 mark, alas, only briefly. (Laschinger did Joe Clark's run in Election 2000. The campaign was widely praised for its original ads and focused attack, but the PCs still came fifth. Laschinger's at .500 again.)

Laschinger has been involved with some other international campaigns and in locales not nearly as exotic. He and his former partner, Martin Goldfarb, were recommended, once again by Mulroney, to help former British prime minister John Major's faltering campaign against Tony Blair in 1997.

"We told them their original strategy was wrong, gave them a new strategy, and they followed it for the last two weeks of the campaign. If they'd done it before, they would have won," Laschinger insists.

Sounds hard to believe, given the massive landslide with which Blair's New Labour Party won.

"When we went over, the Conservatives were fifty points down," Laschinger says. "They only lost by twelve points."

Here comes Laschinger's Political Organizer 101 lecture.

"They had to destroy the enemy," he says. "See, in politics, you have competitors and you have the enemy. And also in business. And if you don't know who the enemy is, you're going to lose. And Major didn't know who the enemy was."

"Who was it?"

"Tony Blair," he says.

"How did they not know that?" I ask.

"Because they were running a campaign that said 'New Danger, New Labour.' Had nothing to do with Tony Blair. They were blaming the party. They were going after the party. The enemy was Tony Blair. And at the time, Tony Blair was not trusted by the public. He was too slick, and he changed all his principles. Don't like this set of principles, I got this. After I did the focus groups all over England, I came back to him and I said, 'You got to put a bullet right in Blair's forehead. Don't go after the party.'"

"Why didn't they listen?"

"They thought it was crazy. And they started to attack Blair the last two weeks of the campaign. The numbers went like this—whoosh." Laschinger's hand sinks like a stone.

"You have to know your enemies in this business."

Perhaps it's a testament to Laschinger's professionalism that after more than thirty years in the business, he appears to have very few.

ONCE MICHAEL MARZOLINI REALIZED HE would never be prime minister, he set his sights on what he figured would be the next best thing.

"My ambition when I was fourteen was to be the pollster to the somebody who would become prime minister," he says.

Marzolini clearly thought he had the credentials. By the time he created the company he now runs, he'd already had ten years of polling experience working for others—and that's not including his public opinion surveying experience from junior high school. But he had two things going against him. First, his idol, Martin Goldfarb, was already the Liberal Party's polling guru. Second, even today, just shy of his forty-fourth birthday, Marzolini has the genetic misfortune of looking more like that school kid from Don Mills Junior High, rather than a serious pollster. So, in 1985, even though early in the campaign, he was the only pollster forecasting an end to the forty-two-year Conservative dynasty in Ontario, few Liberals took him seriously.

"They always said, 'Go see Marty. Marty will give you a job. You'll never be the Liberal pollster,'" he says, with a look on his face that suggests he's still angered at the humiliation of it all. "Well, that's rather motivating."

It wasn't the first time Marzolini's efforts to be part of the Liberal family were rebuffed. Back in 1981, Pierre Trudeau appointed downtown Toronto MP Peter Stollery to the Senate, ostensibly in an effort to get his friend and backroom adviser Jim Coutts into the House of Commons. The riding in which Coutts would run, Spadina, was supposed to be one of the safest Liberal seats anywhere in the country. At the time, Marzolini happened to have an encyclopedic knowledge of each riding in Canada and was particularly familiar with Spadina. He knew the numbers in every polling district. He knew every street name. It led him to believe he had something to contribute to Coutts's effort. When he offered his polling numbers to the Coutts campaign, the campaign manager responded, "Get out of here, kid. Coutts and I have run more campaigns than you've had dinners." Then Coutts proceeded to do the impossible. He lost a riding the Liberals had held since 1945. The NDP's Dan Heap won instead.

On election day, May 2, 1985, the Liberals under David Peterson won more votes than the Tories (38 to 37 per cent), although fewer seats because of the vote splits (fifty-two to forty-eight). The NDP held the balance of power with twenty-five seats. Marzolini felt his prognostications had been vindicated, but ironically, he was still no closer to his dream job. Goldfarb was still "the man."

So with twenty bucks in his pocket, he set up Insight Canada Research, his first significant foray into creating his own polling firm. No bank would touch him. He lived on greasy, take-out fish and chips from a place on Parliament Street near Regent Park and began cultivating clients in the private sector. He continued to crunch numbers and bide his time.

It looked as if he'd have to wait forever. Less than two months after the 1985 Ontario election, the Liberals and New Democrats signed an "accord," overthrew the Conservatives, and installed David Peterson in the premier's office—the first Liberal premier of Ontario since Harry Nixon in 1943. (In a nice homage to the past, Harry's son, Robert Nixon, a former Ontario Liberal leader himself, would serve as Peterson's treasurer.)

The Liberals were so popular, Peterson called an election just two years later, won ninety-five out of 130 seats, and looked as if he was well on his way to starting Ontario's next political dynasty.

Perhaps the most important power any first minister in Canada has is the power to decide when to go back to the polls. American presidents, governors, and legislators are all slaves to the two- or four-year cycle of politics. They can manipulate many things but never the calendar. But prime ministers and premiers have the glorious advantage of being able to choose the timing of their efforts to renew their governments' lives.

In the summer of 1990, David Peterson was still riding high in the polls. Surveys showed him leading the second-place New Democrats by thirty points. The Tories, having gone through two bitter leadership contests after William Davis's retirement, were broke, dispirited, and deeply in the wilderness with Mike Harris as leader.

On July 31, 1990, Michael Marzolini and I found ourselves on the south lawn of Queen's Park as David Peterson was inside the legislature calling yet another election. His government was less than three years old, but he had all sorts of good political reasons for heading back to the polls. I was hosting CBC-TV's live coverage of the election call, and Marzolini, having no official role in the Liberal campaign, was my guest analyst. It was a typical Toronto summer day—too hot, too humid—and before long, both Marzolini and I were ditching our jackets and ties in an effort not to melt under the heat of the weather and the television lights.

None of us knew it then, of course, but that election call would prove to be the worst mistake of David Peterson's political life. His opening news conference was sabotaged by an environmental activist, and that set the tone for a brutal campaign, where Peterson was dogged by protestors wherever he went. Ironically, it also opened a door for Marzolini, because his idol had just committed one of politics' most unpardonable crimes—he'd blown a thirty-point lead.

"Marty was the Liberal pollster," Marzolini says sarcastically. "He was giving them great advice to call an election."

In fairness to Goldfarb, virtually everyone was giving David Peterson the same advice. A recession was coming, the opposition was weak and disorganized, the polls were oh so sweet, and the government seemed extremely popular. Strategically, it looked like a no-brainer. But, of course, it didn't work out that way. Bob Rae staged a shocking upset. David Peterson's political career was over. And soon, too, was Martin Goldfarb's.

Michael Marzolini and I are sitting on the veranda outside his offices in Toronto's chi-chi Yorkville district. As is his custom with visitors who are intending to stay awhile, he offers me a very large, very expensive cigar. Naturally, I decline. But I also figure it would be rude to have him smoking his Romeo y Julieta Churchill all by himself, so I say yes to a much smaller, more modest Monte Cristo. It is a gorgeous, warm, sunny day. The scenery is exquisite.

To see Marzolini in these surroundings is to see how far he's come since we did that election broadcast together eleven years ago. Back then, he was the kid with his face pressed to the glass, hoping against hope to be recognized by someone in Liberal circles. Today, he still looks like the same kid, but he's wearing expensively tailored suits, immaculately pressed shirts, cuff links, and a sharp tie. He looks the very model of a modern major pollster. He is chairman of the board and chief executive officer of the largest Canadian-owned polling company in the country, Pollara. He has five hundred employees working in offices in Toronto, Vancouver, Ottawa, Montreal, and Bathurst, New Brunswick. Although I only associate him with political polling, he tells me in fact 97.5 per cent of his company's revenues are from the corporate sector: airlines, rail and oil companies, telecommunications, financial services, Internet. Last year, the company did more than twenty million dollars in business. And despite all this, Marzolini still has enough of a chip on his shoulder to make for a splendid interview.

"I remember Matt Barrett once complained I was the highest-paid consultant to the Bank of Montreal," Marzolini says of the bank's former chairman and CEO. "My hourly fee was $3,250. And he said, 'How can you justify this?'" That alone might seem a funny question from a banker whose multimillion-dollar annual salary was ample fodder for critics. Marzolini could have referred to that but didn't. "I said, 'Simple. I don't like bankers. In 1985, you were the guys who told me I was worthless, not a good risk and I'd go bankrupt in no time at all.' I got the same from the premier's office."

While Marzolini's corporate accounts may pay the bills, I tell him we're really here to talk about the 2.5 per cent of his business that gets his name in the newspapers on a regular basis—the multitude of campaigns from coast to coast for which he's provided public opinion polling services.

I'm about to discover that one of Marzolini's greatest political victories actually didn't happen on behalf of the Liberal Party. Readers may not recall this, given the abrupt way the voters sent the NDP packing. But three months after the Rae government was elected with just 38 per cent of the total vote, its support in opinion polls took a huge leap to 60 per cent. Ontarians were apparently ecstatic with their socialist experiment. (Finance Minister Floyd Laughren and Premier Rae simultaneously arrived at Question Period the day that poll came out. Laughren enthusiastically said, "Did you see those numbers?" Rae responded, "Don't inhale.")

One of the party's key electoral planks was a pledge to bring in a public auto insurance plan, similar to schemes brought in by previous NDP governments in British Columbia and Manitoba. Leading up to election day, the media were filled with stories from irate drivers who were fit to be tied at their skyrocketing auto insurance premiums. In a province with six million drivers, the issue was potentially explosive. The NDP skillfully championed what seemed to be a cheaper solution for Ontario drivers: take over the business, get the seemingly exorbitant profit margins of the insurance companies out of the mix, and get premiums down.

In the midst of all of this, Marzolini was hired by the Insurance Bureau of Canada, which represented all those companies that were about to lose billions in premiums paid by Ontario drivers. Marzolini had his researchers go into the field and gave the insurance people the bad news: 60 per cent of Ontarians wanted public auto insurance. The NDP had its mandate to take over the business. What the New Democrats weren't prepared for was a nine-month-long, full frontal assault mounted by the insurance companies, with Marzolini's help, to change the government's mind.

The plan culminated with a protest by thousands of women at Queen's Park, women who happened to have clerical jobs with private insurance companies. Did the NDP really want to throw these women onto the unemployment rolls, just as Ontario was about to embark on its worst recession since the Great Depression? The longer the issue festered, the more the government came to realize public auto insurance might not be the panacea it originally thought.

"We made the snowballs and handed them to people to throw," Marzolini says. "In a nine-month period, two and a half million Ontarians changed their minds." It was left to a humbled Bob Rae to tell a phalanx of cameras on the first anniversary of the NDP's election triumph that the government would be backing down on its most popular election promise.

"The industry was happy," Marzolini says matter-of-factly. "They shook my hand. They paid our bill. And they said, 'We'll call you when we have another problem.'"

In this case, coincidentally, Marzolini wasn't unhappy with the outcome. He wasn't a big proponent of public auto insurance. But what happens when a pollster tries to move public opinion towards less noble ends? Marzolini admits he did just that shortly after the insurance issue was resolved. He and his associates put together a strategy for a petrochemical company that ruined the water table (Marzolini won't say where) and was trying to get out of cleaning it up.

"We did a beautiful strategy," he says. "We did great work. Saved the company millions of dollars. We were happy to receive a $60,000 cheque for the work we did. My sister and I looked at each other (his sister Angela is vice-chair of the company), we realized what we had done, and gave the whole damn thing to the Friends of the Earth. We did our job well, were professional, but we felt guilty about that. Now the people we work for are people we have a high degree of respect for."

More than a decade ago, Marzolini pulled the same stunt, but this time in the political realm. A friend of his bet him that he couldn't get a very undesirable candidate elected. He took the bet, perhaps a bit too mindful of the character Richard Gere played in the movie *Power*. That character's attitude was: "My job is to get you in. What you do once you're there is your own concern."

"Well, we got somebody elected to political office who was totally unsuitable to that office," Marzolini says with evident contrition. He won't reveal the candidate's identity. "As I get older, I get more concerned about what people will do. I pick and choose a bit more. He shouldn't have been in. It was a disservice to the pubic. In hindsight, I wouldn't have done it."

Meanwhile, despite federal election losses for the Liberals in 1984 and 1988, and again in Ontario in 1990, it was always understood high up in Liberal circles that Martin Goldfarb would continue to be the party's official pollster, as he had been for more than two decades. Marzolini was allowed to nibble at the edges—he'd begun briefing the federal Liberal caucus in 1990—but essentially it was still Goldfarb's gig.

Mind you, it was hard not to notice Marzolini's improving record on the job. The 1988 election may have been another dud for the Liberals as a party, but for the pollster himself, there was a bit of history in the making. Marzolini's methodology, which he'd always insisted was better than anyone else's, was put to work for CTV News during the election campaign. On election night, Marzolini became the only pollster in Canadian history to pick the popular vote numbers bang on: Conservatives 43 per cent, Liberals 32 per cent, New Democrats 20 per cent.

Over time, Marzolini's improving performance (in sharp contrast with Goldfarb's) began to irritate an increasingly sizeable faction in the party. Brian Tobin, Sergio Marchi, Alfonso Gagliano, and David Dingwall all went to bat for Marzolini from the caucus. And one of Jean Chrétien's closest advisers, Eddie Goldenberg, was urging the newly elected Liberal leader to rethink the file.

So one day in 1992, with the next election still many months away, Chrétien announced to the caucus that Martin Goldfarb had done his last election campaign for the Liberals. Michael Marzolini would be the leader's new pollster. Marzolini was there when the announcement was made.

"I had almost achieved it," Marzolini says, referring to his dream to be the prime minister's pollster. "I had never thought I would replace Marty Goldfarb. Clearly Marty didn't either."

And then, Senator Peter Bosa, a Trudeau appointee who died just a couple of years ago, approached Marzolini after the meeting. "He had tears running down his cheeks. He hugged me and said what a great day it is for Italian Canadians. And then it struck me," Marzolini recalls. "This is important not just to me but a lot of other people as well."

After a small party to celebrate his appointment, Marzolini checked into his Ottawa hotel room for the night. He was dead on his feet, having been through an emotionally draining day. And furthermore, Air Canada had lost his luggage.

"I was very tired when I went to bed that night," Marzolini says. "I remember in my hotel room, I picked up the phone and dialled my grandfather's number: 493-2178."

It was only after he finished dialling that Marzolini realized something he'd forgotten in his state of exhaustion. His maternal grandfather, Cyril Harry Kemp, had been dead for ten years. "I wanted to tell him because he would have been very proud," he says.

It was a tender moment, in rather stark contrast to his first dealings with Chrétien. The first time Marzolini met the new Liberal leader he was ushered into Chrétien's office by Eddie Goldenberg.

"Sir," Goldenberg said, "I'd like you to meet Michael Marzolini. Michael is a pollster."

Chrétien waved Marzolini into his office and over to a sofa.

"I'll always remember that sofa," the pollster recalls. "It was yellow vinyl with a rip in the side of it. I sat on that sofa and waited for him to start speaking. But he just looked at me. I waited, and he seemed to get rather frustrated. He nodded at the sofa and said, 'Well, aren't you going to fix it?'

"There is still some confusion in the federal cabinet about the differences between a pollster and an upholsterer," Marzolini jokes.

Despite the rocky start, staffers in Chrétien's office wanted the two to develop a closer relationship. So they set up lengthy meetings, in three-hour blocks, just to get the Opposition leader and his new pollster to shoot the breeze, talk political history, and become better acquainted.

A week before the 1993 federal election, I called Marzolini to get a read on the campaign.

"What's the big news?" I asked.

"I am looking all over the country," he told me, "and I cannot find any Tory seats."

"What are you talking about, Michael? I know they're going to lose, but surely they're going to win a few dozen, aren't they?"

"Steve, I cannot find any Tory seats."

I started rifling off names of who I thought were the safest Conservative MPs in the country. After each name, Marzolini would repeat the same thing. "Gone. Gone. Gone."

A day or so later, Marzolini had the same conversation with Jean Chrétien and revised his estimate slightly. He told the Liberal leader that two Tories would survive—Jean Charest in Quebec, and Ross Reid in Newfoundland.

On October 25, 1993, the wish of a fourteen-year-old boy from Don Mills, Ontario, came true. Michael Marzolini found himself pollster to the prime minister of Canada. The Liberals were returning to government. And, of course, Marzolini was way off in his projections for the Conservatives. They did win two seats and Charest was one of them. But Elsie Wayne, not Ross Reid, was the other. Chrétien delighted in reminding his pollster that when it came to Tory projections, his margin of error appeared to be 50 per cent.

He couldn't have known it at the time, but Marzolini's worst day in politics would follow close on the heels of his best. Less than two years after becoming the PM's pollster, he found himself the numbers man for another Liberal campaign that couldn't miss. Ontarians were fed up with five years of the NDP, and a return to power for the Liberals, now led by Lyn McLeod of Thunder Bay, seemed a sure bet. Just as in 1990, the Grits had a huge lead in the polls over both Bob Rae's New Democrats and Mike Harris's Conservatives.

I met Marzolini for lunch the day Premier Rae called the election for June 8, 1995. Once or twice a year, Marzolini and I get together to shoot the breeze and gossip about politics. We have an understanding about those get-togethers that we both respect. He may tell me some things he knows as long as I treat that information in confidence. I want that information because I feel it helps me do my job better. He will frequently answer my questions with "I can't tell you that," and while that occasionally frustrates me, I simply have to respect the limits he's imposed. To my knowledge, he's never betrayed the confidence of a client.

I mention all this because at our lunch in the summer of 1995, Marzolini gave me some information which I have never revealed. But he says the story can now be told.

The thing I remember most about that lunch was how nervous he looked. This was not the same guy who was in his glory less than two years before. I assured him the pending election was going to be a cakewalk for his side and he had nothing to worry about. It was obvious the NDP wouldn't be re-elected, and Mike Harris's Common Sense Revolution had been the laughingstock of the chattering classes for a year. Ontarians were a moderate people, not right-wing revolutionaries, and besides, no one had gone from third place to forming a government in seventy years. "Relax, Michael," I told him. "You guys are coming back."

And yet, he was worried. What I didn't know—couldn't have

known—was that Marzolini's polling was showing a deep unrest in the population. The public's fatigue with high taxes was immense. They were fed up with what they perceived to be too many welfare recipients ripping off the system. They felt powerless because they believed crime was as out of control as the province's finances.

Marzolini told me that day the Liberals would not win the election. He said the mood of the electorate was such that an angry, populist-style, bumper-sticker campaign run on so-called "wedge issues"—the likes of which the PCs were planning to wage—would prevail. I told him he was nuts.

You'd think after hearing this man consistently and accurately forecast political developments for ten years, I'd listen to him more carefully. And yet two weeks into the campaign, I was still feeling pretty smug. The Liberal lead was holding. The Tories were still mired in the low twenties in public support.

And then the wheel turned.

"When you're an opposition party in Ontario and the party of the same name is in Ottawa, you're fifteen points handicapped," Marzolini says today. "There was a view fostered by people within the Liberal caucus that it was going to be such an easy win. I thought, 'Can I be the only one who sees this?'"

The night of the leaders' debate, Marzolini and his sister Angela gathered at Pollara's offices to watch the event. "Lyn McLeod performed terrifically, and I thought maybe this isn't going to happen. Maybe I've been wrong and she just has to maintain expectations and she can coast. But I remember at eleven o'clock that night—this is probably the worst five minutes of my political life—we were about to open the champagne but I decided to hold off."

Marzolini's focus groups were starting to report back.

"The people I talked to before the debate, we had a twenty-point lead. The people we talked to, who had watched some of the debate, we were tied. And the people we talked to after the debate, who had watched some of the debate, we're running twenty points behind. I thought, that's it. Game over. Damage control mode. And nobody knew."

Marzolini felt as if there'd been a death in the family, but the rest of the family didn't believe there was a corpse. With two weeks to election day, most Liberal MPPs were still confident of victory.

"Every time I talked to someone it was, 'Yeah, we're still dead.' The campaign people weren't ready for this type of bluntness. Eventually, most of them were throwing up their breakfast."

The choice of beverage for both Marzolini and campaign manager Bob Richardson (now a vice-president at Marzolini's chief competitor, Ipsos-Reid) told the tale of the disaster.

"I started drinking cappuccino the first week of the campaign. By the debate, we'd moved to regular coffee, tea a few days later, then herbal tea the last two weeks, because any drug substance in our stomachs would have had us throwing up. It was that bad."

The bottom line? For the second consecutive election, the Liberals blew a twenty-five-point lead, this time to the PCs. Mike Harris became premier of Ontario. And Michael Marzolini saw it coming all along.

Marzolini ought to know politicians as well as anyone in the country. After all, he estimates he's done polling for almost four hundred candidates at all levels of government. What's the attraction to politics in his view?

"There's a lot to be said for the ego factor," he says. "This is an important job. This is a romantic job. From the campaign, when you throw your hat into the ring, going after the nomination, there's a winner and a loser. The tension, as those numbers come up on election night, it's an addictive type of rush that they get. But behind this is a view to accomplishing something good."

Marzolini believes the vast majority of politicians he's represented are decent people. But of course there are exceptions.

"I could tell you about MPs who have never had as good a job as they have now," he says. "In fact, I once had an MP call me up on the cellphone and tell me, 'Seven years, once I get my pension, I'm outta here,' and back to a certain country where you can live like a king on $20,000 a year."

"Who is it?"

"I won't tell you who, but I doubt you'll be hearing much about him in politics."

"Is he still in?"

"Not for long," he smiles.

The reality of politics today is that the backroom boys are just as big, often bigger names, than the politicians for whom they purport to work. Marzolini and I have a bit of an argument about whether he's a public figure. I say he is.

"I'm not a public figure," he protests, although not too strenuously. "I'm a shy, retiring pollster who quietly exerts only a measure of influence by being an interpreter of those who have the greatest influence. Roger Ailes [former image-maker to U.S. President George Bush] said, 'If I'm ever reincarnated I want to come back as a focus group respondent because they are the most powerful people on God's earth.'"

And then Marzolini tells me something in a more serious tone—something that gives me a greater insight into why he does what he does.

"The pollster is the guardian of civilization's most powerful currency, public opinion," he says. "We are the trustees of the public. If decision-makers are sitting around that table trying to work out what to do, then the public should be there at the table with them. The politicians shouldn't govern by public opinion. That would be wrong. But the public view should always be taken into account."

And what's the lure of public life for him?

"It's a hobby. It's a rush to see the numbers changing so fast. A campaign like 1988, to see the Liberals go up from 23 to 43 per cent in a week, then drop to 36 per cent after another week. This is volatile. It's fascinating."

Marzolini is now at his most animated during our conversation. He's a numbers guy, and in politics, unlike business, you can really see the numbers do amazing things.

"In the corporate sector, you can't get that type of rush—trying to predict and maintain and explain and interpret public opinion during an election campaign. Compare that to sitting with an oil and gas company saying, 'Of the people using your brand, 75 per cent are happy, 25 per cent are not, and you can shift 20 per cent over three years by doing the following.' A good campaign can shift 20 per cent of the vote in two weeks."

I have two final questions for the prime minister's pollster. "When's the next federal election going to be and who's going to win it?"

He smiles. He pauses. "Election in March or April, 2001." (It seems even Marzolini was surprised at the November, 2000, call.) Another long pause. He looks at the beautiful sky over Yorkville. "I'm just going over the odds of majority versus minority government and going back to my conversation with you of 1995."

"Yes, Michael."

"But I wouldn't want to give you those odds while this tape recorder is running."

I shut the machine off. "Twenty per cent chance of Mr. Chrétien winning a third majority government."

As any numbers guy can tell you, those ain't great odds. But they were good enough for Jean Chrétien, who defied all the skeptics and won the trifecta.

It wasn't mentioned in any of the post-election coverage. But you can bet the squire of Yorkville breathed a sigh of relief on election night 2000. After all, Michael Marzolini's childhood dream of being the pollster to the prime minister is still alive.

"I CAN REMEMBER IT AS ONE OF THE MOST exciting nights in politics," says Norman Atkins. The year was 1957 and Atkins had graduated from Acadia in time to participate in what would prove to be one of the country's most historic federal elections. Dalton Camp was responsible for national communications for the PC campaign. He came up with a seemingly simple, yet effective campaign slogan: "It's Time for a Diefenbaker Government." When Prime Minister Louis St. Laurent dropped the writ, that hardly seemed likely. St. Laurent had already won successive majority governments, and there was no reason to suspect things would be different the third time. (The Liberals were so confident, their election slogan was "You Never Had a Government This Good.") But Atkins watched Diefenbaker work his magic in a way neither he nor his brother-in-law had ever seen in a political leader before.

"One night at King's County High School in Kentville, Nova Scotia, the crowd was so large they had to put an amplifying system in the parking lot to handle the spillover," Atkins marvels.

Before the campaign was over, much of the electorate agreed with Dalton Camp. It *was* time for a Diefenbaker government. On June 10, 1957, the Chief won 113 seats, good enough for a minority and the first Conservative government in twenty-seven years.

It was at this point in his life that Norman Atkins made another crucial decision that would forever affect his life in politics, and again, it was rather unorthodox. He was considering whether to enroll in the law school at Dalhousie University—a more traditional entrée into politics—when Uncle Sam came calling. Still an American citizen, Atkins was drafted by the U.S. military, which wanted its two years of service out of him. Interestingly enough, the thought of doing two years in the military disturbed him less than putting in the time required to get the law degree. But what to do?

Atkins met with Dalton Camp and Finlay MacDonald in the home of Len Kitts, then the mayor of Halifax. "I can remember the night," says Atkins. "It turned out to be a very liquid evening," which continued at the famed Lord Nelson Hotel.

Camp and Atkins pulled an all-nighter, discussing Atkins's options, then the pair went to Dalhousie the next day to register.

"Are you happy you're going here?" Camp asked him.

"I'm not a hundred per cent sure I want to take law," Atkins responded.

"If you feel that way, consider this," Camp told him. "I don't know what I'll be doing in two years, but whatever it is, you can be part of it."

Atkins made up his mind right then and there that he wouldn't go to Dal. He put in his two years at Fort Benning, Georgia, and in Schweinfurt, West Germany, then returned in September, 1959, to join Dalton K. Camp and Associates, one of the most influential advertising and political communications firms in Canadian history. His days of being the go-fer for his brother-in-law were over. He was about to get the best seat on the backroom roller-coaster of public life.

Norman Atkins got out of the service in August, 1959, and immediately began working for Dalton Camp. He was a production manager in the advertising business and happily admitted he knew nothing about it.

He did bring some organizational skills learned in the military and was clearly someone Camp thought he could trust, which goes a long way in a business full of cutthroats. (Is this a reference to advertising or politics here?—probably both.)

He did the Nova Scotia and New Brunswick election campaigns of 1960, and three consecutive successful campaigns for Manitoba Premier Duff Roblin, in 1962, 1963, and 1967. Also in 1960, Atkins would meet a man with whom he would have a long-standing and complicated relationship. Brian Mulroney was a student at St. Francis Xavier University and would come to visit Camp, Atkins, and the gang at the Lord Nelson Hotel in Halifax. Atkins remembers Mulroney as a guy who was fascinated by politics and impressed by people who were important in the game. "They were the people he wanted to be connected with," he says. "For me, I was amused by that. I'm not sure I was impressed, but I was amused. No question he was bright. And very sure of himself. He showed maturity and special character and had ambitions to go places. He had a big ego and he wasn't afraid to display it."

In 1962, Camp Associates did the communications strategy for the federal Conservative campaign, which held on to power for Diefenbaker, but they also did the 1963 campaign which was a loser for Dief, and saw the Liberals return to power under Lester Pearson. When Dalton Camp ran for the national presidency of the Tories in 1964, Norman Atkins was his campaign manager. That same year, the agency gave a summer job to the president of the Young Progressive Conservative Association, who impressed everyone with his intelligence and determination. His name was Joe Clark. His assignment was to work on the Fredericton Conference held that September at the University of New Brunswick. Years later, when Bill Davis would hold behind-closed-doors meetings with his closest advisers, Atkins would remember how much of an impression Clark left that summer.

"I was the one at the Park Plaza on the ninth floor saying, 'Watch out for Joe Clark. He could be everyone's second choice.'" And, of course, in 1976 at the PC leadership convention, he won by being just that.

Every year featured another memorable campaign for Atkins. He managed his brother-in-law's bid to become an MP in 1965 in Toronto's Eglinton riding. But Camp was defeated by Mitchell Sharp. The year 1965 was memorable for another reason. Atkins gave up his American citizenship and became a Canadian. ("Not dual citizenship," he points out.)

He was also at the centre of the successful efforts to reassess John Diefenbaker's leadership in 1966. He was the "on-site" chair for Robert Stanfield's successful bid to dump Dief in 1967, and ran Camp's disastrous second bid for a parliamentary seat in Toronto's Don Valley riding in 1968. "That was the Trudeaumania campaign," Atkins recalls. "We got thrashed."

And the worst was still to come. In 1970, Atkins was campaign consultant for George Key's election run on Prince Edward Island. "When the results came in, almost no one would talk to me. I thought my days in politics were over." The Tories won four out of thirty-two seats. However, "I learned more in that election, because one year later I had one of my greatest successes."

Atkins is right. His next campaign would fix his name in the firmament of Canadian political organizers. And ironically, he would have to lose one more before sipping champagne.

When John Robarts announced in late 1970 he was stepping down as premier of Ontario, Atkins was part of a network of close political friends who called themselves the Eglinton Mafia. These were the young Tory turks who'd fought elections, leadership conventions, and tried to dump Dief through the 1960s. Atkins had only met Ontario's then education minister Bill Davis once before.

"We offered to help Billy Davis," says Atkins of the 1971 leadership convention to replace Robarts. "The Davis crowd didn't think they needed our help." Like an army with no Caesar, the Eglinton Mafia found themselves willing and able to do battle, but with no candidate to fight for. Eventually, they convinced Allan Lawrence, a red Tory from St. George riding in downtown Toronto, to run. Lawrence was hardly a campaign team's dream. He was a reluctant candidate up against Davis who was Robarts's not-so-secret choice and the clear favourite. Lawrence also had an odd manner when giving speeches, and at one point almost pulled out of the race altogether. But he did have one thing going for him—the best the Eglinton Mafia had to offer, which was a lot.

"We ran an incredible campaign," says Atkins, not boastfully and with a big smile. "The skill, music, graphics, it all came together and it was exciting." It never disturbed Atkins that his team was clearly backing an inferior horse. "I liked Allan Lawrence and he knew his skills or lack thereof. But in the final days of a campaign you're so committed to success, you don't worry about whether he'd be the best guy for the job."

What should have been a much easier victory for Brampton Billy Davis turned into a four-ballot marathon, which Davis won by only forty-four votes. True, it was a loss for Atkins's side, but the impressiveness of the effort would lead to better things in his future. The Lawrence campaign's slogan was "Winning is just the beginning." In fact, with apologies to Humphrey Bogart and Claude Rains, and the rest of the folks in *Casablanca*, losing that convention was actually the beginning of a beautiful friendship.

After Davis's victory, one of his closest friends and former University of Toronto football buddies, Roy McMurtry, tried to play peacemaker. McMurtry had stayed in close touch with Atkins throughout the leadership fight in hopes of avoiding a bitter split in the party that could affect its hold on power. He got the Davis and Lawrence teams together for a meeting at the National Club in Toronto, and it quickly became apparent that the wounds of the convention would be easily healed.

"I met Billy Davis and you couldn't help but like the man," Atkins says of the evening. He put in a pitch for his candidate, Allan Lawrence, to be deputy premier. "They got a little excited about that, so we had to settle for attorney general."

Meanwhile, as the evening was breaking up, one of Davis's top campaign officials, John Latimer, suggested he take both Davis, Atkins, and others to the Sutton Place Hotel to get further acquainted. "Davis said, 'We may as well go there 'cause there won't be many more nights when I can just go out for a fun evening," Atkins remembers.

With Peter Appleyard providing musical accompaniment on the xylophone, Davis and Atkins hit it off.

"We connected immediately," Atkins says. "First thing I said was, 'Premier, I'm a Stanfield man and I was against the War Measures Act.' He said, 'So was I.' And he made it clear to me that he was a Stanfield person too. We shared hobbies about boating. I told him I was looking for a boat. He had lots of advice. He realized I'd played football. We had so many things in common. That night we really connected.

"The battle was over. But the war was still to come."

By this point, Atkins was cruising in on almost twenty years of working for Tory causes. He'd experienced some wonderful highs such as the Stanfield convention, but also many lows. And he still hadn't truly made a mark, independent of his more famous brother-in-law, not that that was a significant motivating factor for him. So he got together with a friend from British Columbia named Malcolm Wickson, and together, they began to create the template for the newer, more modern campaign of the 1970s. The 1971 Ontario election would be the guinea pig for that plan.

Before long, the new premier sent an emissary to Atkins's office to feel him out on any possible participation in the upcoming election campaign.

"Norm, what would it take to get you to be involved in the Davis organization?" Hugh Macaulay asked. "If we get elected, there could be advertising business."

Atkins seemed a bit miffed at what he thought was too heavy-handed an approach. "Hughey, it doesn't take anything to get me on board," he said. "We're all on the same side. If I can be helpful, I'll be helpful."

Macaulay asked Atkins to come to the premier's office and outline his strategic vision for winning the next election. Atkins unveiled a blueprint that was truly revolutionary by Canadian political advertising standards.

"It was a watershed campaign," he recalls. "We used new concepts never tried in Canada before." Republican pollster Robert Teeter came up from the United States to do research briefings. Polling was never more sophisticated. And Atkins's advertising campaign focused on the leader in an unprecedented fashion. Davis at his cottage. Davis at home. Davis with his family.

"He was a wonderful candidate," Atkins says of the premier. "If he trusted you, he accepted your judgement. It all worked. The whole thing was a remarkable success."

On October 21, 1971, Bill Davis continued the Tory dynasty. Newspaperman Claire Hoy christened Norman Atkins and his team of insiders "The Big Blue Machine." That machine would go on to enjoy future election victories, but according to Atkins, none as sweet as the success of '71.

"Because it was my design," he says with evident pride, thirty years later. "My imprints were all over it."

But politics is a funny game, and over the next few years, Atkins tasted the sweet fruits of almost defeating Pierre Trudeau in 1972, to suffering his worst day in politics in 1974.

"There wasn't a day I went to work where I didn't have a pain in my gut," he says of that '74 campaign. Robert Stanfield wanted to prescribe some tough medicine for the Canadian economy by imposing wage and price controls. Trudeau ridiculed the idea, then after winning the election, brought controls in. However, the issue split the PCs when Stanfield needed to show a unified front. It was heartbreaking for Atkins. "Only two years previous, we'd come from 'The Land Is Strong' to almost upsetting Trudeau," he said, referring to the Liberals' campaign slogan.

But better days were ahead. In fact, Atkins was one of the architects of Brian Mulroney's 211-seat massive majority win in 1984. And how was that night for Atkins? "It was a really exciting night but no more than '71, or the Stanfield leadership in '67. If you've been successful in politics there are too many great nights."

And then Atkins says something that can't possibly be true, but he swears it is. He says he's never taken a fee to run any campaign.

"I wouldn't do a job for the pay because I needed to be able to say 'screw you' if I disagreed with the candidate. I never wanted to be obligated."

And there were occasions when he had to stare down candidates. Perhaps the most infamous example came during the course of the 1984 campaign, when Brian Mulroney thought he was speaking off-the-record to a group of reporters on his campaign bus. Mulroney assumed he was just telling jokes "with the boys" when he referred to a patronage job taken by his old friend, former Liberal MP Bryce Mackasey. "There's no whore like an old whore," Mulroney said of Mackasey. "If I was Bryce, I'd be right in there too with my nose in the trough."

News of the off-colour remark got out, and Mulroney's campaign team had a stormy debate on how to handle the issue.

"One of my most interesting moments was trying to get Mulroney to apologize for the 'old whore' line," Atkins says. It was during a weekend break in Ottawa. "[Mulroney's press secretary] Billy Fox advised the leader to tough it out." Atkins disagreed and described his ensuing phone call with Mulroney as "not a friendly conversation. He knew I was upset. He'd written a wishy-washy, mealy-mouthed apology." Atkins says he finally prevailed on Mulroney to say something much more contrite.

"Brian Mulroney is almost a split personality," he says. "He's very engaging, charming, and has a sincere side. But his public person is something different. He found it very difficult to admit he was wrong on anything, even when he was defending the indefensible."

Finlay MacDonald, Dalton Camp, and Lowell Murray rewrote the statement, and for Mulroney's sake, it's a good thing they did. By coming totally clean on the remark, it allowed Mulroney to go for the jugular against a hapless John Turner in the leader's debate, when Turner inexplicably raised the patronage issue. It was the defining moment of the campaign. From that moment on, the election was over. And Norman Atkins had his front-row seat for the biggest landslide in Canadian electoral history.

After doing Brian Mulroney's successful re-election campaign of 1988, Norman Atkins decided he was campaigned out. He was now an honourable senator from Ontario, having been appointed to the upper chamber by Mulroney strictly for the purposes of running that '88 campaign. But to his surprise and delight, he was now enjoying participating in public life from the Senate chambers. He loved the debates and he dove into the challenge of being elected chairman of the Conservative caucus in 1993 when there were just two MPs, plus the senators.

After helping secure Mulroney's second term, he wrote the prime minister a letter telling him he was finished. The letter, according to Atkins, was not well received. The two haven't spoken in a couple of years, but Atkins insists he has nothing against Mulroney and would happily talk to him tomorrow.

"We weren't close friends but I had the skills he needed. There were times he would have less than the highest regard for me. But he respected my advice whether he liked it or not.

"You can't go through this number of campaigns without paying a price," he says. "I'm a diabetic. I just had a prostate operation [heart-bypass surgery was just around the corner]. I'm burned out. I just don't think Brian Mulroney wanted anyone to withdraw from his cause. And I'm not one of his cronies. But I have enough friends. I don't need the accolades."

He infuriated his long-time friend and former Big Blue Machine colleague John Tory by taking a pass on the 1993 election campaign.

"I'm not in the loop any more and I don't want to be," he says.

He's still hopeful about the Progressive Conservative Party's chances, despite another fifth-place finish in Election 2000.

"We'll get through this," he says. "I don't know how. It may take a change of leadership. I compare it to New Brunswick. Twelve years ago, we were dead. Now we're back. The public are fickle. God knows what it takes to get their support."

And how's this for a surprise? Atkins hasn't been to a Conservative Party function at Queen's Park in more than fifteen years. "I don't feel any close association or feeling to it," he says. "It came and went, and while it was there it was wonderful."

As he looks back on his almost half-century in politics, he seems most grateful that his association with his brother-in-law has given him a chance to know Canada as well as anyone. "Many people go to Harvard and take the Canadian Studies program. I hung around with Dalton Camp and got the same education."

Two years ago, Atkins was on the receiving end of a surprise sixty-fifth birthday party at the Albany Club. The highlight of the evening was the announcement that he'd receive an honorary degree from his beloved alma mater—the last honorary degree Acadia University would grant in the twentieth century.

"If my father could have seen this, he'd be smiling down from heaven," Atkins says. "He adored Acadia."

Finally, referring to those Big Blue Machine years, Atkins says, "People will never have the fun we had. We were all together. We trusted one another. We respected the leader and he respected us. I compare it to the Green Bay Packers. Billy Davis was Vince Lombardi. We were the players. And what a wonderful time it was."

MANY HOUSEHOLDS IN THE TORONTO of the 1940s subscribed to the rule that there were two things you didn't talk about at the dinner table: religion and politics. At David Smith's home—the home of the double PK—they hardly talked about anything else. Smith also had a favourite uncle who lived in the United States, whom he visited regularly as a little kid. He remembers talking to Uncle Wilbur Argue about the thrilling Truman versus Dewey presidential upset in 1948. He recalls driving to California in 1952 to visit relatives and listening to almost every speech from the Republican convention on the radio. That was Eisenhower versus Taft. And he was back in California four years later, watching the Democratic convention, when Adlai Stevenson "threw it open" for delegates to choose the vice-presidential candidate: John Kennedy, Estes Kefauver, or Albert Gore, Sr.

The convention dramas added to Smith's already piqued interest in politics. By the time Smith was ready to go for post-secondary education, Carleton University in the nation's capital seemed such a logical choice. He became president of the Liberal club there and started helping out on campaigns and making contacts. His first campaign was 1963, a good one for Liberals. The country's love affair with John Diefenbaker was over. The Liberals had held Dief to a minority government the year before, then elected Lester Pearson prime minister in '63. Also in that election, Smith would meet a raw, new MP from Shawinigan named Jean Chrétien. Around the same time, Smith became friends with John Turner. The networking and the friendships never stopped.

One of the wackier moments in Smith's early political life came in 1964, a time when Parliament was coming apart because of the debate over a new flag for Canada. Smith had finished his political science degree at Carleton University and was now assistant national director of the party and working the Hill the night of the flag debate. He watched MPs go through gin and rye as if they were in a speakeasy. The debate raged on until two or three in the morning, giving members ample time to get plenty inebriated.

"We set a record that night," Smith says. "When they took the vote, I remember a couple of our guys literally had to be propped up." One Conservative MP had enough of his wits to vote no, then fall right over his front-row desk, face first, in front of the Speaker of the House. "Like a penitent monk in front of an abbot," Smith howls.

Of course, the highlight of the debate was Diefenbaker's strident opposition to losing the Red Ensign. "Dief was wild," Smith says. "He was really worked up about this." At one point in the debate, Dief had reason to get even more worked up. One of his members was so drunk, he accidentally voted with the Liberals in favour of a new flag. The honourable members exploded with laughter, causing the member and his leader considerable embarrassment.

"They say Dief would not speak to him for six months," Smith laughs.

It was no laughing matter for Diefenbaker when Parliament ran the new flag up the flagpole for the first time. Smith was there, noting Dief refused even to look at the new maple leaf. John Turner, who loved parliamentary tradition, thought Dief had crossed the line by showing such disrespect. Pearson, himself, told Smith after adjourning the house, he'd never been so glad to get out of Ottawa. And get out he did, as did Turner. The next day, Turner flew to Tobago for a holiday, far away from the travails of Parliament.

"Turner goes into his hotel," Smith begins, "changes his clothes, gets on the bathing suit, walks down the beach. The first person he walked into was John Diefenbaker. He said he just couldn't believe it."

Smith's first foray into elective politics for himself came after a disappointing loss in the 1972 federal election campaign. Smith was managing the campaign of Toronto MP Ian Wahn, who went down to defeat along with more than forty other Liberal MPs, unable to survive Pierre Trudeau's sudden unpopularity. The election took place on October 30, and somehow, Smith soon realized municipal elections were just around the corner. He was dispirited over losing Ian Wahn's seat and wanted to prove he could run a winning campaign. So he put something together lickety-split and managed to win a seat on Toronto City Council, defeating future Ontario Conservative leader Larry Grossman.

Perhaps the highlight of Smith's six-year tenure in local politics was when the preacher Billy Graham came to town. Graham would be speaking to a full house at Maple Leaf Gardens, and the city wanted just the right person to welcome him. Mayor David Crombie decided David Smith should be that person. After all, he was a PK.

"And I thought, well, this'll be interesting to see if I'm nervous," Smith recalls. "But I wasn't."

In fact, Smith discovered he loved public speaking and had quite a facility for it. "It's almost like an ear for music," he says. "You've gotta be born with it. If you're not born with an ear for music, you can go to one thousand symphony concerts, and you still won't have one."

After Crombie left the mayor's office to run for the PCs federally, Smith decided to run for mayor. His competition would be John Sewell, the iconoclastic, left-wing populist, who wore leather jackets and blue jeans to council meetings and was so fiercely independent, the NDP kicked him out of their municipal caucus. Smith might have had a shot at the job, had another centre-right candidate, Tony O'Donohue, not entered the race as well.

"He came in at the last minute and buggered it all up," Smith says. "I always worked very closely with Crombie. But because I hadn't been a shit disturber, I didn't have as high profile as the other guys." Sewell won a close three-way fight, in which Smith actually placed third.

Fortunately, Smith always had his law firm to go back to. He loved politics, but he didn't need it to pay the bills or maintain his self-esteem. "I've seen too many people that, for a moment, politics became like oxygen," he says. "They're almost like crack cocaine addicts. They just couldn't live without it. And I never wanted to be like that."

Nevertheless, Smith didn't have much time to sit around and stew about losing the mayor's race. A little over a year later, Joe Clark's minority government lost a vote of confidence in the house. Canadians were heading back to the polls, and Liberal insiders wanted David Smith to be their candidate in Don Valley East in the 1980 election. He was, and he won. Along with PK, Smith could now add two new letters beside his name—MP.

Even though he'd already been in and out of Ottawa for almost two decades and had known Pierre Trudeau since 1965, Smith didn't know the prime minister all that well. Very few did. Smith also represented a real swing riding in Toronto, and suspected he'd be in Ottawa for a good time, not a long time. Naturally, he held out hopes for a cabinet job, so he began to watch Trudeau carefully in caucus meetings. He wanted to know what kind of input the prime minister liked and, equally important, what turned him off. Bit by bit, he figured it out.

"One of the first things I learned was, don't get up on your feet too often," Smith says. "When you have something to say—crisp, precise, and to the point, and then sit down. You do that a few times, you'll get his attention. And he'd listen."

One day, the Liberal caucus was debating how much pressure to put on Premier William Davis to make Ontario officially bilingual. Trudeau listened to all the arguments, then pulled this gem of a response out of his repertoire.

"I'm reminded," Trudeau started, "about what Immanuel Kant said about humanity, referring to the *Critique of Pure Reason*." The prime minister then went on to quote, by memory, a couple of paragraphs of the treatise, published in 1781. "On this issue, I've heard you, but I really agree with Kant." And then Trudeau sat down.

Smith was thinking, you crafty devil. Most of these MPs had no idea who Immanuel Kant was, but you could be darned sure nobody was about to admit that in front of Pierre Trudeau. So the MPs started slowly shuffling out of the meeting. Except Smith.

"Prime Minister," he said, "did you know that Immanuel Kant, who lived in Koenigsberg in East Prussia, never travelled more than thirty-five miles from Koenigsberg?"

"How do you know that?" Trudeau asked him.

"Check it out," Smith said. "I'm right."

Six weeks later, Smith found himself at one of Trudeau's "wonderful Wednesday parties," talking to some guy who was very full of himself.

"Where do you work?" Smith asked him.

"PMO," was the curt reply, said with the kind of gravitas reserved for FBI or CIA.

"What do you do there?" Smith asked again.

"I do a variety of things," the stuffed shirt answered. "Just to give you an example of what an eclectic range of activities I'm engaged in, about a month ago, I was asked to go to the library and see if Immanuel Kant had ever travelled more than thirty-five miles from Koenigsberg in East Prussia."

How often does a moment like this present itself in life? Smith went in for the kill.

"I'm the only person in Canada that really knows, other than Mr. Trudeau, why you were asked to do that," he said. "But I'm not gonna tell you." And he walked away.

On another occasion, Trudeau's communications coordinator, Joyce Fairbairn, needed to see Smith. She was in a bit of a panic.

"How many chapters are there in Ecclesiastes?" she asked the PK.

"What are you getting at?" Smith asked back.

"The PM is giving a speech and he wants to use a verse from the Bible," she says. "We can't find it."

"What's it on?"

"Peace, swords, and the ploughshares," she says. "He doesn't want the Isaiah one, he wants the Ecclesiastes one, and we can't find it."

As a PK, Smith could solve the mystery. He told Fairbairn she was looking at the wrong Bible, the King James version, instead of the Catholic one, which has a few extra chapters the Protestants don't really accept.

"You go back to the library, get the Catholic version, and I think you'll find it, maybe around the forty-fourth or forty-fifth chapters," he told her.

"Oh, thank God, thank God!" Fairbairn rejoiced. "We've had three meetings; he told us we were incompetent."

"I'm kinda curious," Smith said. "Why did you come to see me?"

"After the last meeting on this speech," Fairbairn confessed, "he finally threw up his hands and said, 'For God's sake, go and ask David Smith. That little guy'll know."

Smith was clearly building up some credibility with Trudeau and opted to draw on that credibility on the issue of putting God in the Constitution. Initially, there had been a reference to God in the preamble to the new Constitution. But when the provinces raised a fuss about some other aspects of the preamble, Trudeau opted to excise the entire offending passage. The reference to God went with it.

Smith thought this a mistake and told Trudeau so. Trudeau didn't think it was that big a deal, but told Smith, if he thought so, he could do some research and come back with some compelling arguments. So he did. Smith checked the enrollments at every accredited divinity school in the country, then showed Trudeau the facts, denomination by denomination. Then he unrolled a map of Canada for the prime minister and showed him how concentrated those schools were in Western Canada.

"You talk about western alienation," Smith said to Trudeau. "It is little things, little missteps like this that aren't intended. You will just provide ammunition to people who want to portray the Liberals as alien to all of their core family values and religious traditions. It isn't worth it."

Trudeau agreed. Smith promised he could come up with one sentence that could solve the problem. And he did. Trudeau, who rarely handed out compliments to his members, offered one to Smith.

"He told me I was the man that persuaded him to put it in," he says.

While Smith felt he'd figured out the best way to get Trudeau's attention on an issue, he wasn't beyond good old-fashioned "talk at 'em till they drop" politics. Such was Smith's strategy on getting recognition for the disabled in the Constitution. In 1980, Smith had chaired a special parliamentary committee on the disabled and produced a much-discussed report, which, unlike most committee reports, didn't sit gathering dust on some shelf. In the process, Smith established his credentials as a powerful champion of rights for the disabled. When the Liberal caucus debated whom the charter of rights should specifically protect against discrimination, race and religion made the list, but the disabled didn't.

That got Smith into action. Disobeying his own homemade directive about talking too much in caucus, he got up four straight weeks to lecture and hector his colleagues on the matter. Liberal MPs started to groan every time he spoke. Smith was clearly losing his appeal.

One day, Allan MacEachen, as deputy prime minister and finance minister one of the heavy-hitters in caucus, approached Smith.

"David, don't get discouraged on that point you're making," he told him. "Keep it up, because you're right." It was a much-needed shot in the arm. Smith went back to caucus to make his pitch yet again, but this time, the result was different.

"The last time I stood up, Mr. Trudeau said, 'David, okay. We don't want to have to listen to that speech again, we're putting it in.'" Smith laughs.

And that's why section fifteen of the Charter of Rights and Freedoms prohibits discrimination "based on race, national or ethnic origin, colour, religion, sex, age, or *mental or physical disability.*"

It's also why the first line of the charter says: "Whereas Canada is founded upon principles that recognize the supremacy of God and the rule of law..."

"I got it in. I got both those things in," he says proudly. This time, he wasn't laughing.

David Smith enjoyed his share of victories, but life wasn't always rosy on the Hill. For example, somehow he got tabbed with part of the responsibility for selling the National Energy Program in Western Canada. He got sent to Calgary, Edmonton, and Saskatoon to do radio phone-in shows and served as the government's punching bag on a program the West despised. What made things worse was that Smith agreed with the callers. He was never convinced the NEP was a good idea. On the contrary, he thought it fanned the flames of western alienation. Moreover, he felt government intrusions into the private sector didn't really work. And he couldn't say any of that. He was a good Liberal and, as they say in baseball, when the pitcher throws one right at you, he would have to take one for the team.

"This wasn't something that offended conscience," Smith says. "This was something that I just didn't think was worth the battle. It weakened the fabric of the country."

And then there was the time David Smith, in his words, "became number one on Michael Valpy's shit list." Smith infuriated the *Globe and Mail* columnist by sneaking through a bill changing the name of the July first holiday from Dominion Day to Canada Day.

It was an uneventful Friday afternoon in the House and MP Walter Baker, who was on House duty for the Conservatives, was feeling miffed. He'd just been dumped as the party's house leader in favour of the unpleasant Yukon MP Erik Nielsen. So he wasn't feeling particularly inclined to do his party any favours. David Smith knew this and couldn't help but notice most of the Tory MPs were half-asleep at the switch. So Smith introduced the Canada Day bill and urged it be given all three readings. Baker, who under different circumstances might have objected, looked the other way. Most Conservatives were aghast when they suddenly discovered the bill had received third reading and they'd missed it. One Tory MP actually shook his fist in Smith's face. Most Conservatives hated the change because they saw it as a bone tossed by the Liberals to French Canadians and ethnic groups at the expense of legitimate Canadian tradition. The government thought Dominion Day made Canada sound too colonial. Walter Baker, who actually supported the bill, had his revenge for being dumped and enjoyed tweaking his party's nose at the way he'd been treated.

Smith walked up to Trudeau's office. "You're never gonna believe what I just did," he told them. Once Trudeau got the news, he called his contacts in the Senate and instructed them to pass the bill forthwith.

"Did the shit hit the fan!" Smith laughs. But Canada Day it stayed. Michael Valpy wrote columns and started a national campaign trying to have it switched back to Dominion Day, without success. In one column, he describes gathering his children together and telling them the story of David "Puffball" Smith, who besmirched our heritage by denying us the word "Dominion" for July first. David Smith is laughing like hell as he tells the story.

As enjoyable as that escapade was, Smith's best day in politics was probably in the spring of 1982 when he voted in favour of Canada's new Constitution, with an entrenched Charter of Rights and Freedoms. Not just because it was an historic day for the country. Not just because of the significant changes Smith had engineered into the document. More because his mother and sister were in the gallery to see him cast that vote. It was the only time his sister Cay Lindblad, who had lived in California since 1951, ever saw him in the House.

It was also a riotous night in the House, with much of the same environment as the flag debate. Conservative MPs, who opposed the new Constitution and Charter, were standing in front of the Speaker's chair, screaming abuse, raising their fists, and bordering on open rebellion. "I never saw anything like it," says Smith. And this guy's seen a lot.

On August 12, 1983, one of David Smith's dreams came true. Despite the fact he was a John Turner loyalist, Smith was invited by Pierre Trudeau to join the cabinet as the minister responsible for small business and tourism. But Smith's early concerns that his time as an MP would be fun but brief proved to be well-founded. Trudeau retired, Turner took over and promptly lost the 1984 election. One hundred Liberal MPs lost their jobs that night and David Smith was one of them. As he drove to his campaign headquarters to watch the disastrous returns come in, he had a little chat with his then eight-year-old son, Alexander, who was extremely excited to be with his dad and blissfully ignorant of the debacle about to unfold.

"I'm gonna let you in on a secret," Smith told his son. "I think I'm gonna lose tonight."

"Oh no, no, Dad, you're crazy," Alexander said.

"No, I'm gonna lose. And the reason I'm telling you is that I don't want you to feel bad. And you can't say anything. This is a secret between us."

Smith's son kept the secret and the pain of the evening was a little more bearable. Smith's career in elective politics was now over, having lost to the Tory candidate Bill Attewell by twenty points. He'd been a cabinet minister for exactly one year, one month, and four days.

David Smith had spent almost twenty years in Liberal backrooms before becoming an MP. Now he was returning to full-time law and part-time politics. For a guy with direct access to the most powerful people in the country, Smith seems like such an "aw shucks" kinda fella. His jocular stories about rubbing shoulders with prime ministers somehow don't come off as boasting or name-dropping. Liberals who want to get things done often go through David Smith first, figuring a good word from Smith to the prime minister goes a long way.

"Look, I've been amazed every now and then, when ministers will ask me if I would help them get something to happen," he says. Even Eddie Goldenberg, one of Prime Minister Chrétien's closest advisers in the PMO, sometimes suggests Smith put in a plug on certain issues. "Eddie, you're in the office right next door," Smith tells him. Smith doesn't see himself as powerful. Maybe influential on some subjects because he's earned that through almost forty years of bobbing and weaving his way through backroom machinations.

As the man with his finger on the pulse of all things Liberal in Ontario, Smith occasionally finds himself at 24 Sussex Drive with a lengthy list of agenda items to discuss with Prime Minister Chrétien. Getting the PM's attention is another matter. Typically, Smith will arrive at the prime minister's residence with fifteen to twenty items on his list, which require prime ministerial attention. Invariably, before long, Chrétien will change the subject and start reminiscing about old times. Trouble is, Smith can match him story for story in that department, and before long, both men have been meeting for an hour and have completed no business. Eventually, Smith has to interrupt the PM and say, "I'll listen to that story when you address the following matter..." and so it goes.

One time, Chrétien and Smith found themselves on the porch overlooking the Ottawa River, waving to a boat, when suddenly the prime minister saw something that prompted an unusual story.

"That's the exact spot where that guy climbed over the fence and tried to kill me," Chrétien told Smith. "Now I'm gonna show you the whole route."

And he did. Smith followed Chrétien inside as the prime minister picked up the story. "This is where he had to make a decision," Chrétien said. "If he'd turned right, he might have got me. But he turned left, so I was okay." Smith, of course, is laughing his head off as he relives this guided tour of the route of the man who might have killed the PM, if not for an Inuit carving.

Chrétien knew Smith had spent a lot of time at 24 Sussex with previous prime ministers, particularly Lester Pearson, and wanted to know his secret. Why would Pearson have been interested in this kid?

Four hours later, both men finally finished getting through the agenda and it dawned on Chrétien.

"Mr. Pearson didn't have you up here all the time because you had all these positions," he said. "He had you up because you were a PK!" Mystery solved. Both men had a chuckle and liked what the story said about Pearson's character.

Most of what occupies David Smith's backroom activities these days is finding good people to carry the Liberal colours into elections. Despite the fact he seemingly has all the advantages in this game (his party's in power, he can speak for the PM), Smith has never found it more difficult to recruit candidates than now. He blames the Canadian Alliance for its continuous attacks on Canadian institutions.

"Why do they have to exploit this stuff?" Smith asks rhetorically. "You can't have a pension, you can't pay them anything. And then people wonder why you don't get the best and the brightest going into public life. It's just crazy."

Smith recently lost a bid to get an extremely successful businessman into politics.

"In five years, I get a $560,000-a-year U.S. pension indexed for the rest of my life," the executive told Smith.

"Now what do I do?" Smith laughs. "I can't compete with that."

But he tries. Sometimes those efforts result in some delightful foul-ups. Just before the 2000 election campaign, Smith was looking for a candidate to run in Markham riding, just north of Toronto. He wanted someone very competent and high profile because Markham was one of only two ridings in Ontario the Liberals didn't hold. He'd heard the president and chief executive officer of the Markham Stouffville Hospital, Dr. Jim MacLean, might be interested, so he asked Elinor Caplan for a phone number. As a former Ontario health minister and the MP for nearby Thornhill riding, Smith figured Caplan would know how to make contact with MacLean, and in fact, she gave him a number.

Only trouble was, Caplan thought Smith was talking about the Jim MacLean who used to work on her staff at Queen's Park, at the College of Physicians and Surgeons of Ontario, and was the current director of communications for Ontario Liberal leader Dalton McGuinty.

The day before Pierre Trudeau's funeral, MacLean arrived at his office to find two urgent voice mails from Smith. "I thought this was odd because David Smith has never called me in all the years I've known him, and I've known him since he was on Toronto city council," MacLean says. "So I phone him back, get him out of a meeting and say, 'David, it's Jim MacLean returning your call.'"

Smith then began his pitch in earnest. "The prime minister's thinking of calling an election soon," he told MacLean. "We've done some polling in Markham and the numbers on you look great. We think you'd make a terrific candidate." MacLean realized after about fifteen seconds that Smith was pitching the wrong MacLean, but was enjoying the flattery so much, he let him go on for a couple of more minutes before interrupting him. Finally he let the cat out of the bag.

"David, I think you've got the wrong Jim MacLean," the wrong Jim MacLean said.

"Well, who is this?" Smith asked.

"I'm the director of communications for Dalton McGuinty."

"So why are you calling me?" Smith asked again.

"You're the one who left me two voice mails to call," MacLean said. "But I don't think I'm the Jim MacLean you want."

Later that day, after the word had gotten around, McGuinty told *his* Jim MacLean, "Smitty nearly made the biggest mistake of his life thinking you were in any way suitable for office."

"I wouldn't disagree with that, Dalton," MacLean replied.

The next day, Smith ran into McGuinty at Trudeau's funeral and teased him, tongue firmly planted in cheek: "Why are you trying to steal my staff?" All Smith could do was stare at his own shoes.

Today, David Smith contents himself being chairman of Fraser Milner Casgrain, a national law firm with more than five hundred lawyers. He's still trying to find the best and the brightest for his friend Jean Chrétien, offer advice when asked, and play the quintessential backroom boy, to the admiration of some and irritation of others.

Oh yes. Laughing all the way.

THE EIGHTY MINUTES

It was the fall of 1982 when I heard him speak for the first time. He was the headliner at a fundraiser for Otto Jelinek, the Conservative MP for Halton. He may have been well known in Quebec circles, having already contested and lost a bruising fight for the leadership of his party. But as far as the rest of the country was concerned, he'd been out of the public eye for six years.

Canada was in the middle of its second coming with Pierre Trudeau and it wasn't liking what it was seeing. While the country was going through a terrible recession, the prime minister seemed less interested in economic concerns and more interested in pursuing his agenda of constitutional reform. Certainly, that's what Tory partisans in Oakville believed that night in 1982, and the guest speaker played it to the hilt. He whipped the crowd into a frenzy with a rock 'em sock 'em address that threatened to bring the house down. There were still loud rumblings in Tory circles that this man hadn't completely abandoned the notion of leading the Conservative Party some day. But on this day, he played to perfection the part of the loyal visitor, just trying to drum up some money for his friend Otto.

None of the reporters in attendance that night (admittedly a group on the youngish side) knew much about this forty-three-year-old star of the Montreal business community. He was certainly unlike any Conservative leader to whom we had become accustomed. Robert Stanfield. Joe Clark. William Davis. Peter Lougheed. Sterling Lyon. Solid men all. But none with the flair and panache of this guy—and perfect in both official languages to boot.

In fact, we knew so little about him, I sheepishly admitted in a post-speech scrum, that I wasn't completely sure how he pronounced his name. Nobody else was sure either, so I agreed to play the fool and ask.

"It's pronounced Mul-ROO-ney," he said politely with a laugh. "We lost an 'o' on the boat over from Ireland." The scrum continued. We asked the obligatory questions about how Trudeau was doing, whether Clark could come back, whether his leadership aspirations were over, and so on. Then the tape recorders were turned off and he did something unusual. He sat around for a few more minutes and talked shop with some of the reporters. That seemed different as well.

Nearly two decades later, I'd be calling Brian Mulroney at his law office in Montreal in hopes of convincing him to talk about the seductive call of politics, something he understood as well as anyone in the world.

"Mr. Paikin, I'm afraid I don't give interviews," he said cordially in a voice that's now even deeper than it was when he was prime minister.

I knew this wasn't completely true. Mulroney had brought his oratorical skills out of retirement for a few interviews on the tenth anniversary of the death of the Meech Lake Accord. But I also knew two major biographies of Mulroney—by John Sawatsky and Claire Hoy—were written without the benefit of an interview with the man himself.

"I was hoping you'd make an exception in this case," I said. "I feel sure you'll find the subject matter of interest, and I'm approaching it with the care and respect it deserves."

Something must have piqued his curiosity because his next question suggested he might be softening.

"Did Bill Davis give you an interview?" he asked, knowing the former Ontario premier also declines virtually all interview requests.

"Mr. Davis sat down for me twice," I said.

There was a moment's silence on the other end of the phone. "All right. I'm back in Toronto regularly. I'll have Francine set something up," he said, referring to Francine Collins, his very able executive assistant at Ogilvy Renault. We chatted for another minute about the gist of the book, then said goodbye.

Two months later, I visited Brian Mulroney in his hotel suite at the Royal York Hotel in Toronto. Francine had warned me I'd have

David Smith and Prime Minister Lester B. Pearson—both preachers' kids ("PKs").

Peter Lougheed celebrates his first election win, August 30, 1971. (*JEEN POOL*, EDMONTON JOURNAL)

Brothers Daniel and Pierre Marc Johnson both became premiers of Quebec, just like their father.

John Laschinger smiles with newly chosen PC leader Brian Mulroney in the fall of 1983. (JOHN EVANS)

Iona Campagnolo, Canada's first minister of state for amateur fitness and sport, in September, 1976.

The secretary of the cabinet, Ed Stewart (right), swears in Alvin Curling as Ontario's first black cabinet minister in June, 1985. Lieutenant-Governor John Black Aird looks on.

Audrey McLaughlin became the first female leader of a major party in North American history in December, 1989. She is flanked by her mother, Margaret Brown, and NDP stalwart Stanley Knowles.
(PHOTO FEATURES LTD.)

Derwyn Shea (left) and Alan Tonks prepare for a meeting of non-governmental organizations at the United Nations in August, 1994. Shea was representing the World Association of Major Metropolises.

Pollster Michael Marzolini shows Prime Minister Jean Chrétien his latest findings before the PM called the 2000 election. David Smith is on the left, John Rae on the right.

Quebec candidate Anie Perrault and then PC party leader Jean Charest rev up the crowd during the 1997 election campaign.

Elsie Wayne meets South African President Nelson Mandela on September 24, 1998. NDP leader Alexa MacDonough and Prime Minister Jean Chrétien look on.

Lyn McLeod wins the leadership of the Liberal Party of Ontario on February 9, 1992. From left to right are daughters Robin, Kristen, Dara (hugging her) and Dana.

Norman Atkins and his one-time brother-in-law Dalton Camp at Atkins's 65th birthday celebration in June, 1999 at the Air Force Officers' Club, Ottawa.

Eight-year-old Jason Kenney (centre) meets former Prime Minister John Diefenbaker in Regina in 1977. Older brother David looks on.

William Davis roams the floor at the leadership convention in Toronto in January, 1985, bringing an end to his fourteen years as premier of Ontario.

A buoyant Brian Mulroney is mobbed after winning the PC leadership in Ottawa on June 11, 1983.

sixty minutes and no more. He had to dash off to attend an event at the *Toronto Sun*, of which is he now chairman of the board, and he couldn't be late.

The interview must have gone reasonably well because eighty minutes after arriving, with my tape recorder no longer rolling, Brian Mulroney was still doing what Brian Mulroney loves to do—shoot the breeze about politics. It reminded me of that day in Oakville almost twenty years earlier. Except this time, it wasn't a chat with a headliner at a fundraiser. It was with a man who's experienced the highest highs and lowest lows of perhaps anyone who's ever entered public life in Canada. At the beginning of his time in government, no one enjoyed the thrill of victory more than Brian Mulroney. By the time he was finished transforming his country, no one was more despised than Brian Mulroney. Perhaps after eight years of being out of the public spotlight, it's time to reconsider the legacy of Canada's eighteenth prime minister.

BRIAN MULRONEY IS DRESSED IN A CRISP WHITE SHIRT and cuff links, a sharp tie, black loafers, but not wearing his blue suit jacket. He's just returned from Rome. In fact, it seems he's always just flying in from somewhere. It took a long time to pull this meeting together because over the past two months, he's been to England, Ireland, Germany, and France.

We're just two weeks away from the first ever Canadian Alliance leadership convention. At least, it's sort of a convention. The Alliance's one-member, one-vote system may be more democratic, but it has none of the drama of the traditional leadership convention—the kind Mulroney contested twice. It's clear he prefers the old-style system, which broke his heart and made him despondent for several months in 1976, but brought him back into the spotlight and primed for government in 1983.

"I watch these guys," Mulroney says of the Alliance leadership hopefuls. "It's like watching paint dry." He's disappointed none of them appears to have mastered the great stump speech. "It's part of the theatre of democratic discourse," he says.

Politics has changed since Brian Mulroney became leader of the

PC party in 1983. Back then, enthralling the crowd with a dramatic, rousing, stemwinder of an address was a necessary part of a politician's toolkit. Today, the most successful politicians have an almost intentionally dull approach to politics.

Somehow, it became the stuff of Canadian legend that Brian Mulroney wanted to be prime minister since he was four years old. In fact, there's no indication that he had any interest in politics at all before he went to St. Francis Xavier University in Antigonish, Nova Scotia. But once there, he took to it like a duck to water.

"If you're young and you're active in politics, you see the way parties work, sometime during that time frame, I'm sure I said to myself it'd be nice to be prime minister some day," Mulroney says. "But certainly there was no epiphany."

Mulroney's rise in Conservative Party circles is the stuff of which legends are made. When he first got involved in Conservative politics, the party essentially didn't exist in Quebec. By the time the confirmed Tory partisan arrived at Laval University to study law in 1960, the Conservatives had enjoyed precisely one winning campaign in Quebec—Diefenbaker's miraculous but brief landslide in 1958. Before that, the only thing the party had established in that province was a pathetic record.

Mulroney made a name for himself in Quebec, first as a specialist in labour law in Montreal in 1965, then in 1974 as a member of a royal commission investigating crime in the province's construction industry. He was becoming a star. When Robert Stanfield stepped down as national Tory leader, he tried to parlay that stardom by reaching for the brass ring.

Much has been written about Mulroney's first run for the Tory leadership in February, 1976. Most of it is uncomplimentary to the candidate. He was criticized for being far too slick, far too shallow, at thirty-seven years old not nearly seasoned enough, and compensating for that by spending vast sums of money to attract delegate support. Most of all, unlike every other candidate vying for the job, he'd never been elected to anything. Despite all those handicaps, Mulroney made an excellent showing at the convention. He came second on the first ballot, behind Claude Wagner and ahead of Joe Clark.

It was a thrilling convention for spectators, but crushing to Mulroney. It quickly became apparent that he'd fired all his guns on the first ballot and had little growth potential thereafter. Furthermore, he became the target of the other candidates. He watched, heartbroken, as MPs Sinclair Stevens and Flora Macdonald, and even his good friend Lowell Murray from his St. Francis Xavier days, walked right past his section after that first ballot and endorsed Joe Clark. Mulroney lasted until the third ballot, then watched Clark defeat Wagner on the fourth by just sixty-five votes out of more than twenty-three hundred cast.

"It was a rallying to anybody who was a member of caucus as opposed to an outsider," Mulroney says, wincing as he recalls the memory of it. Even after the convention, he never asked any of the MPs why they chose Clark over him, though he must have been dying to.

It took a considerable length of time for Mulroney to get over the wounds of that 1976 convention. Even today, almost a quarter of a century later, he paints a picture of himself as a dejected outsider, who was ignored once it was all over. The fact was, after the convention's dramatic conclusion, the candidates who were MPs returned to Parliament Hill and got on with their job of opposing the Liberals until the next election three years hence.

"There was a new leader in place," Mulroney says. "The caucus members got together daily, did Question Period. They rallied behind the new leader and they had the enjoyment that comes from solidarity after a good fight and a good reunion. I had none of that. I was by myself in Montreal trying to earn a living and pay off the bills. And no one made a great effort to reach out to me from Ottawa."

And who did Mulroney expect to reach out?

"Of course the leader, and then the party apparatus," he says, the sadness still evident in his voice. "I was the only one not part of the parliamentary family, so it was more difficult for me."

(Mulroney is not quite accurate in that assertion. He may have forgotten that Paul Hellyer, one of the leadership aspirants, was actually not part of the caucus at this time, having lost his downtown Toronto seat in the 1974 election. Hellyer was a member of the Ottawa press gallery at the time he decided to contest the Tory leadership.)

As if the isolation weren't enough, there was also the trauma of losing.

"In all candidates for high office there has to be a capacity for self-delusion, otherwise you couldn't do it," he says. "After a while we all believe we are going to win, no matter how hopeless our position is."

Shortly after the convention, Mulroney's wife, Mila, gave birth to the couple's second child. By the summer, he accepted the executive vice-president's job at the Iron Ore Company of Canada. A year later, he was president, overseeing the daily travails of eight thousand employees. More important, he felt certain his political career was now over. At least, that's what he says. He was a commentator on CBC television on election night, May 22, 1979, when he forecast a Conservative victory under Joe Clark.

"I remember very well Joe's victory," he says. "I thought he was very, very good. He showed flashes of his finest qualities. I remember feeling very exhilarated for him, and almost relieved that I could get on with my life and there was no second guessing."

That night, it never occurred to Mulroney that Canadians would be going back to the polls nine months later, that the Tories would blow their first election victory since 1962. "I just thought he'd be there for some time," Mulroney says.

But, of course, he wasn't. Once the clever Liberals learned someone in the Tory camp couldn't count, the government fell on a vote of non-confidence, and Pierre Trudeau was welcoming everyone to the 1980s. It was a mistake that would haunt Clark for the rest of his life.

History tells us at this point, the knives began to become unsheathed for Clark, and it was all being orchestrated by the boy from Baie Comeau. It's at this point in our interview that Mulroney really gets animated. He does not like the way history has portrayed his conduct, leading up to the review of Clark's leadership on January 28, 1983 in Winnipeg.

"I voted for Clark and so did my wife," he insists. Mulroney thinks journalists have ignored the facts because his alleged regicide against Clark simply made for a better story. Mulroney wasn't an MP. He came from a province which, at this point, had elected *one* Tory MP (Roch LaSalle). Clark's office controlled the party fundraising apparatus and organization at the convention. Plus, Mulroney held a news conference with Clark announcing his fealty to the leader (a much-discussed event which critics charge portrayed Mulroney at his most cynical—supporting Clark publicly, while at the same time undermining him privately.)

"To have a convention in Winnipeg in the middle of the winter, and how I somehow organized a convention against Clark?" Mulroney asks incredulously. "Well, if the stupidity of that statement doesn't strike you immediately, you should get out of journalism right away. It's pretty preposterous."

Does Mulroney have a case? He says that in the memoirs of both former PC cabinet minister John Crosbie and former William Davis aide Eddie Goodman, there is ample evidence to show the plot to get Clark was widespread.

"This was an Ontario operation," Mulroney says. "Everybody knows that. Davis was sitting on the largest majority government in the largest province. If the Ontario Progressive Conservative Party had wanted Joe Clark re-elected with a large majority, he'd have been re-elected. And he wasn't."

The history of this time will show that Premier Bill Davis did have some significant problems with Clark. But Davis also made a public statement of support for the Tory leader, and according to Eddie Goodman's memoirs, "remained loyal to him throughout the convention."

However, Mulroney is right that Newfoundland and Ontario ultimately did Clark in. The Newfoundlanders were hoping John Crosbie would emerge as an alternative to Clark. And pollsters discovered only 60 per cent of the Ontario delegation supported Clark. Clearly, not enough of them followed Premier Davis's lead on the leadership review issue.

Then, in one of the seminal moments in Canadian political history, Joe Clark counted the votes at that leadership review and determined that 66.9 per cent support wasn't good enough. It was the second major miscalculation of his life.

But if none of what you've heard so far is convincing enough, Mulroney has saved the best for last.

"To show you how preposterous it really was," he begins, "some weeks before that convention, I had to close down the town of Schefferville [Quebec]. If you can think of a more disastrous launch for a political career than to do this, willfully knowing you were going to go into politics, it's nothing short of lunacy."

In fact, Mulroney says he left the Winnipeg convention and immediately went to Florida for a week to begin preparing for parliamentary hearings ordered by the Quebec National Assembly into the shutting down of Schefferville as a result of the closure of the iron ore mines.

However, with Clark's call for a new leadership contest, Mulroney was back in the game. And this time, he would not be denied. He changed virtually everything he did from his 1976 run. Instead of presenting a gaudy, flashy campaign, he went for understated substance. He met delegates in small groups, away from the television cameras. He looked more comfortable in his own skin and exuded winnability, something Tories were desperate for after the 1979 interregnum.

Mulroney also made the most compelling argument of the campaign. He told his fellow Tories there were 102 constituencies in Canada where the French-speaking population comprised at least 15 per cent of the voters. In the previous election, the Liberals had won one hundred of those ridings. The French fortress had to be penetrated, and Mulroney claimed he was the only one who could do it.

On June 11, 1983, the majority of delegates at the PC leadership convention evidently agreed. Mulroney captured the prize that had eluded him so painfully seven years earlier. He defeated Joe Clark, who led on every ballot except the last one. Mulroney won it on the fourth ballot and became leader of the Progressive Conservative Party of Canada, something he'd dreamed of since his days at St. Francis Xavier.

Then, fifteen months later, he made good on his boast about delivering the French-Canadian vote, particularly in Quebec. He took fifty-eight of the seventy-five Quebec seats (eight more than Diefenbaker captured in '58) en route to the biggest majority government in Canadian history. And it almost certainly wouldn't have happened if not for a magic moment that lasted perhaps half a minute in duration but changed the course of Canadian history.

Leaders' debates are always played up by the parties and the media as if they were heavyweight-title bouts. In fact, they're almost always anti-climactic. There's rarely the defining moment everyone seeks. But the second leaders' debate in the 1984 campaign broke all the rules.

Most commentators agreed Mulroney had won the first debate, in French, on points. No knockout blow but a solid performance. The Tory leader figured if he could turn the trick again, he'd have a shot at chipping away at the Liberals' lead. He'd gotten himself into trouble earlier in the campaign by making some ill-advised comments about patronage. And during the second debate, in English, John Turner intended to make him pay for it. Turner brandished a copy of the Montreal *Gazette*, intending to bring Mulroney's comments to the attention of the viewers.

Mulroney's initial reaction was to cry foul. Props were expressly forbidden by the debate rules. But he held his fire and decided to see where Turner intended to go with the offensive. Sure enough, Turner wanted to spit Mulroney's unfortunate words right back at him. It was a decision which would cost him his job.

"When John said that, I counter-punched," recalls Mulroney, who found it outrageous that Turner would raise the patronage issue, given the orgy of partisan appointments Turner had just made at Pierre Trudeau's behest. "But at that point in time, I was just trying to rag the puck," he says, employing the familiar hockey term for not trying to score, simply trying to avoid being scored upon.

Then John Turner put up his hands and said he had no option when he made those appointments.

"As soon as he said that, I came alive," Mulroney says, reliving the moment. In the most electrifying exchange of any televised debate in Canadian history, the PC leader told Turner he *did* have an option. He could have said no, Mr. Trudeau, I won't make those patronage appointments because they're not good for Canada. He accused Turner of a disavowal of leadership.

"It was a very rapid-fire exchange," Mulroney says. "I'm sure it didn't last any more than ten seconds. But it was a devastating ten seconds." And unlike most memorable lines in debates, it hadn't been rehearsed ahead of time. It was spontaneous.

Mulroney and Mila rode back to Stornaway, the Opposition leader's home, "I think you just hit it out of the park," she told him.

Mulroney was bouncing off the ceiling. He flipped on CKO, the national all-news radio station, and listened to the phone calls come in from all over the country. There was little doubt the callers thought he'd wiped the floor with Turner.

The next day, he flew to Sherbrooke to meet his Quebec candidates, "And you could tell the earth had just moved," he says. After a long day, he arrived at the Connaught Hotel in Hamilton at one o'clock in the morning to a boisterous throng of supporters. He and Mila went up to their suite and met with Allan Gregg, the campaign pollster.

"We've just looked at the overnights," Gregg told him. "You've just been responsible for the most radical change in modern Canadian political history."

Ten seconds. Election over.

Some might argue that Mulroney's victory was actually less impressive than Diefenbaker's. The House of Commons was smaller in 1958, so Dief's Tories captured almost 79 per cent of the seats in the Commons, compared to Mulroney's nearly 75 per cent. However, by another yardstick—the margin of victory—Mulroney comes out ahead. He bested John Turner's Liberals by 171 seats. Dief's lead over Lester Pearson's Liberals was 161 seats. Regardless, it was a hell of a debut from a guy who'd never been elected to any public office before becoming party leader.

"Bill Davis always said your first election is the one you always remember," Mulroney says. "It was a great day, no doubt about it. I got the results in my hometown. I had done what I told that party I was going to do. Take them from opposition to government, and in a big way."

One of Mulroney's first thoughts was, "Two hundred and eleven seats—what a huge responsibility. Then another thought occurred to him.

"It's better than *one* hundred and eleven, which is where the Conservatives had ended up most of their lives."

Three weeks after election day, Brian Mulroney became Canada's eighteenth prime minister. He adored the job. His first cabinet meeting. His first time entering the House as prime minister, the government's first budget, his first federal-provincial conference. His first G-7 summit.

"It is very, very heady and very exciting," he says. "When you're new, it's an extraordinarily challenging job. One of the reasons is the geography of the country. It's so huge. Mrs. Thatcher used to say, 'In an hour, I can get anywhere in the kingdom, and Brian can't get to the airport.'"

Mulroney was also different from Thatcher and other world leaders inasmuch as his family was still growing. He and Mila already had three children when he became prime minister. A fourth child was born a year later. The childhood Mulroney's offspring enjoyed was light-years away from what the prime minister himself had experienced in Baie Comeau. He was constantly mindful of that contrast.

"I used to tell the kids at Harrington Lake [the prime minister's retreat], 'None of this belongs to us. When Daddy's finished with this, we're going back to Montreal and start all over again.' They had a very clear understanding of that from the beginning," he says.

Having said that, Mila Mulroney insisted the kids be involved in everything the first couple did. Occasionally, the prime minister would be on the second floor of the residence with a foreign visitor late in the afternoon, perhaps Ronald Reagan or Mikhail Gorbachev. It was typical for the kids to barge in and tell the assembled dignitaries about their day at school.

"The only calls I told my staff to interrupt my cabinet meetings for were from the children," Mulroney adds. "They'd call up and say, 'I want to talk to my dad.' I would leave the meeting and take the call."

And what would the kids want to discuss with the highest-ranking politician in the land?

"Mommy's in Toronto tonight and we think you should take us to the movies," was a typical request.

Obviously, with such an overwhelming mandate, Mulroney was able to enjoy a bit of a honeymoon. But it was surprisingly short, considering the size of the victory. The Parliament Hill media had real problems with his presidentializing the prime ministership. He put too many cronies, who weren't up to the job, in important positions. He had cabinet ministers disappoint him through incompetence, or in some cases, by being the subject of a public inquiry or a criminal investigation. And through it all, there was something about Mulroney's personality that just rubbed too many people the wrong way. Claire Hoy, one of the prime minister's harshest critics, described it this way in his book *Friends in High Places*: "Watching Mulroney, one got the feeling that beneath the plastic exterior of the studied politician there was an impenetrable layer of more plastic."

Mulroney also disappointed "small-c" conservatives, who felt he failed in his efforts to bring down Canada's annual budget deficits. Mulroney acknowledges whatever progress was made against reducing the deficit came as much through tax increases as spending cuts. At one point during his final year in office, the deficit hit thirty-four billion dollars, which seemed like an outrageously high number for a government committed to fiscal prudence.

However, that charge doesn't tell the entire story. By 1990, the deficit as a percentage of the country's gross domestic product had been cut in half. Even with the recession of the early 1990s, it was still down by one-third from what the Conservatives inherited from the Liberals.

"There would be no recognition of the importance of deficits without Brian Mulroney," says Stanley Hartt, his one-time chief of staff, now chairman of Salomon Smith Barney Canada Inc.

"The best thing we did was get people to change their attitudes towards deficits," echoes Michael Wilson, the former finance minister, who says polls at the time showed just one-tenth of one per cent of the public was concerned about deficits. "Everybody figured there's a bottomless pit of cash in Ottawa. Now people know there's no free lunch. In 1984 that wasn't the case."

The political landscape of the country was totally different then as well. Back in 1984, both opposition parties—the Liberals and the New Democrats—were hounding the government to spend more. Every suggested spending cut was met by cries of Armageddon. After the Liberals took over in 1993, they had the luxury of having the

Reform Party in opposition, harassing them to cut spending and taxes harder and faster.

"Brian Mulroney and I had this discussion a number of times," Wilson says. "He said, 'We're not here for the power. We're here to do things. We are here to make changes and leave the job in a certain finite time. We wanted to be able to go away and say we made a difference. People can disagree with us but that was the driver."

(Ironically, for all his loyalty to Mulroney, Michael Wilson seemed to have more in common with Joe Clark. He was a cabinet minister in Clark's short-lived government. The two also shared a rare family connection. Both Clark and Wilson each had a grandfather who became mayor of Bay City, Michigan. Despite that, Wilson was the first contender to leap to Mulroney's box after the first ballot of the 1983 PC leadership convention.)

While he was prime minister, Brian Mulroney always gave the impression he cared far too much about being loved and admired rather than respected and trusted. Phone calls by assistants to journalists who'd written unflattering pieces became par for the course.

Today, Mulroney claims that two years into his first mandate he gave up the pursuit of immediate popularity, concentrating instead on the longer view. He realized he was governing in, as he calls it, "a decade of convulsive change." Communism collapsed, globalization took off, George Bush went from 91 per cent approval ratings to out of a job within a year. Margaret Thatcher was turfed out by her own caucus. The Socialists were rejected in France. The entire system almost collapsed in Japan and did collapse in the Soviet Union.

"In some important ways," he now says, "the pursuit of popularity and the achievement of great things is antithetical. Harry Truman left office as the most unpopular president in the history of the United States. Forty years later, he's viewed as the fifth-greatest president in the history of the republic. The greatest prime minister in the history of the world, Winston Churchill, was driven from office and humiliated after saving the United Kingdom from destruction and single-handedly warning about the Nazis. That's democracy.

"You want to be friendly with everyone. It's a natural human instinct," he continues. "After a while you realize this is impossible. If we were a government that was going to do historic things, then we were going to have to do it ourselves and damn the consequences in terms of public opinion."

And the forces lined up against him were formidable, starting with the media, continuing on with special interest groups, trade unions, the bureaucrats, universities, and the list goes on. Clearly, Mulroney feels his government was singled out for special condemnation. Why?

"In part because of the size of our majority, in part because of our ideology, which they thought was aberrant and abhorrent," he says. "If you're not a Liberal or a socialist in Ottawa, you're in for trying times."

Brian Mulroney had managed to put together a significant list of enemies during his first four years in office. And yet, on November 21, 1988, he was re-elected by Canadians with a second consecutive majority government. Enough Canadians, though clearly not the majority, were prepared to take a leap of faith on Mulroney's free trade pact with the United States, ensuring his re-election with 169 seats.

In a sense, Mulroney's second election win was even more of an achievement than his first, even though the seat count was much lower. It had been thirty-five years since any prime minister had won back-to-back majority governments. And no Conservative prime minister had turned the trick since Sir John A. Macdonald almost one hundred years earlier.

"Look at the opponents we managed to rally in the free trade debate," he says proudly. "Pretty hard to improve on that. As Franklin Roosevelt said of Al Smith (the Democratic Party's standard-bearer for president in 1928), 'I love him for the enemies he's made.' And judged by that criteria, I was widely loved!" Mulroney loves telling the story and punctuates it with an uproarious laugh.

If Mulroney's first term was historic because of the size of his victory, his second term was even more so for the economic issues he tackled: free trade, the goods and services tax (GST), and waging war on inflation.

"We knew it was going to be very troublesome and supremely difficult," he says. "I decided to do them both right away, right in the face of a recession, and at the same time, to appoint a governor of the

Bank of Canada to wring inflation out of the system. Now that trilogy is no prescription for popularity. But it was a prescription for the complete modernization of the new Canadian economy."

Two McGill University professors evidently agree. Al Riggs and Tom Velks last year updated a 1993 study and concluded, "Brian Mulroney remains the man to beat." Using eighteen different indices measuring economic performance, the pair found Mulroney had the best economic record in the last half-century. The findings also consider the state of the economy when each prime minister assumed power and contrasts the record with his predecessor.

"I can't tell you I was offended at being ranked number one," Mulroney deadpans.

Throughout the interview, Mulroney has tried his best to be statesmanlike, but here he can't resist a partisan shot.

"And the current guy ranked *last*," he says, referring to Jean Chrétien. "As *they* said, dead last."

(Mulroney is being accurate here, however, the authors also point out Chrétien's record is still incomplete.)

"We did big things," Mulroney adds, continuing the contrast with Chrétien. "If you're the prime minister and you decide you're not going to do something major because you might fail, then you've just abdicated responsibility. Of course you're going to fail from time to time. But you have to take stands. And that's what we did."

Does he have no regrets about free trade or the GST?

"Without those policies, Paul Martin and Jean Chrétien are up a tree," he says emphatically. "You tell Paul Martin you're going to cancel the GST today, he'll tell you to go jump off a bridge."

Mulroney is now clearly in his glory, happily recounting how controversial, yet permanent, free trade and the GST are today. And a majority of Canadians seem to agree. In last year's annual year-end survey, *Maclean's* magazine found 71 per cent of Canadians agreed the country should sign free trade agreements with many other countries. Only 17 per cent disagreed. *Maclean's* concludes, "Free trade has simply become part of the Canadian economic fabric."

But these accounts pale in comparison to Brian Mulroney's worst day in public life.

"When I got word that contrary to his formal signing of a constitutional document..." He pauses dramatically. "The arrogance of a man who had given his word."

The ghost of Clyde Wells still haunts Brian Mulroney. Wells's decision not to put Mulroney's beloved Meech Lake Constitutional Accord before the Newfoundland House of Assembly for a vote still rankles.

"What about Manitoba?" I ask. "They didn't pass it either."

"Manitoba was solvable," he insists, and leaves it there.

Former Saskatchewan premier Allan Blakeney disagrees. "Meech failed because of the chutzpah of Mulroney," he says.

Obviously, Mulroney disagrees. In June, 1990, he ventured to Newfoundland, along with premiers David Peterson, Grant Devine, and Frank McKenna, all of whom put forward their best case for ratification before the House of Assembly.

"If it had gone to a vote, who could complain?" Mulroney says. "That's democracy." He still sounds infuriated at the way Meech failed, using dramatic language in describing the former Newfoundland premier.

"Did he honour his signature or dishonour it?" Mulroney asks rhetorically. He speculates Wells declined to allow the vote not because of events in Manitoba, but because Wells was afraid the accord would pass.

Soon after Meech's demise, Mulroney got a call from Clyde Wells, looking for federal dollars to help support Newfoundland's efforts to develop the Hibernia oil fields. Perhaps surprisingly, Mulroney said yes.

"I did it because I thought it was right," he says. "He [Wells] had usurped the rights of the people of Newfoundland. That was a profound act of arrogance. For me to have engaged in retribution against the people of Newfoundland for something that he had done would perhaps have been understandable but just as wrong as he had been."

So Mulroney offered Newfoundland $2.8 billion in loan guarantees to develop the Hibernia oil fields. It's a measure of the influence the prime minister had over his Quebec MPs that he was able to convince them to okay the offer. After Meech's failure, Clyde Wells was seen as public enemy number one in Quebec. Yet somehow, Mulroney avoided an intra-caucus bloodbath on the issue.

"You can have a lot of failings as prime minister," he says. "But vindictiveness shouldn't be one of them."

Unlike Jean Chrétien, Mulroney says it was always his intention to get out of politics after two terms as prime minister.

"You get to think it's a birthright if you keep going on," he says. "I'm just going to keep running 'cause I like playing golf? That's not a good enough reason," he says sarcastically, again in a not-so-thinly-veiled reference to Chrétien.

"I thought I'd exhaust my energy and agenda in two terms, nine years. And in fact, I did. I left, having done everything I tried to do. I succeeded in some, and I failed in others. But I had no more ideas. I didn't have the freshness of 1983 any more. I had spent my capital on a great cause for Canada."

There were other historic achievements during the latter stages of Mulroney's second mandate: the North American Free Trade Agreement, which added Mexico to a now continent-wide deal; and the Charlottetown Accord, another landmark constitutional agreement reached in August, 1992, which had the backing of both opposition leaders, all ten premiers, the head of the Assembly of First Nations, and two former prime ministers. Yet the Canadian public rejected it in a nation-wide referendum.

The trouble with engaging on those major files so late in his mandate was, of course, transition. Mulroney would be leaving his successor little time to improve the party's fortunes. Still, he figured a vigorous, knock-down-drag-'em-out leadership campaign, waged by many of the stars of his cabinet, would solve that problem. He'd fought two of those kinds of conventions, and both times, the new leader won the ensuing election. He hoped the 1993 affair would feature the likes of Kim Campbell, Barbara McDougall, Jean Charest, Michael Wilson, Tom Hockin, Otto Jelinek, Bernard Valcourt, and Perrin Beatty for starters. He'd shuffled his cabinet to enhance the chances of some of those ministers. He put McDougall into foreign affairs to raise her profile. He knew Wilson would be too much associated with the recession if left in finance, so Mulroney created a new posting for him—industry and international trade. He liked Campbell enough to promote her to the justice portfolio in rather short order.

But Mulroney's hopes for a convention that would showcase all that Tory talent were quickly dashed. Campbell sprinted to such a huge, apparently insurmountable lead, that just one high-profile minister, Jean Charest, only in his late thirties, dared challenge her. All the other "stars" took a pass.

"The beauty of a brutal leadership campaign is that if you are still standing at the end of it, chances are you can rally the party around you, and you'll do well at an election campaign," Mulroney says, explaining his preference. "You're a personality. Your physical strength, mental agility, campaigning skills, eloquence, all of these skills are brought to bear and are contrasted with your competitors. The media is lethal and ruthless and so are your competitors. That's the strange beauty of an aggressive and tough leadership campaign which a coronation would not serve."

However, Mulroney's former cabinet mates and the convention delegates clearly disagreed. They didn't want a bloodbath. Even though the Campbell–Charest contest did get very nasty, the outcome was never in doubt.

By the time Kim Campbell replaced Mulroney in the summer of 1993 as leader of the PC Party, there were just a few months left before the new prime minister had to call an election. In her autobiography Campbell constantly bemoans the fact that she didn't have enough time to put her own stamp on the job. The result, of course, was the worst drubbing the Tories had received in history.

"Brian Mulroney has to take some responsibility for it," says Norman Atkins about that 1993 election result. "He left his departure too late."

The debate will endure forever as to who's more responsible for that '93 debacle—the new prime minister, who ran a mediocre campaign, or the former prime minister, who was wildly unpopular upon leaving office. There's little doubt as to where Mulroney stands on the issue.

"I've always contended and acknowledged she was carrying water for us," he says of Campbell. "But I went out of my way to ensure that everything was done to give her the greatest advantages that we could," he says. "She had time. I worked very closely in the days after to bring the party together in support of her."

Mulroney says a significant chunk of Jean Charest's organization wanted to quit the party, so bad were the wounds after the leadership convention. That certainly didn't help. But as for his role?

"I don't think there's a single thing my wife and I failed to do to ensure for her the most comfortable of sendoffs," he says. "It was June. She had until the fall to call the election. The big nation-builders were in place. And to her great credit, she brought the party back to a very favourable situation, just what we expected would happen."

In fact, Campbell's personal popularity *was* high. "Our internal polls showed her widely ahead of Mr. Chrétien on every criterion of leadership," Mulroney says. While the party ran behind its new leader in popularity, Campbell had still managed to get the Tories into a very competitive position. The Gallup poll on August 19, 1993, put the Liberals at 49 per cent, the PCs at 36 per cent, the NDP at 8 per cent, and the Reform Party at 7 per cent. The Tories under Campbell even led the Bloc Québécois 47 to 28 per cent in Quebec.

Even if the former prime minister's popularity was an unspoken issue lurking just below the surface for Canadians, Mulroney points out it's every new leader's job to improve on the outgoing regime's record.

"Trudeau took over a bad situation from Mr. Pearson and made it better," he says. "Ralph Klein took over a very bad situation [from Don Getty]. Within months he made it better and became premier. Sometimes it works, sometimes it doesn't. The transition was remarkably smooth. I can't remember Kim ever saying anything to Mila or me except the most profound thank you for everything we had done."

However, once Campbell called the election, the public saw, according to Mulroney, a tentative leader, who for some reason was unable to articulate the government's accomplishments. Mulroney says his successor should have been boasting about the newly restructured and modernized economy which would go on to lead the world in job creation. Instead, on day one of the campaign, she predicted double-digit unemployment until the end of the decade.

What should she have said?

"We have laid the foundations for an export-driven recovery in a modernized Canadian economy," Mulroney offers. "And on this foundation, as your new prime minister, I am going to build a mansion for you. That mansion will be high job creation, deficit elimination, lower taxes, and smaller government."

What did Mulroney think when he saw Campbell's approach?

"When I didn't see that kind of attitude, I was disappointed," he admits. He thought Campbell's missteps began to chip away at her confidence. "I'm not trying in any way to suggest that a new leader taking over in those circumstances didn't have a tough job ahead of him or her," he says. "But in this case it didn't succeed."

Instead, the PC Party blew apart. The fragile coalition Mulroney had masterfully put together—western populists, Ontario Tories, and Quebec nationalists—was gone. At this writing, the once-proud Progressive Conservative Party of Canada is a shell of its former self, in fact, on life-support systems. And Brian Mulroney does have to wear much of that, although he doesn't see the situation in quite such dire terms.

"Joe's saved the party and things are going to be okay," he insists. "It doesn't mean we won't talk to other parties, as Stanley [Hartt, his former chief of staff] would say, 'mergers and acquisitions.' But the Conservative Party will be around 133 years from today.

"I might even still be the leader," he laughs.

Have Canadians changed their views on Mulroney all these years later? Major General Lewis MacKenzie, a Conservative candidate in the 1997 election, was stunned at what he discovered on the hustings. He had mostly favourable encounters with voters until the day after Jean Charest, the then PC leader, admitted to having consulted Mulroney during the campaign, as if that were one of the seven deadly sins.

"Tories from way back would just about throw you off their front porch after that," MacKenzie says. "They couldn't believe Charest would get involved with Mulroney. The hatred for him was still visceral."

I tell Mulroney the story and he's not surprised.

"Preston Manning drove his party to success by demonizing and brutalizing Brian Mulroney and his record," he says. "We were crooks. We were from Quebec, and he was going to clean up this mess. The West was getting shafted, glued, screwed, and tattooed."

Mulroney says the truth is, the public is much kinder to him these days than his old friends in the national press gallery would believe.

"They're of the view that people are throwing tomatoes at me on the streets," he says. To the contrary, "People are asking for autographs, shaking hands, wishing me well. When my daughter got married, a huge crowd gathered in front of the church for hours on a cold day. When we got out, there was huge applause. When we go into restaurants, we sometimes get standing ovations. It's nice.

"If you want to see what the reaction is, what's really going on, forget this bullshit. You walk down the street with me in Toronto any time you want. You watch and see what happens. I'll tell you it would curl your hair. And remember this, if a tomato comes flying through the air, it was intended for you!" he says with a hearty laugh.

Mulroney says the days of his poring over every newspaper article about him are long since over. He still misses his Wednesday caucus meetings, and the energy he'd soak up into his pores from his many MPs. For a man who was almost always very low in the polls (except at election time), Mulroney always managed to maintain the loyalty and affection of his caucus, a remarkable achievement in today's often vicious politics.

He misses the cut and thrust of Parliament, the campaigning, the speeches. "I even loved the hecklers," he says. "I can't say there's very much I miss because of the following—I was given the opportunity to stay in office long enough to achieve what I thought was right." That is something many prime ministers—Kim Campbell, John Turner, and Joe Clark to name but a few—never got.

How much is Brian Mulroney plugged into politics these days? Not much, he insists. He does travel an enormous amount for the many businesses he serves. From his home base as senior partner at the Montreal law firm Ogilvy Renault, he is also a director of Barrick Gold, TrizecHahn, and Sun Media in Toronto; Archer Daniels Midland in Decatur, Illinois; Cendant Corporation in New York; Quebecor Inc., Cognicase Inc., and Telesystems Ltd. in Montreal. And the list doesn't end there. Mulroney also acts as senior counsellor to Hicks, Muse, Tate and Furst, a global private equity fund in Dallas, whose head, Tom Hicks, owns the Dallas Stars and Texas

Rangers. Mulroney is also chairman of Forbes Global in New York, a member of the international advisory councils of Power Corporation of Canada, Bombardier Inc. Aerospace Group, the China International Trust and Investment Corporation in Beijing; and the Chase Manhattan Corporation, Violy, Byorum & Partners, and VS&A Communications Partners III, all of New York; plus Independant Newspapers, PLC in Dublin, and General Enterprise Management Services Limited in the British Virgin Islands.

And those are only his business interests. He also sits as a trustee of the Montreal Heart Institute, Freedom Forum, the George Bush Presidential Library, and is affiliated with programs at the Université de Montréal, Stanford University, and Vanderbilt University.

It's without question the most impressive post-political resumé ever crafted by a Canadian politician.

I tell Brian Mulroney I can't imagine him not active in politics.

"*Il faut tourner la page,*" he says, a reminder of one of his favourite expressions when he was in office. "You've gotta turn the page." To the extent he keeps up to date on the goings-on in Parliament, it's thanks to the efforts of Francine Collins, who clips newspaper articles for him.

Just to show me how little he follows it all, Mulroney tells me a story about a seatmate he had on a recent flight.

"According to the newspapers you're on every board," the man said to him.

"Yeah, I'm doing okay," Mulroney responds. "What do you do?"

"I'm in politics," he says.

"Oh yeah? What do you do?" Mulroney asks.

"I'm in the cabinet," the seatmate answers.

Mulroney bursts out laughing. "There was a time I would have known the guy's wife, the names of his kids. Now I'm out of the country 60 per cent of the time."

Ironically, Mulroney's gravest moments in politics came after he'd left office. The Liberal government was investigating the former prime minister for allegedly accepting five million dollars in kickbacks from the sale of Airbus jets to Air Canada. The story later collapsed and an embarrassed government had to apologize to Mulroney and pay him $2.1 million in costs.

The day after the formal apology, Prime Minister Chrétien's office was on the phone to Mulroney's law office. "The prime minister would like to call Mr. Mulroney tomorrow," the voice said. "At what time would he be ready to accept a call from the prime minister?" Francine Collins contacted Mulroney, who was out of the country, heard his answer, and returned the PMO's phone call.

The answer was, "Never."

I ask how the prime minister took that response.

"I could care less," Mulroney says, still clearly hurt by the episode. "I had to live through that. It did hurt my wife, my children, and myself. But it's part of politics. We've dealt with it and moved on."

Brian Mulroney looks at his watch. "Whoa, I have to go," he says. I check mine and I see he's given me eighty minutes—twenty more than Francine budgeted. I turn off my tape recorder and thank him for his time. Even then, with time having run out, Mulroney spares another few minutes for some political gossip about the old times. As I collect my belongings, he delights in sharing some stories the only way Mulroney can—enthusiastically and with a big belly laugh.

I leave Mulroney's suite at the Royal York Hotel, considering the legacy of this man so full of contradictions. Reviled, yet re-elected. A Tory opposition leader who said pick me and I'll win. They did, and he did.

"If you're the leader of an opposition party," he tells me, "there is one criterion and one criterion alone by which you are judged. Did you win? That's all."

Since Confederation, the tens of millions of Canadians who have lived in our country have seen just twenty politicians become prime minister. Nine inherited the job, and only two of them—St. Laurent and Trudeau—won mandates of their own.

Like it or not, Brian Mulroney is one of only thirteen men in Canadian history to have won an election and one of only six prime ministers to have won consecutive majority governments—a rather exclusive club.

Did he win?

Yes, he did.

THE INSPIRATION

Once upon a time, a twenty-year-old kid from North York decided he'd had enough of southern Ontario. His father, Sam, was a successful real-estate developer in the increasingly prosperous suburbs outside Toronto. But the family business held no interest for him. So Greg Sorbara joined the Company of Young Canadians, Prime Minister Lester Pearson's answer to America's Peace Corps. He moved to the mountains of British Columbia to start building communities. It was the thing to do for a generation of young kids who were idealistic and full of energy for a country that had just passed its one hundredth birthday.

"I was a dropout, a back to the lander," Sorbara recalls. It was an inspirational time for him. He fell in love with a woman, also from southern Ontario, named Kate Barlow. For two people who had turned their backs on doing the establishment thing, their next move was very traditional—they decided to get married.

Sorbara had always had an interest in public service, but never thought of himself as a future politician. Having said that, he was deeply fascinated with a politician who had burst onto the political scene with a dashing style and handsome looks. And ironically, it wasn't Pierre Trudeau. It was John F. Kennedy, whose story Sorbara followed on television with complete fascination, starting with Kennedy's winning the Democratic presidential nomination. The Kennedy story had a profound impact on Sorbara, who was just fourteen at the time.

"For years after, I was particularly fascinated with the big convention, when the beehive rejects the old queen bee and picks a new queen bee," he says. "It's a very important part of the way politics renews itself," he says.

As Trudeau's first term was coming to an end, Sorbara started musing about running in the 1972 election for the NDP in British Columbia. He asked his wife what she thought of the idea.

"And she said to me, 'Why in God's name…'" Sorbara pauses here, realizing that's not completely accurate. "Actually, she said, 'Why the fuck would anyone vote for you? You've never done anything.'"

A harsh judgement perhaps, but not altogether incorrect. So Sorbara resolved to get some credentials, just in case one day, he might actually consider himself worthy of being a candidate. The idea was to return to Ontario, become a lawyer, then hightail it back to the mountains of Nelson, B.C., and maybe become active in politics.

But a funny thing happened on the way to the Rockies. Pierre Trudeau retired, forcing the Liberals into a leadership convention in the summer of 1984. Sorbara, mindful of the one leadership convention he remembered fondly—JFK's in 1960—wanted in. He contacted a local politician who arranged for him to have delegate status at this, his first ever convention.

"I wandered around in awe and wonder, thinking, this is really bizarre," Sorbara says. "I don't know anyone here. And I'm going to help select the next prime minister of Canada."

He started the convention uncommitted but ended up supporting Jean Chrétien, who lost on the second ballot to John Turner in one of the least dramatic conventions of the last half-century. But something must have happened to Greg Sorbara that weekend in Ottawa, because five months later representatives of the Ontario Liberal Party courted him to run in the next provincial election and he was listening. They wanted him to run in his home riding of York North, which had sent Conservatives to Queen's Park for the past forty-two straight years.

"I thought, you know what, I probably have to do this," Sorbara remembers. "It had been in the back of my mind for a really long time."

For three months he thought about it, then told his wife of his decision.

"How dare you! How could you?" came the response from his wife.

"Don't worry," he said. "I can't win this thing. This is a Tory area."

Like most developers, the Sorbaras supported the party in power, and in Ontario, that meant the PCs, who were always in power. And the party truly had a stranglehold on politics in York Region. The MPP for the previous seventeen years, Bill Hodgson, was a Tory. One of his sons was director of engineering for the region. Every subdivision application had to go through him. Another son worked in the Ministry of Municipal Affairs and Housing. And Greg Sorbara told his family he wanted to challenge all that.

"You're running for the Liberals?" his brother Joe asked. "Are you crazy? Do you realize the Hodgsons control development in this area?"

Nevertheless, Sorbara pointed to the chestnut tree outside the family's farmhouse. It was late February, 1985. The election would be called the following month for May 2.

"I said to my wife, 'Before the blossoms are out on that tree, this will all be over. So don't worry too much about it.' That was my story to her," he says.

What Sorbara *really* thought he must have kept to himself, because if he'd shared his true feelings with his wife, she'd have gone wild. Both his province and his riding were changing. David Peterson, he figured, was a more logical successor to Bill Davis than was Frank Miller. Peterson was in the tradition of younger, middle-of-the-road leaders. Miller was too right wing, and didn't represent a generational change (in fact, he was a few years older than Davis). And locally, the man Sorbara would try to defeat was a seventy-two-year-old backbencher from the northern, Waspier part of the riding, whereas increasing numbers of people were Italian Canadians living in communities such as Woodbridge in the south.

Sorbara thought, "I can speak to those people in a way he can't. I actually think I have a shot at this, if I'm cut out for it."

The Tories must have thought that too, because in the middle of the campaign another Sorbara brother, Ed, received an anonymous, threatening phone call.

"Your brother's doing rather well in this campaign," the voice at the other end of the phone said. "Do you ever want to develop one more piece of land in York Region? Do you know what the consequences might be?" Fortunately, the threat was never acted upon. Sorbara later speculated it was an overzealous Conservative campaign worker trying to play the heavy.

Sorbara's campaign team did some polling at the start of the campaign and discovered his name recognition was a whopping 1 per cent. In other words, in the most populous riding in the province, virtually no one had heard of him. On election day, Sorbara's campaign manager, Steve Budaci, congratulated his candidate on running an excellent race. The Sorbara name was now better known. But Budaci told him he was still going to lose by five thousand votes.

Sorbara's response: "That's just great, Steve, but I've been going door to door, and you're full of shit."

As it turned out, the former flower child from the mountains of British Columbia *won* the campaign by five thousand votes. And the adventure did not end, as he'd promised his wife, when the blossoms came out on the chestnut tree. In fact, the Sorbara family would watch those blossoms fall off and die, then reappear ten more times before Greg Sorbara's career as an elected politician was over. And even then, it really wasn't over.

When the Liberals under David Peterson took over the government in the summer of 1985, Sorbara was thirty-nine years old. He walked through the front doors of Queen's Park and right to the cabinet table. You could say this election worked out a tad better than his previous attempt—an unsuccessful run for treasurer of the student council when he was fifteen.

To say Sorbara was a novice at politics was a huge understatement. Unlike most politicians, he hadn't spent any time coming up through the ranks of the party. He didn't understand how political parties were organized, how the legislature worked, or how a minister runs a ministry. His learning curve looked like the Alps and he loved it.

"It's just one of those times in your life where you learn, and absorb, at a tremendous pace," he says. "We were constantly developing skills at a really rapid rate."

He was also developing a healthy respect for the job. One has to remember, this was 1985—before the recession, before Meech Lake, before the public's hatred of politicians exploded.

"I believe fundamentally to my core, that it's important work," Sorbara says. "The individual politician's work is not that important, just like the individual guy on the assembly line isn't all that important. But the assembly line together produces the product. The work collectively is tremendously important. I had a deputy minister once say it as graphically as anyone. 'You've gotta remember that democracy is what we use to keep the losers from taking up arms and shooting their neighbours.'"

Sorbara's first portfolio was the Ministry of Colleges and Universities. About a year into the job, he led a mission to the Middle East to firm up a deal that one of his Conservative predecessors, Bette Stephenson, had set up. The Ontario government was selling educational services to several countries in the region—building new universities, and teaching the local governments how to administer them.

"I got off the plane, and the Canadian ambassador was waiting," Sorbara recalls. "He's in a total panic that this new government, with this new kid, is going to really screw up this deal." The group visited five countries in ten days and opened the new medical school at the University of Oman. Military guards followed them everywhere. It looked as if Sorbara and his group were receiving the same kind of attention an American president might enjoy. "All the streets were closed so the Ontario minister and his entourage could go through," he says. "And for a day that's quite nice. What really satisfied me was that the same ambassador who met me at the outset of the mission said, at its completion, 'You did a brilliant job of handling these dignitaries.' And that made me feel really good."

One thing Greg Sorbara quickly discovered about public life was that not every day was like a mission to the Middle East. There were bad days too, particularly in the Liberals' second term. The party had won an astonishing ninety-five out of 130 seats in the

1987 election. The expectations and scrutiny on the government increased exponentially. After two years of mostly rave notices and an unusual level of satisfaction in the electorate, the Liberals were finally experiencing the other side of politics: nastier headlines, larger missteps by cabinet ministers, and policies that increasingly lost public support. Only two years into his second term, David Peterson went around the cabinet table, soliciting opinions on when the Liberals should seek re-election. It seemed a little early to be going back to the polls, but there were solid strategic reasons for doing so. Most ministers weren't anxious to get back on the hustings, accurately figuring the early call would result in a bruising campaign. But ultimately the attitude was, let's get it over with.

Cabinet minutes will show there was only one minister who, to the end, was begging the premier not to call an early election. It was the same minister who, five years earlier, sensed something was changing in York Region and across the province.

"David Peterson and all his ministers decided, yes, this is a good idea, and I was the last one to say, 'Sorry, Premier, I cannot agree with this decision,' Sorbara recalls. "I didn't think we were going to lose. But I thought we were going to get punched rather severely and we'd lose a lot of good members. I was also on the side of his wife and his mother, who were also giving him that advice, so I was in good company."

On September 6, 1990, more than sixty Liberal MPPs lost their jobs, as the Liberal government went down in flames. But Greg Sorbara kept his seat that night, and within a year and a half would enjoy his greatest moment in politics, a moment which, in some respects, he'd been anticipating since he was fourteen years old.

Sorbara was at Copps Coliseum in Hamilton, one of six Liberal MPPs trying to become the new queen bee of the Liberal hive. Five thousand party members had gathered to determine whether he was ready for prime time.

"It almost goes back to Kennedy," he says. "I always wanted to give that speech. I wanted to stand there in that position. It's like you're an actor and you go to a play, and you say you want on that stage and play that role for a while. I'd always wondered about the level of anxiety that arises in the body in anticipation of such a moment."

But the road to realizing this political dream was awfully bumpy. The night before the speech, Sorbara only slept for about two hours, because he was in a constant battle with his speech writers over what to say.

"The problem with Greg was he never intended to give a coherent speech," says Allan Golombek, one of the speech writers. "The speech he wanted to give wouldn't get people cheering or create any momentum."

Golombek came to fear that Sorbara, after waiting decades to give that speech, just didn't understand the convention psychology. Sorbara wanted to wow the delegates with the force of his ideas. Golombek wanted the candidate to blow them away with his charisma and rabble-rousing populism. Golombek remembered the 1984 federal Liberal leadership convention in Ottawa, when Jean Chrétien took aim at Conservative leader Brian Mulroney by saying, "Brian, do not adjust your set. What you see is what you're going to get."

"The crowd went absolutely wild," Golombek says, "but Greg hated that line."

The debate between candidate and speech writer was getting too intense. "I ended up feeling I was babysitting a spoiled child," Golombek says.

There was no love lost on Sorbara's end either. "I finally had to call my campaign manager and say, 'Keep that asshole away from me, I'm trying to decide on what to say and I'm running out of time.'"

Golombek offered one last admonition. "If you give the speech you want to give, they're not going to cheer," he said.

"Does it matter if they cheer?" Sorbara asked.

"Does it matter if you win?" Golombek shot back.

The next day, the day of The Speech, Sorbara was sitting in his section of the arena, listening to his competitors' orations. And he was still tinkering away. By the time he got to the podium, he had five pages with hand-scribbled notes all over them. His campaign team's advice was dancing around in his head. Be powerful enough to capture the undecided votes. But not over the top. You're speaking to a television audience as well. Make eye contact with the crowd so everyone will think you're looking directly at them.

The irony, of course, was that it didn't matter whether Sorbara spoke as well as former president John F. Kennedy or former Maple Leaf captain "Teeder" Kennedy. He couldn't win the convention. And he'd known it for weeks.

"I did want to be the leader," he says. "I did want to be the premier. But I thought, you're not going to make it and you've got to go through all this campaigning. But you know what? I have to do it anyway. Because I have to give the speech. I have to do that performance, because politics in so many of its dimensions is public performance."

Sorbara gave the speech. "The level of anxiety I felt was unique," he says. "I had never felt it before or since. It's an anxiety that creates energy. You feel 'at one' with the speech."

Sorbara thought it was one of the best he'd ever given. Golombek didn't. "I wish I had a tape recording of that speech because it made no sense," he says. "People came up to me and said, 'Scoop, tell me you didn't write that speech.'"

Sorbara's old campaign manager, Steve Budaci, who was a delegate at the convention, didn't like the speech either. He found it too scripted. "It really wasn't Greg," he says. "From my vantage point, I thought the speech was mediocre." After waiting more than thirty years to give the speech of his life, Sorbara had to content himself with the fact that there was no "Ask not what your country can do for you..." in his address. Historians would not be quoting him for years to come. However, in fairness, one columnist, Thomas Walkom of the *Toronto Star*, called Sorbara's speech the best one of the bunch at that convention.

Nevertheless, the next day, Sorbara showed surprising strength, lasting until the fourth ballot. He came third behind Lyn McLeod and Murray Elston. He had to drop out.

Ironically, with all of the drama and preparation that went into the speech, it probably wasn't the best one Sorbara delivered that weekend. After he dropped off the ballot, he gathered all his supporters together in one section of the coliseum. Because the hall had gone strangely quiet and the seats were configured on an incline, Sorbara could talk to all his supporters very intimately, without screaming.

Then he gave the speech perhaps he should have given the night before. He told the delegates he wasn't going to declare his support for either candidate on the last ballot, and urged them to vote their consciences as well. He spoke in a deeply personal way about what the quest for the leadership meant to him and the entire team.

"It was from the heart, from the soul, off the cuff," recalls Budaci. "That was one of the finest speeches that I think he's ever delivered. Greg had, and still has, the Trudeau talent of being able to captivate an audience and talk off the cuff. I've seen it over and over again."

And then something quite unusual happened on the fifth and final ballot, which Lyn McLeod won and on which Sorbara was absent. Twenty-three delegates spoiled their ballots, an unusually high number for a final vote. No one could figure it out, until Greg Sorbara woke up the next morning and found twenty-three pink flamingos on the front lawn of his home—one for each of the twenty-three delegates who were so moved by Sorbara's "other" speech they could not bring themselves to vote for either of the two finalists, but who wanted to make a statement nonetheless.

One of Sorbara's delegates, Rose Vecchiarelli, spearheaded the spoiled-ballot effort and the pink flamingos. "We still wanted to vote for Greg," she says. "It was an emotional thing. And those flamingos, they were the last leg to stand on." Just like those twenty-three delegates.

For most people, life goes back to normal the day after a leadership convention. Not so for the candidates. It can take two or three years before the candidate stops saying, 'If only I'd done this,' or 'What if I'd done that,' and Sorbara was no exception. He also got to a point after the convention where he didn't want to be a politician any more.

"I wanted to have the success of rebuilding the party, restating its values and presenting it to the public," he says. "I didn't make it. I quickly came to the conclusion that Lyn McLeod wasn't going to win the 1995 election. Mike Harris was going to win it. People told me, 'You're crazy, you don't know what you're talking about.' I smelled it a long way away. And I thought, I don't want to be in opposition for another five years."

The lure of The Life for Sorbara meant an almost religious-like devotion to the job. When he was in cabinet or running for the party leadership, public life took up virtually all his time.

"I remember so clearly my wife saying to me, 'The children are growing up and you're missing it. It's really exciting what's going on and you're missing it 'cause you're never here, and when you're here, you're unwinding.' As it lures your life, it takes your life. By 1994, I was thinking, there are other things, I'm getting older, and I should taste some of it."

Sorbara served out his term and didn't seek re-election in 1995. He'd promised his wife that his political adventure would be over by the time the blossoms came out on the chestnut tree at their farm. He was off by about ten years. But in a marvellous bit of synchronicity, the old family farm was now a new subdivision. As Greg Sorbara's political career was coming to an end, so too was that chestnut tree, which succumbed to a chainsaw in the name of progress.

He was finished with politics, for now. But that didn't mean politics was finished with him. After Liberal MP Sergio Marchi resigned in August, 1999, to become Canada's new ambassador to the World Trade Organization in Geneva, Sorbara's phone started ringing again. Marchi's riding wasn't too far away from Sorbara's former stomping grounds, and his Italian heritage would no doubt be an asset.

"I got a whole bunch of phone calls from people saying, 'This is your opportunity to go federally,'" he says. "That's a quintessentially Canadian phrase: 'Go federally.' And my response was always the same—this is your opportunity to go fuck yourself."

Life in the private sector wasn't too bad for Sorbara. He did some work for the family real-estate development business. He replaced his passion for public life with two private projects—owning the St. Catharines Stompers minor-league baseball team and doing a land-development deal in the Czech Republic. He recently sold his interest in both ventures, and all the kids are out of the house now. Moreover, he's a grandfather. So with all the extra time on his hands, what did he return to?

Politics, of course. He eased his way back in by becoming president of the Ontario Liberal Party "till further notice," offering advice to leader Dalton McGuinty and filling up the party's coffers in anticipation of the next election.

And then, after sitting out two consecutive provincial elections and enjoying his view from the sidelines, Sorbara succumbed to the seductive call of politics he could no longer deny. When PC cabinet minister Al Palladini died suddenly of a heart attack in March, 2001, Sorbara opted to run in the ensuing by-election, which would take place in what was essentially his former riding. He claims he didn't want to do it. He claims he couldn't withstand the pressure his leader and his party put on him to try to make a small Liberal dent in the "905" fortress that has given every seat to the Tories for two consecutive elections. Actually, he put it somewhat more graphically. Sorbara suggested that McGuinty had put the gonads of the Liberal Party president in a vice grip, promising to squeeze harder and harder until the reluctant candidate said yes.

So Sorbara said yes. And on June 28, 2001, the voters of Vaughan-King-Aurora did likewise by an almost 10,000-vote margin.

"There's nothing in the private sector that is quite as important," Sorbara says of The Life. "The heady part of politics is stimulating in a way that nothing in the private sector can match. It's just not there."

THE POWER

A well-known veteran of Canadian politics was at Number 10 Downing Street, enjoying the company of Britain's prime minister, Margaret Thatcher. It was his third visit to the prime ministerial residence. Just to make conversation, he looked around at the august surroundings and said to Thatcher, "Madam Prime Minister, are you still enjoying all of this?"

She turned around with a big smile and said, "Of course! Where else would I have such great power?"

Michael Marzolini, the chairman and CEO of the market research firm Pollara, remembers taking a guided tour of the facilities of one of the most successful pollsters in the United States. Richard Wirthlin was showing off his massive computer system and basking in the glory of being the pollster to Ronald Reagan.

He said to Marzolini, "I can press any button in this room, and I can get anybody elected to any job in this country."

"Have you ever thought about pressing a button and electing yourself to the Senate?" Marzolini asked him.

"And give up all this power?" Wirthlin asked incredulously.

The prime minister and the pollster both used a word almost no Canadian politician would be caught dead uttering—power. Even our most brazen politicians are loath to talk about the joys of exercising power, preferring instead to talk about the burdens of responsibility. It seems that in today's age, it's acceptable to call one's opponents liars, criminals, or idiots. But don't accuse them of enjoying power. Virtually every Canadian politician is embarrassed to admit he or she has power, exercises it, or relishes it.

"We never ever used the word 'power.' In fact, we banned it," says Peter Lougheed, the former Alberta premier. "We worked on the concept that we're trustees for the people, there for a limited period of time."

William Davis shudders when asked whether he enjoyed exercising power.

"I'm the antithesis of that," the former Ontario premier says. "I do not accept the word. It's not what I sought."

The modesty expressed by those first ministers is in stark contrast to the conventional wisdom as to why people get into politics. University of Toronto historian and author Michael Bliss recalls why his contemporaries ran for office in the 1960s.

"To tell you the truth, I want power," they'd say to him. "And office meant wielding power over other people. They won't say that today, however. Now they say, 'We all want to make a difference.'"

"The implication that you like to wield power, meaning you like to see yourself influencing other individuals by bending them to your will? That, I'd like to think, is not me," says Allan Blakeney, the former Saskatchewan premier. "But by organizing a plan, seeing it happen, seeing the results, if that's wielding power, then I put myself in the category of saying yes indeed."

Blakeney's successor, Roy Romanow, insists premiers don't have the kind of power citizens perceive they do. Subcommittees of cabinet vet major policy initiatives. Ministers have their eye on their own departments rather than on the government's overall message. Caucus members, when they want to, can also dampen the premier's power.

"You have so many checks and balances on you," says Romanow. "So exercising power doesn't have some sort of a wild west, open corral nature to it. It's disciplined by so many constraints. It's a very cluttered chessboard of moving major policy decisions forward."

Are New Democrats, in particular, averse to wielding power? I asked Bob Rae, premier of Ontario for one term, whether he found power intoxicating.

"Well, in my case it was so brief that it hardly became habit-forming," he laughs. However, Rae quickly noticed the power of the premier in even the smallest incidents.

"You do get used to going into a meeting and people are waiting for you to get there. And when does the meeting start? It starts when you get there, Premier, that's when it starts."

Former NDP leader Audrey McLaughlin has noticed a distinct difference in the way the two genders respond to the call to office. When she asks women if they'd be interested in running, they're unsure they can handle the responsibility.

"When I talk to men about it, they would often say, 'Gee, it would be really interesting to have that power,'" she says.

Some politicians have discovered how much power they have quite by accident. In 1985, Alvin Curling became Ontario's first Liberal housing minister in forty-two years. As he got off the elevator to enter his new office, he looked at the pictures of former housing ministers on the outer wall and jokingly said to his deputy minister, "Golly, what a way to greet me every morning, seeing all these Tories!"

The next day, Curling showed up for work and all the pictures were gone. "I thought, that's power. That's really power!"

Pierre Marc Johnson was one of three men named Johnson to wield power in the premier's office in Quebec.

"The notion of power for me is you're entrusted by the population with an instrument where you make executive orders and adopt legislation," he says. "And that's what it's about. If you think it's about anything else, having a chauffeur and a bodyguard, uh-uh," he chuckles, shaking his head. "That might come with the job but who cares. The real thing is the possibility to change reality."

Johnson, himself, became a cabinet minister in René Lévesque's Parti Québécois government just two days past his thirtieth birthday. He's one of the few politicians who admits to having enjoyed wielding power, while acknowledging some of his colleagues couldn't.

"Exercising power is like booze or money," he says. "Some people just can't take it. Some people become radically transformed. That either brings the best or the worst out of someone. You can become extremely superficial, extremely isolated."

Tom Long has been hanging around politicians since he was a teenager. He's seen the type Johnson describes.

"I worry a little bit about people who gain their self-worth out of exercising what they think is power, because it's very transitory," he says. Long has seen numerous examples of hotshots who think they're powerful. "They think the reason that people are returning their calls is because of their incredible intrinsic attractiveness." Until they lose their jobs. "Then you find out that life unfortunately isn't like that. Politics is a fundamentally humbling business. Generally the wheel turns and you end up on the other side. There is a utility to the golden rule."

David Peterson agrees. From 1985 to 1990, he was one of the most popular politicians in the country. Then he lost an election and his name fell off invitation lists with a thud.

"If you think you're getting invited 'cause you're a great guy, you're wrong," Peterson says. "Your self-esteem should not rest on perceived success or failure in your chosen job. I think a lot of politicians can't get over that. They think they still deserve it somehow or other. That's an endemic hazard in the business."

In conversations with nearly one hundred Canadian politicians, only the smallest handful acknowledge that power *is* all it's cracked up to be.

"It's not the lifestyle that's all that attractive. You don't do the job for the climate, that's for sure," says Peterson. "Our parliamentary system gives the first minister and cabinet unbelievable power. I think if you're smart, you've got to be very humble. Because being a dictator doesn't last very long unless you exercise that power well and sensitively."

Did Peterson enjoy exercising power?

"Loved it," he says unambiguously. "I remember sitting down in the chair in the premier's office for the first time and I felt terribly comfortable and I said to myself, I can do this. I was never once intimidated. I felt I had the power to do what I considered good."

Peterson doesn't seem any more power-crazed than any other politician. He just seems more open to discussing the joys of being a first minister. Sometimes, politicians have more power than they realize, but they're afraid to use it. In 1997, Jean Chrétien's Liberals won a second consecutive majority with 155 seats. That constituted just a four-seat cushion over the opposition. On several occasions, Liberal MPs voted against their consciences and their own track records on issues because they feared the boss's retribution.

"The imperial power of the prime minister in our system and his ability to crush, with virtually no resistance, dissent and the conscience of his own members of Parliament...," says Canadian Alliance MP Jason Kenney, his voice trailing off in disgust. "It's about power, its retention and concentration."

Kenney says if a handful of Liberal backbenchers in that thirty-sixth Parliament had bound together, they could have held the balance of power. Used intelligently, they could have nudged the prime minister into increasing the power of ordinary MPs or other reforms. Kenney says, instead, they did nothing.

"These people folded like a cheap deck of cards," he says.

Personally, Kenney respects many of those on the other side of the aisle. In their private conversations with him, Liberal MPs admit they are fearful about exercising what power they may have.

"You don't understand the degree of pressure that can be exerted on us," one of them told Kenney. "We have to keep our powder dry, so we can fight on another issue."

Kenney says he's been told if MPs exercise too much independence, the prime minister will refuse to sign their nomination papers.

"But at some point you have to draw the line or give up the notion that you actually have a conscience," Kenney says. "That's what allows the total concentration of power. It's the refusal of individual members to bind together. And just a handful could really change the system."

Kenney's least favourite example was a court case which rendered some child pornography legal. Sixty-five Liberal MPs signed a letter to Prime Minister Chrétien, asking him to use the "notwithstanding clause" of the Charter of Rights and Freedoms to overturn the court decision. When the Reform Party proposed a motion to do just that, all but three MPs buckled to pressure from the PMO and voted against their own petition.

"This was not an ideological issue," Kenney says. "The NDP and the Bloc Québécois supported us."

Despite the feeling that ordinary MPs have no power at all, nearly every Liberal backbencher ran for re-election in 2000. Why?

"This is a pretty good life," says Carolyn Bennett, Liberal MP for St. Paul's. "I get to influence lots of things. Some ministers don't get to decide anything."

Bennett admits some of her colleagues on the backbench are big-time suck-ups to the PMO in hopes of some day getting into cabinet.

"If you spend your life trying to get into cabinet, you can get nothing done," she says.

Still, the quest for almost every parliamentarian is to sit on the executive council and feel as if you're at the centre of where it all happens. That was certainly what was pulsating through Larry Grossman's veins when he was under consideration for a big job in 1977. Rumours were rampant that Bill Davis was going to shuffle his cabinet. Grossman wanted to be near a phone just in case the call came. But he also had a funeral in his riding that he had to attend. So he left the widow's home phone number with the premier's office just in case. As Grossman and his wife were in line to express their condolences, he noticed a message on a nearby table with his name on it and the phone number of the premier's office. Grossman saw the note, turned to his wife, and said, "Forget the widow. Where's a phone?" He made the call and learned he would be Ontario's next consumer minister.

But aren't ministers, unlike backbenchers, in charge? Aren't they decision-makers?

"They're in charge until they're in trouble," laughs Carolyn Bennett. "Then the PMO and PCO (Privy Council Office) take over. Then you're in cabinet and you've got no power at all."

Bennett genuinely believes ordinary MPs can wield influence, if not power. She calls them an "early warning system" for cabinet ministers. For example, she cites a time when Paul Martin invited a small group of backbenchers to talk to him about one issue. Martin took notes. So did his staffers. After the meeting, one of those staffers called Bennett for some further recommended reading. "That's how we wield influence in Ottawa," Bennett says of the city she describes as "twenty-four square miles surrounded by reality."

Perhaps, but there's certainly another view of how power is exercised in a large caucus.

"The party is just a collection of people fighting for power," says David Goyette, the former political consultant. "The first time a politician goes to a caucus meeting, they learn their hands will be tied. It is not democratic in any sense. You're basically told what's going to happen, and it doesn't matter what you say. They're slaves to the party and are told what to do. And if they don't do what they're told, they're penalized."

Goyette says the upside of that equation is that many politicians decide to give up chasing the dream of making cabinet and become effective members for their constituents because their ridings are the only places they can be king or queen. They can get potholes fixed, forms filled out, or workers' compensation claims filled. Goyette thinks most backbenchers "take satisfaction in convincing themselves that the voters think they're important, that they are in constant contact with the premier or prime minister, even though they certainly aren't."

Even if power is too concentrated in the first minister's office, there's apparently enough that spills out, making the politician's job worth having.

"It's the ability to make things happen," says Dennis Timbrell, a former Ontario cabinet minister. "To pick up the newspaper in the morning and say, that's not right, and pick up the phone and go into a cabinet meeting or go into a caucus meeting and do something about it. There's nothing like it. It's the ultimate high. You're not going to find anything else like it in the private sector."

THE EPILOGUE

Having now read a few hundred pages characterizing many different experiences in public life, you may be asking yourself whether I have told these stories with a sufficiently critical voice.

Let me be clear. Yes, I have met politicians who are corrupt, evil, vain, ignorant, incompetent, and a whole bunch of other terrible things. But I have also encountered many who are inspiring. Some of them live lives of such intense drama on a daily basis, one can't help but admire them. Like it or not, they do blaze trails. They do have important jobs. And when they get things done—even the small, seemingly insignificant things—they can change our lives. For some, as you've seen, politics has become the family business. Others get into politics for the most altruistic of reasons. That's not to say they're absent of ego or haven't learned how to play hardball. It is to say they are truly motivated by noble causes, and haven't entered politics as a stepping stone to something more lucrative after it's all over.

You've met the politicians who've yearned for The Life since they were teenagers, and others who were simply attracted to the game out of a sense of public spiritedness and because they discovered they were good at it.

Of course, there are those who have found themselves chewed up and spit out by rules of engagement which can be extremely harsh and unforgiving. And yet, they run again, and again, and again.

On September 6, 1990, Ontario voters were handing Premier David Peterson the shock of his political life. Peterson's astonishing landslide victory three years earlier was disintegrating, to be replaced by the province's first ever NDP government under Premier Bob Rae.

Lyn McLeod, a Liberal cabinet minister, who survived the shellacking and eventually became Peterson's successor, watched the debacle unfold from her campaign headquarters in Thunder Bay. At one point in the evening, McLeod's oldest daughter, Dana, asked, "Why would you want anyone you love to do this?"

Dana, I hope this book has answered your question.

THE BACK OF THE BOOK

During the summer of 1999, I received a letter out of the blue from the Bukowski Agency. Did I ever want to write a book? I responded yes I did, but I doubted anyone would be interested in publishing what I wanted to write about. Write an outline anyway, they insisted. I thought it would be a huge waste of time, but I did it anyway. The next thing I knew, literary agent Denise Bukowski was convincing me of the merits of the idea. I thought she was well-intentioned but simply wrong. People like to hate politicians. Who cares about what drives them?

Nevertheless, Denise put me in touch with Cynthia Good, the president and publisher of Penguin Books Canada. I don't think I have ever hit it off so well and so quickly with (a) someone I'd never met before, and (b) someone in a position to play a major role in my life for the next two years. She lives, breathes, and adores publishing books written by Canadian writers. She will never know how much I have appreciated her infectious enthusiasm, wonderful advice, and confidence in me throughout the two years we spent making *The Life* a reality.

In one sense, this book took so long to write because I was holding down a very full-time job, co-hosting *Studio 2* and *Diplomatic Immunity* on TVOntario. I tried as hard as it was humanly possible not to let the execution of this project interfere with my duties at TVO. I think I was *mostly* successful. Nevertheless, I owe a huge debt of thanks to *Studio 2*'s executive producer Doug Grant for his understanding. However, Doug, my gratitude to you has limits. I was not able to convince the publisher to entitle this book *Doug Grant and Other Legends I Have Known*, although I'm sure that will make a fine book some day.

Thanks also to: Craig I.W. Marlatt, the website manager for www.craigmarlatt.com. His ability to come up with the most arcane facts so quickly saved me hours of time in the library; Sally Ritchie, for her invaluable research and timely suggestions during moments of particular panic; Wodek Szemberg, a constant sounding board at all hours of the day and night; Tim Murphy, for his insightful assistance in understanding politics from our different vantage points; Mary Adachi, copy editor extraordinaire, whose remarkable sharpness improved this rookie's first effort; and Sandra Tooze, whose rare combination of gentle nature, yet lazer-like eye for detail, caught many mistakes the author missed. Their advice made this book better than it might have been. Of course, the responsibility for the book's shortcomings is all mine.

And finally, on a personal note, I want to thank Dr. Roberto and Caroline Grosso for allowing me to write part of this book at their beautiful cottage on Manitoulin Island; my parents, Marnie and Larry Paikin, who nurtured in me my own love of The Life; my brother, Jeff, who follows politics not a whit, and certainly won't read this book, but he is my only sibling and I love him; my three sons, Zachary, Henry, and Teddy, any one of whom would make a magnificent prime minister or premier, and who already make their father so proud every day by exhibiting the best qualities politicians should have; and finally, to Francesca Grosso, who put up with my intolerable absences—never very happily—but did so because she knew how important writing a book was to me. She transcribed many of my interviews. She redefined the word "supportive." Even if this book sells no copies, the fact that she is still in my life is victory enough.

I am fortunate, indeed, to know all of these people.

Oh, and one more thank you. To Frank Sinatra. Just... because.

THE NAME INDEX